# SPIRAL GUIDE

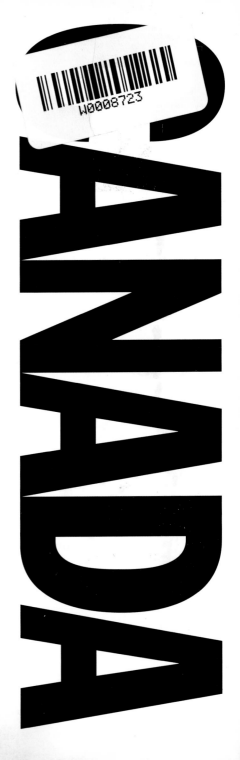

# CANADA

**AA**
**Publishing**

# Contents

Written by Penny Phenix

Magazine section by Paul Waters
The North by Jenni Davis
Copy edited by Sarah Hudson
Verified by Rebecca Marks and Anna Phenix
Indexed by Marie Lorimer
Editorial Management by Allen Stidwill

Published by AA Publishing, a trading name of Automobile
Association Developments Limited, whose registered office is
Southwood East, Apollo Rise, Farnborough, Hampshire GU14 0JW.
Registered number 1878835.

ISBN 0 7495 4536 4

The contents of this publication are believed correct at the time of
printing. Nevertheless, AA Publishing accept no responsibility for
errors, omissions or changes in the details given, or for the conse-
quences of readers' reliance on this information. This does not
affect your statutory rights. Assessments of the attractions, hotels
and restaurants are based upon the author's own experience and
contain subjective opinions that may not reflect the publisher's opin-
ion or a reader's experience. We have tried to ensure accuracy, but
things do change, so please let us know if you have any comments or
corrections.

A CIP catalogue record for this book is available from the
British Library.

Cover design and binding style by permission of AA Publishing
Color separation by Leo Reprographics
Printed and bound in China by Leo Paper Products

Find out more about AA Publishing and the wide range of travel
publications and services the AA provides by visiting our website at
www.theAA.com/bookshop

A01999
Mapping produced from Canada data © Tele Atlas N.V. 2005

*the magazine*

# Best of Canada

## Best cities

**Canada** has three great metropolises: west to east, Vancouver, Toronto and Montréal. All three make the "best-of" charts for different reasons.

**Vancouver** (➤ 54–57) wins hands down for setting, framed by the Coastal Mountains to the north and the fertile Fraser River Delta to the south. Its west end fronts on English Bay, and it has both the best urban green space in Canada – Stanley Park – and the best urban ski resort – Grouse Mountain.

**Toronto**'s (➤ 103–106) surroundings on the other hand are, well, dull (aside from the lake), but no one goes to Toronto for the scenery. In the last 30 years, the city has emerged as the cultural center of Canada and one of the most multi-cultural cities on Earth. It has Canada's best street market (Kensington), some of its best restaurants and first-rate dance and opera companies. After New York and London, this is also the world's most important center for English-language theater.

**Montréal** (➤ 122–125) is something completely different – or, *quelque chose complètement different*. One of the largest French-speaking cities in the world, it has Canada's most adventurous restaurants, best nightlife, best-dressed street crowds and most magnificent cathedrals and churches. It also has a history that stretches back to 1638 – positively paleolithic by Canadian standards.

### Most Unusual Names

Newfoundland wins for the delightful villages of Heart's Desire, Heart's Delight and Heart's Content. Some other place names in the province – Come-by-Chance, Blow-Me-Down and Run-by-Guess, for example – hint mistakenly at a devil-may-care attitude to the art of navigation by local mariners.

Cosmopolitan street life is a great attraction in Montreal

Vancouver's setting between the ocean and the mountains is nothing short of spectacular

Cobblestones and French Colonial architecture in Québec City's Place Royale

## Best small town

Following strict orders from back home, colonists in **Lunenburg** (➤ 156), Nova Scotia, ignored the steep landscape and laid out their town of multicolored wooden houses according to a rigid grid. The result is a delightful triumph of order over common sense.

## Best walled city

Not only the best, but the *only* walled city (in the whole of North America), **Québec City** (➤ 126–128) is a beautifully preserved piece of New France.

## Best wilderness

Canada's wilderness begins just a few miles from some of the country's biggest cities and ends at the edge of the polar ice-cap. It includes soaring mountains, thunderous rivers, endless stretches of lichen-covered tundra and about a quarter of the world's fresh water. And much of it is surprisingly easy to get to.

The best wilderness for beginners is Quebec's **Mont Tremblant National Park** (➤ 134). Its 1,510sq km (583sq miles) of mountains, lakes and rushing rivers are just a couple of hours north of Montréal.

Just as dramatic is **Kluane National Park** (➤ 191), a mountainous, 21,980sq-km (8,486sq-mile) reserve on the western edge of Yukon territory. Its peaks include Canada's highest – Mount Logan at 5,959m (19,545ft) and it is home to grizzly bears and sure-footed Dall sheep.

Mont Tremblant offers year-round activities in easy reach of Montréal

## Best road trips

Nothing beats the **Cabot Trail** (➤ 188–190) that wraps around the mountainous northern end of Cape Breton Island, Nova Scotia. In the west, Alberta's **Icefields Parkway** (➤ 180–181) lacks Cape Breton's ocean vistas but makes up for it with bigger mountains, wolves and mountain goats.

In the north, the gravel-surfaced **Dempster Highway** (➤ 173) starts near Dawson City, Yukon and runs 750km (465 miles) to Inuvik on the Beaufort Sea, 200km (125 miles) north of the Arctic Circle (which means 24-hour daylight in summer).

## Best ferry ride

No contest: It's the spectacular southbound trip on B. C. Ferries' *Queen of Chilliwack* from **Bella Coola to Port Hardy**.

**The Dempster Highway crosses a wild and remote landscape**

## Best music

**Natalie MacMaster** (below), one of Nova Scotia's world-famous fiddlers, is at the forefront of the Celtic music revival. Toronto's **Tragically Hip**, now at last making some inroads internationally, remain Canada's favorite rock band.

## Best beach

On the east coast, long strips of pink and white sand ringed by dunes and wild rose bushes make up much of the 40km (25 miles) of coastline within the **Prince Edward Island National Park** (▶ 150). The island also claims to have the warmest seawater north of the Carolinas. Out west, the water that breaks ashore on **Vancouver Island's Long Beach** (▶ 53) is decidedly chillier, but both the waves and the surrounding landscape are far more dramatic.

# Just say hockey

It's difficult for outsiders to grasp the true ferocity of Canada's national sport. To begin with, it's played not with a ball or a shuttlecock, but a puck – an inch-thick disc of granite-hard black rubber that can fly at speeds of up to 145kph (90mph) when properly "slapshot." It's one reason why hockey players strap on about 9kg (20lb) of plastic armor before they take to the ice, and why goalies wear enough pads to deflect anything short of a scud-missile.

It's also why in the 1950s and '60s, when helmets were rare even at the high-school level and faceguards unheard of, that Canada was known as the "land of the

**Fast and furious (literally), hockey is a national obsession**

### Information
www.canadianhockey.ca and www.nhl.com are the best sites to find out how to see a game.

toothless forechecker." A well-directed puck can harvest a whole row of incisors and canines in a single, blinding moment of pain. Is it any wonder that legendary goalie Glenn Hall ducked into the bathroom to vomit before every single one of the 764 maskless games he played during his National Hockey League career?

But the puck is the least of it. This is a game, remember, played by guys (and these days, girls) with steel blades attached to their feet and 1.5m (5ft) sticks in their hands on a cold, hard and unforgiving surface. And it's perfectly legal – in the men's game anyway – for a 115kg (250lb) defenseman to slam a stickhandling forward into the boards that line the rink with enough force to shatter the chassis on a tank. And fight! The guys in the professional leagues drop their gloves and pound at each other with such regularity that it's a favorite joke of sports fans to say: "I went to a boxing match and a hockey game broke out."

But in spite of the brawls, bruises and dental bills, there's not a boy over six (or under 80) who doesn't sometimes fantasize about playing left wing for one of the 30 teams in the National Hockey League.

Kids are as young as six when they begin trying to live that fantasy in thousands of local arenas across the country, padded and helmeted from head to foot so even their

### Get the Name Right
Canadians call their game simply hockey, not ice hockey. The game played on the grass in England is referred to as field hockey in North America.

**Hockey skills are learned from an early age**

parents have to identify them by the numbers on their jerseys. Increasingly the faces behind those masks belong to girls, who often play on the same teams as their male counterparts until their early teens, when the male leagues begin to allow bodychecking.

In summer, the best kids and those with rich parents go to hockey camps to get tips from the pros. The rest play street hockey, a lightly padded version of the real thing, featuring a ball instead of a puck and a lightweight goal that can be moved out of the way whenever a car drives by.

Few of these enthusiasts ever make it into the professional leagues, or even on to the elite junior teams that feed players into the pros. But they all dream a little, including the girls: Canada's senior women's team won eight consecutive world championships between 1990 and 2004.

And the game – despite its ferocity and the expense of the equipment – is fun. How else to explain all the guys in their 30s, 40s and 50s who book time in local arenas – often at midnight or later – to play refereeless games before empty stands. There's more to it all than blood and glory.

## National Hockey League
Only six Canadian cities – Montréal, Ottawa, Toronto, Edmonton, Calgary and Vancouver – have teams in the National Hockey League. The other 24 teams are American, but more than half the players are Canadians.

## Olympic Triumph
In the 2002 Salt Lake City Winter Olympics, Canada won gold in both men's and women's hockey – which for many Canadians were the only medals that counted.

## Origins
There are angry disputes over where hockey started, but most experts agree the first real game with rules and referees was played on Montréal's Victoria Skating Rink on March 3, 1875, between McGill University and a team called the Victorias. McGill won 2–1.

# The Cry of

# the Wild

If Africa's animals are noted for ferocity and Australia's for weirdness, the signal characteristic of Canada's has to be gregariousness. There are exceptions, of course. Few mammals are more solitary (or fiercer) than the polar bear, and his cousin the grizzly is about as sociable as a badger with toothache.

**Snow Geese**
Among Canada's most social creatures are the snow

**Above: the gray wolf is more often heard than seen**

**Below: orcas are year-round residents off the BC coast**

geese. Every spring and fall, great clouds of these graceful white birds descend on the marshy fields along the St. Lawrence River in southern Québec. They spend several days there each season, resting and stocking up on calories before continuing their journey, either to their summer breeding grounds

near Baffin Island or their
winter home in the southern
United States. By day they
search for food, but every
evening they gather by the
thousands in the fields along
the river, squatting in noisy
contentment in the damp
stubble, chattering and
gabbling with gusto.

## Caribou

The North American reindeer,
the caribou, are perhaps the
most outgoing of all
Canadian animals. In the
summertime they gather in
herds that can number into
the tens of thousands.
They're big travelers, too,
migrating sometimes
as much as
5,000km (3,000
miles) a year in
search of food and
breeding grounds.
In winter, the caribou
manages to live almost
entirely on lichens,
thanks to a stagger-
ingly efficient diges-
tive system.
  Caribou once
ranged as far
south as the
state of Maine,

but most of them now live on
the tundra or among the
sparse woodlands of northern
Québec and Ontario. There
is, however, a herd of them in
Québec's Gaspé Provincial
Park, the only place where
caribou, deer and moose
coexist.

## Beavers

The beaver, Canada's national
animal, is positively subur-

**Main picture:
magnificent,
and dangerous,
polar bears can
be seen (safely)
in the wild at
Churchill,
Manitoba**

ban in its pursuits, living in tight-knit family groups and spending its days engaged in endless home-improvement projects. It constructs long wooden dams across streams and brooks and then builds its snug wooden lodges in the middle of the ponds that form behind the dams. It's a high-maintenance way of life that requires constant dedication.

Canadians like to think the beaver exemplifies all the best qualities of the the national character: discretion, industriousness and family devotion. The unvarnished truth, however, is that the beaver is a national emblem because slaughtering this toothy little rodent was Canada's first major industry. In fact, some Canadians still make a living trapping beavers and other fur-bearing animals – an economic fact of life that sometimes shocks the sensitive. International protests against the spring seal hunt in the Gulf of St. Lawrence, for example, are a regular event on the enviromentalists' calendar.

*the beaver exemplifies all the best qualities of the national character*

**Marine Mammals**
Harp seals – the prey in this enterprise – are a gregarious bunch, too, gathering by the tens of thousands on the icefields to give birth. Sealers prowl among them, clubbing the pups and stripping them of their silvery pelts. It's a gruesome picture, all right, but seals are not an endangered species and to those who kill them to make a living for their families, they're just another marine resource like cod or herring.

Efforts to make the seals a tourist attraction have been only marginally successful. The number of people ready to pay big money to be helicoptered out to an ice floe in March or April is somewhat limited.

Whales, however, have become an unqualified success as a tourist attraction. Fishermen and other entrepreneurs make a tidy extra income taking tourists out to see orcas and grays on the Pacific coast and right whales, minkes, belugas, finbacks and even blues on the Atlantic coast.

It is perhaps fitting that one of Canada's most popular destinations for whale-watchers is the same Gulf of St. Lawrence that is so deadly for the seals.

# Klondike Days

Then I ducked my head and the lights went out,

And two guns blazed in the dark;

And a woman screamed, and the lights went up,

And two men lay stiff and stark.

Pitched on his head, and pumped full of lead,

Was Dangerous Dan McGrew,

While the man from the creeks lay clutched to the breast

Of the lady that's known as Lou.'

From "The Shooting of Dan McGrew" (1907),
by Robert Service (1874–1958)

## Gold Rush

The Klondike Gold Rush began on August 17, 1896, when George Carmack, Tagish Charlie and Skookum Jim struck it rich on Bonanza Creek. At least 35,000 Gold-Rush stampeders descended on the town, making it the largest Canadian city west of Winnipeg. In 1900 the Yukon goldfields produced more than 1,077,500 ounces in nuggets and dust.

**No hardship seemed too great for those who had caught gold fever**

**Makeshift settlements rose and fell with the fortunes of gold seekers**

"The Shooting of Dan McGrew" is perhaps the most famous poem ever written in Canada. For many romantics it captures the very spirit of the Klondike Gold Rush that in the early days of the 20th century made the remote Yukon settlement of Dawson City (►168–169) one of the richest towns on Earth. Indeed, the writer – bank clerk Robert Service – knew Yukon well. He lived there in those halcyon days when men were men and women were less than entirely honest.

And his setting was certainly perfect for a shoot-'em-up tale. Even today, Dawson City is an almost perfectly preserved Wild West town of wooden sidewalks, gingerbread architecture and bars with batwing doors. But Service's story was a work of almost pure imagination. Dawson City was, in spite of the gamblers, fast women and criminals it attracted, a law-abiding place.

## Robert Service

Robert Service's most famous poem was inspired by an actual shooting – of sorts. One night, he slipped into the bank where he worked to spend a few quiet hours writing. Unfortunately (or fortunately from a poetic point of view), his arrival startled the bank guard who took a shot at him, by mistake.

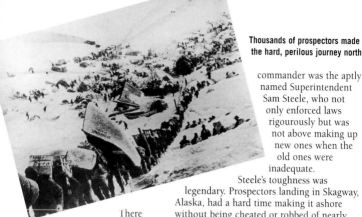

Thousands of prospectors made the hard, perilous journey north

commander was the aptly named Superintendent Sam Steele, who not only enforced laws rigourously but was not above making up new ones when the old ones were inadequate.

Steele's toughness was legendary. Prospectors landing in Skagway, Alaska, had a hard time making it ashore without being cheated or robbed of nearly everything they'd brought with them. But once across the Canadian border into Yukon, it was said a sourdough (old-time prospector) could leave his pack by the side of the trail for days and return to find it undisturbed.

There were few robberies, no shootings and no murders. In fact, guns weren't even allowed in town.

Credit for the town's probity belongs to a tiny detachment of incorruptible policemen. They were members of the Northwest Mounted Police, the red-coated force that became the modern Royal Canadian Mounted Police. Their

Steele was a firm believer in upholding the Sabbath. Dawson City's bars, brothels and casinos operated full tilt 24 hours a day every day except Sunday. One minute before midnight on Saturday night, the people would clear out of the saloons and casinos. The owners would leave the lights on and a Mountie would walk by each bar to make sure they were all empty. Then they'd turn off the lights and close down until one minute past midnight on Monday morning.

But Steele was more than just an honest cop. He also established and chaired Yukon's first board of health, chaired a board of license commissioners and supervized the winter mail service.

When "the Lion of the North" finally left Yukon, thousands of Dawsonites lined the wharves to bid him farewell. For two years he had been the only law on the very edge of civilization, a position that a more venal man could have used to make himself very rich with a minimum of effort. But when Steele left, he was no richer than when he arrived, save for the purse of gold nuggets the town's leading citizens presented him in appreciation for his services.

**Glittering grains being weighed to pay for provisions**

## Sam Steele

After his Yukon service, Sam Steele (1849–1919) commanded the Strathcona's Horse in the Boer War in South Africa. From 1901 to 1906 he took charge of the South African Constabulary, styled after the Northwest Mounted Police. During World War I he was promoted to Major-General, commanding Canadian forces in England.

# The Women of New France

It's not very politically correct to say it, but Montréal (➤ 122–125) has been described as Canada's most feminine city. People say that largely because it's undeniably romantic, with sidewalk cafés, narrow, cobbled streets and a mountain park smack in the middle that's perfect for springtime courtships.

But the city's femininity goes a lot deeper than a little surface romance. Montréal owes its very existence to a pair of formidable females. The first was Jeanne Mance, the daughter of a French lawyer who for the first

**The Musée M. d'Youville honors the founder of the Grey Nuns Hospital**

**Portrait of Marguerite de Youville at Montréal's Musée M. d'Youville**

sweeping France. Instead of entering a convent, however, she abandoned her home in Champagne and sailed off across the Atlantic with a group of pious settlers to found a Catholic colony in the Canadian wilderness. This, remember, was in an age when proper young women were expected to learn needlepoint, marry well and have babies, or if they were religiously inclined, to disappear genteely into some cloister and learn to sing hymns. Traipsing halfway round the world to found colonies was not on the list of recommended occupations.

Jeanne and her 53 companions landed in Canada in May 1642 to establish Ville Marie – the colony that became Montréal – in a clearing on the shore of the St. Lawrence River. They were thousands of miles from home, hundreds of miles from the nearest European colony, amid less than friendly natives.

But against all odds, Ville Marie endured. That same year, Jeanne opened a very humble hospital in her own home where she treated both natives and settlers. Two years later she moved the hospital to larger quarters on rue St. Paul.

34 years of her life led a perfectly conventional existence. Then in 1640, her father died and Jeanne, still single and without marital prospects, was caught up in the religious fervor that was

**Maison St.-Gabriel, now the Montréal Heritage Museum, was built in 1668**

Until her death in 1673, Jeanne worked tirelessly for the colony's success. She made three gruelling voyages back to France to recruit nurses and teachers for the fledgling city and to raise money for defense and construction. Her efforts earned her the title of Co-founder of Montréal.

The second formidable Frenchwoman in Montréal's history was Marguerite Bourgeoys, Canada's first schoolteacher. She, too, was captivated by the idea of establishing a truly Christian community in the New World and in 1653, left her home in Troyes for Ville Marie. She opened her first school in 1657 and returned twice to France to recruit women to help her. To ensure greater freedom, Marguerite founded the Congrégation de Notre Dame, an uncloistered community that still exists. Not only did they teach the children of colonists and First Nations, they also trained the Filles du Roy (Daughters of the King) – girls of good but poor families sent from France to be the wives and mothers of New France.

The third remarkable female, Marguerite d'Youville (1701–1771), was born in Canada and, in fact, became the country's first native-born saint. A holy life, however, is not always a happy one. Marguerite was orphaned in her youth and married off at 21 to an adulterous whiskey trader who treated her abominably. Widowed at 29, with three young children, she set out to alleviate the misery of others. Marguerite rescued a foundering hospital

A pious pose captures the devotion of Marguerite Bourgeoys

from ruin in which to make a home for the city's down-and-outers. She founded a religious order to help her, called the Sisters of Charity, who became universally known – as they still are today – as the Soeurs Grises (Grey Nuns). Marguerite d'Youville was canonized by Pope John Paul II in 1990.

## Hôtel Dieu Hospital

The hospital that Jeanne Mance founded – Hôtel Dieu – is still a major medical facility in Montréal. It's now run by the Québec provincial government, but nuns of the Religieuses Hospitallières Saint-Joseph – the order that Jeanne recruited – still have a residence and a museum next door.

## Congrégation de Notre Dame

Marguerite Bourgeoys' Congrégation de Notre Dame still has nearly 1,500 sisters working in seven Canadian provinces, three American states, Japan and Central America. In Montréal, the order runs Villa Maria, a private girls' school, and Marianopolis, a coed pre-university college.

# Canada's cookin'

The late Fernand Lachance often admitted that he was doubtful when a customer in his snackbar in rural Québec asked him to dump gravy and cheese curds into his bag of french fries. "That'll just make a heck of a mess," he protested, using the very French-Canadian word for mess – *poutine*. That was in 1957. Now *poutine* is a favorite in hamburger joints and snack bars across Canada. Even big chains like Burger King and McDonald's feature it occasionally. There are several different versions – the Italian one, for example, uses spaghetti sauce and Parmesan – but the original is still best: hot french fries covered in rubbery cheese curds smothered with dark, glue-like gravy.

If that's not enough to make your arteries crackle, you could try another great Québec contribution to popular cuisine – the smoked-meat sandwich. This features a tall stack of smoked, spiced beef brisket squeezed between two pieces of rye bread. The dish, a Montréal icon, originated with Jewish immigrants from Romania who flooded into Montréal in the late 19th and early 20th centuries.

The origins of *poutine* and smoked meat reflect the nature of most Canadian food – a hodgepodge of ethnic imports tempered by local tastes. It began with the French settlers, who lived on a hearty diet of *fèves-au-lard* (baked beans), thick pea soup and *tortière*, a kind of meat pie flavored with cloves and other spices – all of which are still popular.

But much of Canada's most distinctive food is purely indigenous. It was

**Imaginatively presented poached salmon with fiddleheads**

the First Nations who discovered how to turn the sap of the sugar maple into syrup and today Canada produces more than 70 percent of the world's supply. Traditional springtime sugaring-off celebrations have become a year-round industry, with *cabanes-à-sucres* (sugar shacks) all over eastern Canada offering feasts of ham, beans, pancakes, potatoes and even eggs – all cooked in and flavored with maple syrup.

On the west coast, it was the indigenous Haida and Sechelt people who taught white settlers how to catch the king and coho salmon, and more importantly, how to barbecue them on cedar planks over hot coals. This sweetly succulent dish is still British Columbia's tastiest contribution to Canadian cuisine.

First Nations, too, were the first to harvest fiddleheads in the wetlands of the Atlantic coast. These coiled young leaves of the ostrich fern are delicately delicious steamed and served with melted butter. They partner well with a more robust Atlantic product, the cod tongues and cod cheeks so beloved of Newfoundlanders. Rolled in crumbs and fried or baked with a little onion and salt, they taste a little like a poor man's shellfish.

**Prime cuts of succulent beef are never better than when served straight from the barbecue**

In Québec, French culture blends with Canada's national traits of friendliness and enthusiasm

# jaser avec

.... or "chat with the folks"....

## CANADIAN FRENCH

In the late 1990s, an odd word crept into the lexicon of California's "Valley girls," joining the notorious "omigod" and the ubiquitous "like." The word was "fiche" (pronounced *feesch*), and it meant "scram" or "beat it." Teen girls used it mostly to discourage nerdy males. The word's precise origin remains a mystery, but the best guess of California's pop-etymologists is that it came from French Canada, and was an abbreviation of *Fiche moi la paix*, more literally "Leave me in peace," but roughly translated as "scram" or "beat it."

The word's appearance among the nubile denizens of the San Bernardino Valley is a testament to the vigor of Canadian French. Upper-class Parisians might sniff contemptuously at the broad accents and unbuttoned pronunciation of their Canadian cousins, but the fact is the language is flourishing – and probably would be even without the province of Québec's laws limiting the public use of other languages.

And it is, in some ways, more French than the language you hear in Paris these days. Most Québecers, for example, still get their medication at the *pharmacie*, not *le drugstore*, and go camping on the *fin de semaine* rather than *le weekend*. They might, however, go both places in their *char* rather than their *voiture*, and a romantic male might bring his *blonde* (girlfriend) camping – even if she's a brunette. (A female, incidentally, would bring her *chum*.)

Not all Canadians, of course, speak French the same way – any more than Albertans and Newfoundlanders speak the same brand of English. There's a world of difference between the private-school French spoken in subur-

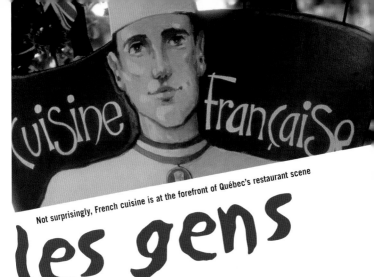

Not surprisingly, French cuisine is at the forefront of Québec's restaurant scene

# les gens

ban Outremont, for example, and the consonant-challenged *joual* of less prosperous parts (the dialect gets its name from the way its users pronounce *cheval*, the French word for "horse"). Acadian French, of the Maritime Provinces, is different again.

Generally though, Canadian French tends to be less formal than that spoken in France. Canadian francophones – especially those under 30 – lapse quickly into the familiar *tu* and *toi*, reserving the formal *vous* for things

like job interviews. All of which makes it a pretty friendly language to pick up. A quick glance through your high-school *grammaire*, and you'll be ready to drop into a St. Denis Street bistro to *jaser avec les gens* (chat with the folks) and maybe cough up a few *piastres* (dollars) to buy a round or two. When you leave, be sure to *donner un bec* (a friendly, two-cheek kiss) to your new friends.

The tricolor and Québec provincial flag fly proudly here

## Uniquely Canadian expressions

*À cet heure* (pronounced *asteur*): Now.
*Dépanneur*: A convenience store (used by all language groups in Québec).
*En plâtre*: Clumsy (literally translates as "in plaster"), as in *te bien en plâtre* – you are so clumsy. (Acadian)
*Niaiseux*: An irrritatingly stupid person or situation.
*Plate*, as in (*c'est plate*): Means either boring or disagreeable.
*Prends tes jambes*: literally, "take your legs," meaning "run like hell." (Acadian)
*Tanné*: Exasperated, as in *je suis tanné*.

### Chuckwagon Races

The Calgary Stampede's most hair-raising
events are the chuckwagon races. Four fully-
loaded wagons, each pulled by eight horses
with a single outrider thunder around the
track at a breakneck pace. Spills are
frequent; thrills are guaranteed.

# *stivals*

The chuckwagon races at the Calgary Stampede are among the most exciting events in the country

Let's face it: Just about anyone can organize a festival in the summer when the sun is warm, the sky is blue and everyone's in the mood to dance barefoot in the grass. The real test is to throw an outdoor party in winter when it's cold enough to make your nostrils crackle and your spit freeze before it hits the ground.

Canadians are as good as anyone at the first, with enough festivals, fairs and celebrations to fill just about every day in July and August. But they really excel at the second.

The granddaddy of Canada's cold-weather celebrations is the Carnaval de Québec, which traces its roots to the 19th century when Québec City's devout colonists prepared for Lent with a last loud blowout – literally a "farewell to meat," or "carne vale" in Latin. Lent may have gone out of fashion, but carnival hasn't. Today's 17-day festival might be more family oriented than its Rio counterpart (and revelers are certainly more thoroughly covered) but the fun is still uninhibited, thanks to liberal doses of a concoction called caribou (equal parts grain alcohol and sweet, red wine, with maybe a dash of brandy).

Snow, ice and subzero temperatures add a dimension of endurance to the carnival's glit-

It's not just music at the Montréal Jazz Festival

tering nighttime parade through the narrow, cobbled streets of Old Québec. The same streets serve as a course for one of North America's most unusual dogsled races, and a gallery for some of the world's most talented ice sculptors. The most unusual event, though, is the "canoe race" across the St. Lawrence River. The craft involved are actually double-ended boats that five-person crews paddle, haul and push through, around and over the ice floes choking the river.

Dozens of cities and towns across the country have similar winter festivals, and one of the most successful is Ottawa's two-week Winterlude in February, a family-focused festival that's largely centered on the "world's largest ice rink" – a 7.8-km (4.8-mile) stretch of the frozen Rideau Canal.

Ottawa is at its most colorful, however, in spring, when it celebrates the Tulip Festival, which originated in a little royal gratitude. In the fall of 1945, Princess Juliana of the Netherlands gave Ottawa 100,000 tulip bulbs to show her appreciation for the safe haven she and her family found there during World War II. Ever since, the National Capital Region has gone just a little tulip nuts every May, with tulip-themed fashion shows, boat

parades and fireworks – not to mention the millions of tulips in every imaginable color – more than 300,000 on Parliament Hill alone.

The early-summer obsession in nearby Montréal is jazz, and has been ever since the city staged its first annual International Jazz Festival in 1979. That relatively modest street party has since grown into the world's largest jazz celebration, attracting over the years such stars as Count Basie, Ella Fitzgerald, Wynton Marsalis and Diana Krall. The festival's big galas have ticket prices to match, but true to the original street-party vision, most of the 400 concerts are free, with big outdoor sound stages set up in downtown Montréal.

In early September the festival focus shifts to Toronto, when you can't walk down Bloor Street without bumping into a director, an actor or a screenwriter. The city's full of them for the Toronto International Film

## Ice breakers

The boat race across the ice-choked St. Lawrence River during Québec City's winter carnival harks back to the days before large-span bridges when the North-Shore city relied on daring boatmen to keep communication with the South Shore open.

The streets of Montréal are jam packed for the Jazz Festival

**First Nations events keep tribal culture alive**

Festival, one of the most important on the continent. More than 300 movies from 60 countries are screened over the ten days of the festival, and it attracts such film-makers as Bille August, Terry Gilliam, Gus Van Sant and John Sayles, not to mention Canadians Atom Egoyan and Denys Arcand, and stars like Kevin Bacon, Orlando Bloom, Sandra Bullock, Matt Dillon, Dustin Hoffman, Bob Hoskins and Sean Penn.

Over on the east coast every October Nova Scotia's scenic Cape Breton Island hosts the Celtic Colours Festival – 10 days of concerts and dances that features musicians from all over the Celtic world, including Brittany,

Scotland, Wales and Ireland. But much of the considerable talent on display is local. Many Cape Bretoners are descended from immigrant Scots, and they've not only kept alive the music, they have produced some of the world's best fiddlers.

Music hardly figures in what Calgarians call the "greatest show on Earth." An exaggeration, maybe, but the Calgary Stampede is the world's biggest rodeo and the greatest outdoor show in Canada. For 10 days in July it draws cowboys from all over the world hoping for a share of the more than $1 million in prizes by busting broncos, riding bulls and roping calves. The spectacle attracts more than a million visitors each year, and they all seem to have a Stetson and cowboy boots, even if they work as accountants or lawyers the rest of the year.

# first nations art

Jean-Louis Newashish, an Atikamekw Indian from the Québec village of Manawan, still makes traditional canoes the old fashioned way, sewing sheets of birchbark to hand-cut cedar frames with cords of spruce roots. He decorates them by hand, too, with little motifs along the gunwales and a carefully etched Indian head, beaver or eagle on the bow.

A 4m (13ft) canoe – a 400-hour project – costs about $6,000, but it's worth every dime. A Newashish canoe isn't just a superbly maneuverable watercraft; it's a work of art that would

look almost as good hanging in your living room as it would crossing a lake at sunset.

The saga of Canada's relations with its aboriginal peoples – the Inuit of the far north and the dozens of Indian nations farther south – has been pretty dismal, often marked by distrust, prejudice and betrayal. Although Canada is one of the world's most prosperous countries, many of its First Nations people live in remote, squalid reservations where violence and substance-abuse are endemic. But Mr. Newashish's modest endeavor is a hopeful sign of a new pride emerging among Canada's aboriginals as they rediscover the richness of their cultures and find ways to adapt them to the 21st century.

It probably began in the 1950s, when the world discovered the fluid beauty created by Inuit artists out of soapstone and ivory. Their works have almost become a Canadian cliché like maple syrup and hockey fights. But their success with collectors helped transform the economies of many northern communities, and opened the door for other groups.

On the west coast, for example, native artists drew on the mythology of such Pacific nations as the Haida and the Squamish for inspiration. One of the most successful was the late Bill Reid, whose red-and-black prints of such spiritually significant creatures as the raven, the eagle and the orca are almost shockingly vivid. He also carved totems and, like Mr. Newashish far to the east,

Opposite and above: first Nations carvings represent stylized images of everyday life

Left: a Newashish canoe at the Canadian Museum of Civilization in Gatineau

built canoes. Not birchbark, but oceangoing cedar dug-outs decorated with intricately carved Haida designs.

The Museum of Anthropology (▶ 56) in Vancouver has some excellent exhibits, but one of the greatest monuments to the revival of native culture is the First Peoples' Gallery in the Canadian Museum of Civilization in Gatineau, Québec (▶ 98). Its extensive collection of Indian and Inuit arts includes one of Mr. Reid's canoes and the finest assembly of totem poles in the country. Equally impressive is the museum building itself, a huge structure with few straight lines that looks as if it were formed by the forces of nature rather than construction crews. It, too, is the work of an aboriginal artist – Douglas Cardinal, a Blackfoot from the plains of Alberta and one of Canada's leading architects.

# *Did You Know...?*

### It's big!
Canada, at nearly 10 million sq km (3.8 million sq miles) is the second-largest country in the world – bigger than both the U.S. and China and outsized only by Russia.

### C'est énorme
Québec – the largest of Canada's 10 provinces at 1.5 million sq km (579,000 sq miles) and the heart of French Canada – is nearly three times the size of France.

### Banting and Best
Two Canadians – Frederick Banting and Charles Best – gave diabetics around the world new hope in 1921 when they isolated insulin.

### Water, water...
Canada's lakes and rivers contain about 20 percent of the world's fresh water supply. Unfortunately for thirsty cities in the south and the US, 60 percent of it flows north.

### Royal Canada
Canada is a monarchy. The official head of state is the reigning monarch of Britain, represented in Canada by a Governor-General appointed by the federal government in Ottawa.

### Train lag
Scottish-Canadian railroad engineer Sir Sandford Fleming is responsible for jet lag. In 1878, he devized standard time zones to simplify train scheduling. Previously rail companies had to contend with hundreds of different local times.

### Sporting hero?
George Retzlaff, the first producer of C.B.C.'s Hockey Night in Canada, invented that staple of sports broadcasting – the "instant replay." He used a new "hot processor" in 1956 to develop a recording of a goal within 30 seconds.

### ...it's Superman!
The Man of Steel is half Canadian. Toronto-born Joe Shuster dreamed up the idea of Superman with his high-school pal, Jerry Seigel, of Cleveland, Ohio. Superman's girlfriend in the movies was played by the all-Canadian Margot Kidder.

### ...it's Superlative!
Man-made attractions include the world's largest Easter egg (in Vegreville, Alberta), the world's largest lobster (in Shediac, New Brunswick) and the world's largest elk (in Oranole, Manitoba).

### Winnipeg the Pooh
The real-life bear that inspired A.A. Milne's Winnie the Pooh stories was born in Canada. In fact, his name is short for Winnipeg, the capital of Manitoba.

# Finding Your Feet

# First Two Hours

## Arriving in Canada
There are scheduled international flights to all of the airports listed below, with linking flights to many domestic airports. All the airports listed below offer full transportation services, duty-free shops, currency exchange facilities and bookstores, and most are completely wheelchair accessible. In addition to airport taxes and security charges, some Canadian airports levy an Airport Improvement Fee (usually $10–15 per person) on departing international passengers, and this must be paid directly to the airport.

## Vancouver International Airport
- **Vancouver International Airport** is 6.5km (4 miles) south of the city in the suburb of Richmond.
- The **Airporter bus** (www.yvrairporter.com) links the airport with the city's major hotels, the cruise ship terminal and the downtown bus depot/train station. Buses depart from the International and Domestic arrivals level every 20 minutes 9 am–8 pm, half-hourly from 9 pm–11.30 pm. One-way fare $12, child $5, family $24. **Public buses** are also available: No. 424 picks up at the domestic terminal, 100 and 98B from the Airport Bus Terminal. Fares depend on destination, and you need the exact amount in cash. There are also **courtesy shuttles** to some hotels.
- Licensed **taxis** line up outside the terminals 24 hours a day, and are metered. The fare to downtown is about $25, assuming no traffic hold-ups. Wheelchair-accessible taxis are also available.
- **Car rental** agencies with desks at the airport include Alamo, Avis, Budget, Hertz, National and Thrifty. Discount, Dollar and Enterprise have offices nearby and will pick up.

## Calgary International Airport
- The **airport** is 17.5km (11 miles) northeast of downtown Calgary, about a half-hour drive.
- A number of companies operate **shuttle buses** to various destinations. Airport Shuttle Express Ltd (www.airportshuttleexpress.com) operate five- and ten-seat vehicles at about half the cost of a taxi into downtown Calgary, and shuttles to various ski resorts. Their airport check-in counter is on the Arrivals level. Calgary Transit bus 57 serves the airport.
- **Car rental** agencies with desks in the airport include Alamo, Avis, Budget, Hertz, National and Thrifty. Discount, Dollar and Enterprise have locations nearby.

## Ottawa: Macdonald-Cartier International Airport
- **Ottawa Airport** is 17.5km (11 miles) from downtown.
- Shuttle **buses** operate between the airport and downtown ($9 one way). There is also the hotel shuttle to various downtown hotel locations, which runs every half hour between 5.35 am and 12.05 am ($12 one way, $10 each for a party of two, $9 each for a party of three; under 16s free).
- **Taxis** to downtown cost around $30.
- **Car rental** Alamo/National, Avis, Budget, Enterprise and Hertz all have desks in the Arrivals area.

# Toronto: Pearson International Airport

- **Pearson International** is 29km (18 miles) northwest of downtown.
- Shuttle **buses** leave for Toronto's major hotels every half hour from 6 am–12:10 am ($12.50 one way).
- **Taxis** cost around $40, including taxes, to downtown. Toronto taxi drivers aren't all familiar with the entire city, so unless you are headed for a major hotel or landmark building you will probably need to tell them the street address and its nearest major intersection.
- **Car rental** agencies are located in the parking garages of terminals 1 (basement level), 2 and 3 (ground level). Companies include Alamo/National, Avis, Budget, Dollar/Thrifty and Hertz. Discount and Enterprise are not located in the airport, but will pick up and drop off there by arrangement.

# Montréal: Pierre Elliott Trudeau International Airport

- Montréal's **former Dorval Airport** is undergoing a complete transformation. Renamed to honor the former prime minister, it is operational, but work will be ongoing through 2006. It is on Montréal island, 22.5km (14 miles) southwest of downtown.
- A **bus** shuttle service, L'Aérobus, links the airport with downtown (and with Mirabel Airport). The one-way fare to downtown is $12 (child $8.25); transfer to Mirabel is free for passengers making flight connections within 15 hours.
- A **taxi** to downtown will cost around $30, and around $70 to Mirabel Airport.
- For **car rental**, Alamo, Avis, Budget, Hertz, National and Thrifty all have desks in the airport.

# Halifax International Airport

- With a multi-million dollar improvement completed in 2003, **Halifax International Airport** now offers greatly enhanced facilities. It is about 40km (26 miles) north of downtown, off exit 6 of Highway 102. The drive by car to downtown takes 30–45 minutes, depending on traffic conditions.
- The **AirBus shuttle bus** runs to downtown at regular intervals from about 8 am to 11 pm daily ($12 one way). Services to other Nova Scotia and Prince Edward Island destinations are also available (tel: 902/873-1223 for information).
- **Taxis** wait outside the arrivals building, and the fare to downtown is about $40.
- **Car rental** desks in the airport are operated by Alamo/National, Avis, Budget, Enterprise, Thrifty/Dollar and Hertz.

## Tourist Information Offices

Each province and territory has a main tourism office, in addition to numerous information points in the towns and cities.
- **Alberta**: Travel Alberta, Suite 760, 999 - 8 Street SW, Calgary, Alberta T2R 1J5, tel: 403/509-2590; www.travelalberta.com
- **British Columbia**: Tourism British Columbia, Box 9830, Southern Provincial Government, Victoria, British Columbia V8W 9W5, tel: 250/387-1642; www.HelloBC.com
- **Manitoba**: Travel Manitoba, 155 Carlton Street, 7th Floor, Winnipeg R3C 3H8, tel: 204/945-3796; www.travelmanitoba.com
- **New Brunswick**: Department of Tourism and Parks, PO Box 6000, Fredericton, New Brunswick E3B 5H1, tel: 506/457-6701; www.TourismNewBrunswick.ca

- **Newfoundland & Labrador**: Department of Tourism, Culture and Recreation, PO Box 8700, 2nd Floor, West Block, Confederation Building, Higgins Line, St. John's, Newfoundland, tel: 709/729-2830; www.gov.nl.ca
- **Northwest Territories**: NWT Arctic Tourism, Box 610, Yellowknife, Northwest Territories X1A 2N5, tel: 867/873-7200; www.nwttravel.nt.ca
- **Nova Scotia**: Nova Scotia Tourism and Culture, PO Box 456, Halifax, Nova Scotia B3J 2R5, tel: 902/425-5781; www.novascotia.com
- **Nunavut**: Nunavut Tourism, Box 1450, Iqaluit, Nunavut X0A 0H0, tel: 867/979-6551; www.nunavutTourism.com
- **Ontario**: Ontario Tourism, 10th Floor, Hearst Block, 900 Bay Street, Toronto, Ontario M7A 2E1, tel: 800/668-2746; www.ontariotravel.net
- **Prince Edward Island**: Tourism PEI, PO Box 940, Charlottetown, Prince Edward Island C1A 7M5, tel: 902/368-4444; www.peiplay.com
- **Québec**: Tourism Québec, PO Box 979, Montréal, Québec H3C 2W3, tel: 800/363-7777; www.bonjourquebec.com
- **Saskatchewan**: Tourism Saskatchewan, 1922 Park Street, Regina, Saskatchewan S4P 3V7, tel: 306/787-2300; www.sasktourism.com
- **Yukon**: Tourism Yukon, PO Box 2803, Whitehorse, Yukon Y1A 2C6, tel: 867/667-5034; www.touryukon.com

---

**Prices**
The cost of admission for museums and places of interest mentioned in the text is indicated by the following price categories
**Inexpensive** – under $4   **Moderate** – $5–$9   **Expensive** – more than $10

---

# Getting Around

## By Plane
Canada is a huge country, but it is not difficult to get around if you have the time. There's a network of domestic flights linking large and small towns and cities, plus some of the remote areas of the north. Domestic airlines include:

- **Air Canada Jazz** and **Tango**: two subsidiaries of the national airline, offering a range of services to around 70 Canadian destinations; www.aircanadajazz.com and www.flytango.com/en/
- **Air North**: links Vancouver, Calgary, Edmonton, Yukon, Northwest Territories and Alaska; www.airnorth.uk.net
- **Canadian North**: access to communities throughout the north from Calgary, Edmonton and Ottawa; www.canadiannorth.com
- **First Air**: flights to destinations in the north from Edmonton, Winnipeg, Ottawa and Montréal; www.firstair.ca
- **Jetsgo**: a low-cost airline linking most major cities in Canada; www.jetsgo.net
- **Westjet**: scheduled flights to domestic airports; www.westjet.com
- **ZIP**: low-fare Air Canada subsidiary, but operating independently in western Canada; www.4321zip.com

## By Train
The national rail company is **VIA Rail** (www.viarail.ca; in the UK, tel: 0845 644553), which operates an efficient, clean and comfortable service on its

comprehensive network. The famous transcontinental route offers a scenic journey of a lifetime in beautifully restored trains with observation cars. Economy and First-Class options are available, and you can purchase a **Canrail Pass** allowing 12 days of unlimited Economy travel within a 30-day period. Obtain tickets as far in advance as possible as seats reserved for Canrail Pass holders can be limited on some services. Special offers are frequently available on scheduled services.

**Scenic tours** include the fabulous **Rocky Mountaineer Railtours** (www.rockymountaineer.com) and **Skeena** route in the west. Great trips to take in eastern Canada include those run by the **Acadian Railway Company** (www.acadianrailway.com) and **Québec North Shore & Labrador Railway** (tel: 418/962-9411), while northern Ontario offers the **Algoma Central Railway** (www.agawacanyontourtrain.com) and **Ontario Northland** (www.northernontariotrains.com), which takes you to the edge of the Arctic. In the north, the **White Pass and Yukon Railway** (www.whitepassrailroad.com) is a spectacular narrow-gauge trip to Skagway, Alaska.

Many of Canada's major cities have a **rapid-transit** light railway system, including Calgary and Vancouver; Toronto's GO (Government of Ontario) Trains provide an excellent service to commuter satellite towns on double-decker trains.

**Subway** (métro; underground) systems are an important part of getting around in Toronto and Montréal, and both link to their underground shopping areas. Maps can be picked up at any subway station, or from tourist information offices.

## By Bus

Long-distance buses are a good budget option for seeing Canada – more comfortable than you might imagine, with air-conditioning and washrooms. **Greyhound Canada** (www.greyhound.ca) links Toronto with cities in western Canada and offers good leg-room, movies, music and snacks. There are many provincial bus companies offering intercity and local routes. Look in the *Yellow Pages*, or ask at tourist information offices.

The **Canada Pass** buys you 7, 10, 15, 21, 30, 45 or 60 days of unlimited travel on certain Greyhound and regional bus company services, plus Via Rail's Ottawa–Montréal and Toronto–Montréal routes. A **Rout-Pass** (www.routpass.com) will give you access to more than 35 intercity bus companies that operate in Ontario and Québec. It covers 15 consecutive days, and is available mid-April to mid-November.

## By Boat

### Cruises

A number of companies operate cruises on the Pacific and Atlantic coasts and along the St. Lawrence Seaway, including **Cunard** (www.cunard.com), **Holland America** (www.hollandamerica.com), **Norwegian Cruise Lines** (www.uk.ncl.com), **Princess Cruises** (www.princesscruises.co.uk), and **St. Lawrence River Cruise Lines Inc**. (www.stlawrencecruiselines.com). For lake and river cruises in the Canadian interior, contact the relevant tourist information office for details.

### Ferries

There are various ferry services giving access to offshore islands, or for hopping between coastal settlements. Advance booking is recommended for some services, particularly at peak times.
- Alaska Marine Highway (www.akferry.com) sail from Bellingham and Prince Rupert along the Inside Passage to Alaska.

- **Aquabus** (www.aquabus.bc.ca) and **Granville Island Ferries** (www.granvilleislandferries.bc.ca) operate passenger ferries around False Creek in downtown Vancouver, including commuter services and sightseeing trips.
- **BC Ferries** (www.bcferries.com) have daily services from Vancouver to Vancouver Island and the Gulf Islands, plus an Inside Passage service (► 178–179) and the scenic Bella Coola–Port Hardy service (► 8).
- **Black Ball Transport Inc** (www.cohoferry.com), **Victoria Clipper** (www.victoriaclipper.com) and **Victoria Express** (www.victoriaexpress.com) all offer services from Victoria, British Columbia to various destinations.
- **Bay and NFL Ferries** (www.nfl-bay.com) run services from Wood Island, Prince Edward Island to Caribou, Nova Scotia and from St. John, New Brunswick to Digby, Nova Scotia.
- **Marine Atlantic** (www.marine-atlantic.ca/index.html) provides access to Newfoundland from Cape Breton Island, Nova Scotia.
- **Ferries Services Newfoundland and Labrador** (tel: 709/535-6872) link Newfoundland with Labrador.
- **The Woodward Group** (tel: 1-800/563-6353) runs a service between St. Barbe, Newfoundland and Blanc Sablon, Québec.
- **Ontario Northland Ferries** (www.ontc.on.ca) have services from Tobermory to Montoulin Island and from Kindsville and Leamington to Pelee Island.

## By Taxi

Taxis are widely available in all towns and cities and can be picked up at taxi stands or booked by telephone. In Toronto (where you can also hail cabs on the street downtown) not all drivers are familiar with the entire city – you will need to tell them the street address *and* the nearest major intersection.

## Car Rental

Car rental is quite expensive in Canada, and there may be restrictions. Some companies will not let you take the vehicle outside the province in which it was rented, and if you want to drop off at a different location, surcharges can be extremely high. Make sure you get an unlimited mileage deal and full insurance coverage.

## Driving

Public transportation is best in downtown areas, or for covering long distances in a shortest time, but a car is invaluable everywhere else.

---

**Rules of the road**
- **Drive on the right** and overtake on the left, but on multilane highways you can overtake on any side – before changing lanes watch out for vehicles zipping past you on either side.
- Unless there's a sign indicating otherwise, you can **turn right on a red light**, as long as the road is clear. Always come to a complete stop first.
- At **four-way stops** (indicated by a black-and-white sign) whoever gets to the junction first gets to go first, then the other vehicles take their respective turn.
- At traffic lights, a **flashing green light** lets you turn left across the highway (sometimes you get a green arrow instead).
- **Road conditions** are generally good – though winter weather can cause potholes and cracked edges – and traffic is light once you get out of the cities. There are some unpaved roads in more remote areas.

# Accommodations

The recommended places to stay in this guide have been carefully selected to offer a cross-section of prices and styles, and each has been inspected and approved by the American Automobile Association (AAA). For details of the grading system, see page 40. Further information is available by visiting www.aaa.com. The selections in this book range from city hotels and upscale resorts of the highest international standard to bed-and-breakfasts in historic homes, plus simple motels and housekeeping (self-catering) cottages. Standards of accommodations are generally high and Canadians are renowned for their friendly hospitality. The AAA categorise the types of accommodations in the following way:

## Hotels
These vary in size, but all offer a full range of services, including a variety of eating options, stores, conference amenities and recreational activities.

## Resorts
Generally in the luxury bracket, resorts are aimed specifically at the vacation market and provide a variety of restaurants and an excellent range of leisure amenities, such as a golf course, or access to winter sports areas.

## Motels
Generally low-rise, with convenient parking, motels offer limited services – for instance, many have no restaurant or public areas and no recreational facilities, though this is not always the case. They are usually located close to main highways, but can be quite close to downtown areas.

## Bed-and-Breakfasts
A home-away-from-home atmosphere is usually the norm, and most will be owner-operated with friendly, personal service. A Continental or full hot breakfast is included in the room rate. Many bed-and-breakfasts are in interesting historic buildings or cozy family homes.

## Country Inns
These are similar in style to bed-and-breakfas, but are usually larger in scale with spacious public areas, and they will have a dining facility that serves at least breakfast and dinner.

## Lodges
Typically a low-rise building, often of rustic architecture and decor and with a restaurant. There are also fishing and hunting lodges, often in remote wilderness locations, that specialize in vacations for enthusiasts and organize the activities.

## Ranches
Offering entertainment and recreation with a Western theme, ranches usually provide all-inclusive packages to cover meals and activities such as horseback-riding and barbecues.

## Cottages
Usually a group of individual units in a rural location. They will incorporate a living area, cooking facilities and one or more bedrooms, and often have a verandah and/or lawned area with a barbecue.

## Condominiums/Apartments

Aimed at the vacation or extended-stay market, these consist primarily of a suite with living room, full kitchen, eating area and one or more bedrooms; studio apartments may combine the sleeping and living area.

## Hostels

Most of the major cities have low-cost hostel lodgings, usually in dormitories, but they may have some double and family rooms. They generally have cooking facilities, communal areas where you can get to know other hostelers. Barbecues and tours are sometimes on offer.

## University Residences

Some universities rent out their student accommodations during the long summer break. These usually take the form of single or double rooms with private bathrooms and a shared kitchen. They are fairly basic, but comfortable, and offer a budget option in a downtown (or close by) location.

## Reservations

Making reservations is advisable, particularly if you have special requirements or are touring Canada's vast empty spaces, but even in cities, you might have difficulty finding what you want at the last minute if there's a convention in town or a big festival taking place. You can often get the best room rates by reserving early. On the other hand, if you just show up somewhere and a room is available, you may well be able to strike a last-minute deal. It's always worth asking if any discounts or special offers are available (and mention the fact if you are a AAA or CAA member).

## AAA Diamond Ratings

The listings in this guide have all been inspected and approved by the American Automobile Association and use the following ratings system.

The ultimate in luxury and sophistication, these places are first class and the physical attributes are extraordinary in every manner. Often renowned, they offer a world-class and opulent experience. Staff offer meticulous service and exceed all expectations, while maintaining an impeccable standard of excellence. Many personalized services and amenities enhance an unmatched level of comfort.

Upscale establishments in which accommodations are refined and stylish. There's an enhanced level of quality throughout, and an extensive array of amenities combined with a high degree of hospitality, service and attention to detail. Highly proficient staff demonstrates a profound desire to meet or exceed guest expectations. Many of Canada's prominent, historic hotels are included in this category.

These places appeal to travelers with comprehensive needs, and have a distinguished style, including superior furnishings, amenities and level of comfort provided. Service is typically semi-formal and proficient.

More than basic lodgings, these establishments exhibit modest enhancements to the overall style, service and decor. They are usually informal and room rates offer good value.

Essentially, this category includes the no-frills accommodations that appeal to the budget-minded traveler, meeting the basic needs of comfort, cleanliness and hospitality.

# Food and Drink

Canada is one of the most multi-ethnic nations in the world, and this is reflected in the range of cuisines available in most cities. Standards are generally high and portions generous and, particularly to visitors from Europe, prices are very reasonable. Service is invariably friendly and efficient.

Home-grown, top-quality ingredients of all kinds, including organically grown produce, is plentiful: the Atlantic, Pacific and Arctic oceans provide wonderful seafood – notably east-coast lobsters and mussels and Alaskan king crabs; rivers are full of salmon at spawning time and lakes have some unusual freshwater fish. There's prime beef and pork (though lamb is not particularly plentiful here) and game including venison, bison and caribou. The southern climate is perfect for growing fruit and vegetables of every kind – juicy peaches and berries, grapes for Niagara and Okanagan wineries, several succulent varieties of corn (peaches-and-cream is one of the best), the famous Prince Edward Island potato and, of course, maple syrup.

## Restaurants
Types of restaurant vary enormously, with top-class establishments matching the best that the rest of the world has to offer. There is every kind of national theme you can imagine, together with traditional Western-style steak-houses. Lots of places have sidewalk or terrace seating to make the most of the summer weather, and all the major cities (and Niagara Falls) have revolving restaurants to show off their best views. Some restaurants offer table d'hôte, a set menu with a set price, a less expensive option than the à la carte menu.

## Bistros and Cafés
These tend to be informal, with simple but good food at reasonable prices, though some of the chic designer cafés in swanky downtown areas can be more pricey. Generally, though, this category includes lively cosmopolitan eateries full of noise and bustle, cozy cafés with a grandma's parlor atmosphere, and the quintessential 1950s-style diner. Victoria, British Columbia, is also famous for its English-style tearooms.

## Pubs and Bars
Food is increasingly on offer in pubs and bars, in the form of down-to-earth standards such as burgers, nachos, pasta, and fish and chips. Some offer more sophisticated fare, and brewpubs are a particularly attractive option, serving ales made on the premises.

## Opening Hours
- Generally **lunch** is served between noon and 3 pm.
- Sunday **brunch** is very popular and is usually available from 10:30 or 11 am until about 3:30 pm.
- **Dinner** service begins around 6 or 7 pm.
- Big cities have many restaurants that **stay open late** into the night, but in more rural areas and small towns, they usually close at 9 pm.
- Outside these general hours, some places open at 6:30 am for **breakfast**, and there's even occasional **24-hour service**.

### Reservations
It is always a good idea to reserve a table if the time or the place is important, but some places do not accept reservations – you just have to show up and wait if necessary.

### Payment
If you are planning on splitting the restaurant check between members of your party, you can let the wait staff know this, and they will be happy to issue separate checks. Make sure in advance that your credit or debit card is acceptable if you plan to pay by this method. Remember that taxes are additional to the menu prices.

### Tipping
The standard restaurant tip is 10–15 percent, but it's edging more towards 15 percent. You will generally get the option of adding it to your credit card payment. Tips are expected throughout the industry, even in pubs and the most inexpensive diners, where wages for wait staff are calculated on the basis that tips will bring it up to an acceptable level. Service is generally of a high standard in Canada, but if it is ever disappointing, you retain the right not to tip.

### What to Drink
- **Wine** is expensive in Canada, particularly the ones imported from Europe and the US, but there are some excellent domestic varieties from the wineries of the Niagara region and BC's Okanagan Valley that are well worth trying.
- In addition to the huge **brewing** giants Molson and Labatts, there are a number of microbreweries and brewpubs producing English-style ales. If you're in the Atlantic Provinces, sample the excellent beer from the Alexander Keith Brewery in Halifax.
- When it comes to **liquor**, Canadian Club is the national distillation. And if someone tells you to drink Canada Dry, it's not a challenge – they'll be referring to the ginger ale mixer.

### What to Eat
For an introduction to the idiosyncracies of Canadian cuisine, ➤ 22–23.

# Shopping

Canada is an incredible place to shop, not just for the huge and comprehensive range of goods available, but also for the friendly and helpful service, the constant availability of places to rest and get a bite to eat, easy parking (outside downtown areas, at least) and prices that are generally very attractive to visitors from abroad.

### Arts and Crafts
Outstanding hand-made items produced by First Nations and Inuit artists and artisans are to be found in stores and galleries throughout the country, including **native-run outlets** on reservations. These will offer a range of wonderful carvings in wood and soapstone, suede and leather clothing and moccasins, jewelry, drums and dreamcatchers (➤ 30–31).

Crafts introduced by the early **pioneers** from Europe include quilts, hooked rugs and household items, and these are available in many small-town specialty stores, as well as some of the living history "villages."

- **Art galleries**, such as the National Gallery of Canada (➤ 98) and Toronto's Art Gallery of Ontario (➤ 106), usually have a good selection of prints of paintings by First Nations artists and the Group of Seven (seven Canadian artists whose landscape paintings of Canadian scenes are particularly inspirational). They make excellent souvenirs.
- **Modern crafts**, including ceramics, glass and jewelry are also widely available, and local tourist offices can tell you where to find workshops and stores producing good-quality items.

## Clothing and Fashion
Not surprisingly, there are excellent ranges of **outdoor and winter-sports wear** designed to withstand extreme cold, and these are cheaper in the city malls than in the upscale mountain resorts. Canada has a number of accomplished and imaginative **fashion designers**, too, whose creations are available alongside international labels in the chic city boutiques.

## Shopping Malls
The fact that Canada has the two largest malls in the world – **West Edmonton Mall** in Edmonton, Alberta (➤ 82) and **Metrotown** in Burnaby, British Columbia (➤ 70) – give an idea of how important shopping is here. There are malls everywhere, even in quite small communities, and in the major cities they are huge, completely undercover to beat the winter weather, and generally surrounded by large parking lots. Often, malls also include movie theaters as well as the usual restaurants.

In addition to the regular malls, there are outlet malls full of big-name stores selling at discounted prices. You can get up to 70 percent off discontinued lines and surplus stock from designer clothing and sports footwear to household items and electronics.

## Markets
Market shopping is very popular, and all the major cities have permanent market locations where producers and wholesalers offer mountains of fresh fruit and vegetables, deli items, clothing, arts and crafts, often accompanied by street entertainers and the aroma of roasting coffee and food from nearby restaurants.

Check out the **Granville Island Public Market** in Vancouver, the **Forks Market** in Winnipeg, Ottawa's **Byward Market**, Toronto's **St. Lawrence Market**, **Maisonneuve**, **Jean-Talon** and **Atwater** markets in Montréal, the **Public Market** in Québec City, and **Boyce's Farmers' Market** in Fredericton, New Brunswick.

**Flea markets** are popular, too, most of them temporary but regular on a specific site. **Dr. Flea** in Toronto is in a permanent building, every weekend, and includes a farmers' market.

## Opening Hours
Stores are usually open Monday to Saturday from 9 or 10 am to 5:30 or 6 pm, with late opening on Thursday and Friday, and on Sunday from noon. However, times vary and big city stores may open well into the evening most days. The malls usually stay open until between 7:30 and 9 pm.

## Credit Cards
Canada is a plastic society, and credit and debit cards are widely accepted. However, it's always best to check whether your particular card is accepted before you get too far with your purchases. Some retailers use the system whereby you enter your four-digit security PIN into a machine rather than sign a sales docket, so you'll need to memorize your number.

# Entertainment

There's a rich cultural life in Canada and the arts in all their forms are strenuously and enthusiastically promoted at all levels, from national opera and ballet companies and provincial orchestras to small-town theaters. Nightlife includes live music venues, jazz and blues clubs, nightclubs and casinos with Las Vegas-style shows.

## Toronto
The **entertainment capital** of the country, Toronto has a thriving theater district hosting all the big Broadway-style blockbusters, magnificent state-of-the-art concert halls, intimate theaters and arts centers producing less mainstream works, stadiums for megastar rock concerts, and an internationally famous comedy club. It's also home to some of the best live music venues in the country, cool jazz clubs and the hottest dance clubs.

## Montréal
Montréal adds a touch of French *je-ne-sais-quoi* to its nightlife. Many theater productions are in French and you'd need a good grasp of the language to get the best out of the experience. There are English-language productions, too, and some movies are shown in their original language.

### The Best of the Rest
**Vancouver** is also very lively, with an excellent theater and music scene, and the provincial capitals of the **Prairies** also have plenty to offer, from their own symphony orchestras to the country music that suits their thriving cowboy culture. The cities of the **Maritimes** are smaller and quieter, perhaps a tad less sophisticated, but are not devoid of good theater, nightclubs and live music, and they have a world-famous heritage of Celtic-style fiddle music and dance. The **North** tends to fall back on its Gold Rush heritage, with vaudeville-style saloon shows and the like, and the most spectacular entertainment here might well be watching the *aurora borealis* while you keep warm with a mug of hot chocolate.

### Festivals
Thousands of festivals take place throughout the country every month, celebrating just about everything – the arts, food and drink, national cultures, sports, wildlife, even the winter weather. To find out what's on where contact the relevant tourist information offices.

### Spectator Sports
**Hockey** and **curling** are the winter obsessions, with **baseball**, **Canadian football** and **basketball** taking over in summer. There's healthy rivalry, plenty of vocal support and a good atmosphere among the crowds at the stadiums. There are **racetracks** within easy reach of all the major cities for thorough-bred and harness racing – Toronto's Woodbine track hosts the major classic races. The **Canadian Golf Open** is held at a different course each year (details from the Royal Canadian Golf Association, www.rcga.org).

### Tickets
A number of theaters, stadiums and sport venues use **Ticketmaster** to sell tickets for events. Buy online at www.ticketmaster.ca or check them out in the *Yellow Pages*. The face value of tickets generally includes national and provincial taxes.

# British Columbia
# and the Rockies

# Getting Your Bearings

At first glance British Columbia seems to have it all, and in-depth exploration only reinforces that first impression. In addition to the beautiful and historic provincial capital of Victoria there's the vibrant city of Vancouver – both cities are consistently on the list of best places in the world to live – plus interesting towns and small artsy enclaves dotted around the interior and islands. There's history here, too, with a strong First Nations culture and reminders of the early pioneers and Gold-Rush days.

Hiking in the mountains of the West is well rewarded

The landscapes in BC are spectacular – magnificent mountains, the wilderness areas of the north, rain forests, hot springs, rolling ranchlands and river valleys, vineyards producing first-class wines, and the orchards of the Okanagan, which is one of North America's premier fruit-growing regions. The Pacific coastline, with its forested fjords, wide inlets, islands and the legendary Inside Passage, offers some of the best scuba-diving sites in the world, superb whale-watching, scenic coastal cruises, and unspoiled beaches. This chapter also encompasses the part of the province of Alberta that lies within the Rocky Mountains.

British Columbia is the only province in Canada where the average winter temperatures remain above freezing point, and yet up in the Rockies and Coast Mountains the winter sports are excellent. Whistler is the most famous ski resort, heading a list of places where you can enjoy downhill and cross-country (Nordic) skiing, snowboarding, dog-sledding and extreme sports. Summer activities include great golf, horseback riding, river-rafting and coastal cruises, wildlife safaris and hiking.

Cultural life is diverse and absorbing, encompassing the full range of arts, entertainment and nightlife. Vancouver and Victoria are the hotspots, with year-round programs that include all kinds of festivals, an opera season, world-class classical performances and a variety of theater productions. There is also a huge range of dance clubs, jazz and blues venues, live rock and comedy clubs. Night or day in BC and the Rockies, you could stay for ever and not see everything.

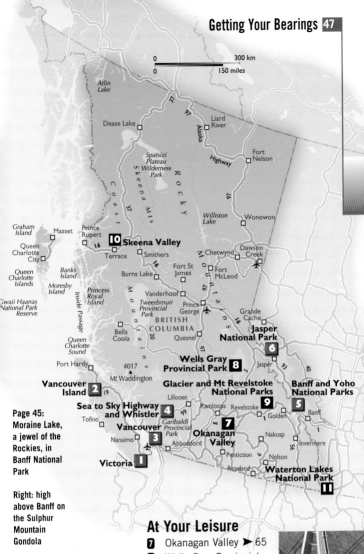

0   300 km

0   150 miles

Atlin Lake

Dease Lake

Liard River

Alaska   Highway

Fort Nelson

Spatsizi Plateau Wilderness Park

Skeena Mts

R O C K Y

Williston Lake

Wonowon

Coast

Graham Island

Masset

Prince Rupert

**10 Skeena Valley**

Queen Charlotte City

Queen Charlotte Islands

Banks Island

Moresby Island

Terrace

Smithers

Chetwynd

Dawson Creek

Gwaii Haanas National Park Reserve

Princess Royal Island

Inside Passage

Burns Lake

Fort St James

Fort McLeod

Vanderhoof

Tweedsmuir Provincial Park

Prince George

M o u n t a i n s

BRITISH COLUMBIA

Grande Cache

**Jasper National Park 6**

Bella Coola

Quesnel

Queen Charlotte Sound

Port Hardy

4017 ▲ Mt Waddington

**Wells Gray Provincial Park 8**

Jasper

**Vancouver Island 2**

**Glacier and Mt Revelstoke National Parks**

**Banff and Yoho National Parks**

**Sea to Sky Highway and Whistler 4**

Lillooet

Kamloops

Revelstoke

**9**

Golden

Banff

**5**

Tofino

**Vancouver 3**

Garibaldi Provincial Park

**7**

**Okanagan Valley**

Nanaimo

Abbotsford

Nakusp

Invermere

Penticton

Nelson

**Victoria 1**

Rossland

**Waterton Lakes National Park**

**11**

Page 45: Moraine Lake, a jewel of the Rockies, in Banff National Park

Right: high above Banff on the Sulphur Mountain Gondola

Breathtakingly beautiful, this region incorporates vibrant cities, fascinating First Nations heritage and outdoor activities in superlative national parks.

# BC and the Rockies in Seven Days

## Day 1

**Morning** Start at Vancouver Island, with an exploration of **1** Victoria (➤ 50–51). Stroll along the waterfront walk around the Inner Harbour, then head for the **Royal British Columbia Museum** and Thunderbird Park.

**Lunch** Visit the Pacific Restaurant and Terrace on Belleville Street (250/380-4458) for creative West Coast cuisine.

**Afternoon** Take a quick look around the **Maritime Museum**, then head down to the harbor for a sightseeing cruise. Back on land, go for afternoon tea at the Fairmont Empress Hotel (➤ 67), a Victoria institution. Walk it off by doing a bit of browsing in the city's attractive shopping streets.

**Evening** Catch a show at one of Victoria's excellent theaters and pop into the Sticky Wicket Pub (➤ 51) for a beer.

## Day 2

**Morning** Head out of Victoria to explore the rest of **2** Vancouver Island (➤ 52–53) via Oak Bay and **Butchart Gardens**, then continue up to Duncan.

**Lunch** Try to attend the noon salmon barbecue at the **Quw'utsun Cultural and Conference Centre** (➤ 52) and stay on to tour the exhibits there.

**Afternoon** Drive up through Nanaimo and Port Alberni and head for Tofino (➤ 53), out on the west coast. Take a stroll on **Long Beach**.

**Evening** Have a meal and stay overnight at the Wickanninish Inn (tel: 250/725-3100 or 800/333-4604; $$$).

## Day 3

**Morning** Start out early for the drive back down to Nanaimo, and catch the ferry to **3** Vancouver (➤ 54–57). From the ferry terminal make your way to Granville Island.

**Lunch** Have lunch at the Dockside Restaurant at the Granville Island Hotel (➤ 67).

**Afternoon** Spend a leisurely afternoon strolling around Granville Island, browsing its arts and crafts and soaking up the atmosphere. Find a sidewalk café for a break.

**Evening** Sample some of Vancouver's famous nightlife, and have dinner at the Blue Water Café on Hamilton Street (tel: 604/688-8078; $$$).

# Day 4

**Morning** Still in Vancouver, visit the excellent **Museum of Anthropology**, then head over to Chinatown for a stroll around the **Dr. Sun Yat-Sen Classical Chinese Garden**.
**Lunch** Enjoy an authentic Chinese lunch at one of the many restaurants in Chinatown.
**Afternoon** Drive the **4 Sea to Sky Highway** (► 58–59) up to **Whistler** (► 59) and take the Whistler Village Gondola to the top of Whistler Mountain. Relax over a cup of tea on one of the sundecks and enjoy the view.
**Evening** If the Fairmont Chateau Whistler hotel (tel:1-800/684-6344 is beyond your budget, stay elsewhere and just come here for dinner.

# Day 5

**Morning** Drive back to Vancouver and fly to Banff, then rent a car to explore **5 Banff and Yoho National Parks** (► 60–62).
**Lunch** Feast on buffalo steak or wild salmon at the rustic Buffalo Mountain Lodge (tel: 403/410-7414) on Tunnel Mountain Road.
**Afternoon** Visit the **Cave and Basin National Historic Site**, then take the **Sulphur Mountain Gondola** for spectacular views and a hike in the mountains.
**Evening** Have an early evening soak in **Banff Hot Springs**, and enjoy a relaxing evening in the town of Banff.

# Day 6

**Morning** Set out as early as possible on the **Bow Valley Parkway** to **Lake Louise**(► 61). After soaking up the view before the tour-bus crowds arrive, pick up some picnic provisions in Lake Louise Village, then take the **Icefields Parkway** north (► 180–181).
**Lunch** There are picnic tables and restrooms at Bow Lake, Herbert Lake, Saskatchewan Crossing and Coleman on the Icefields Parkway.
**Afternoon** Stop at the Icefields Centre for a pre-booked (tel: 877/423-7433) "Snocoach" trip (expensive) onto the Athabasca Glacier, then continue north to **Jasper**.
**Evening** Treat yourself to a night at the Fairmont Jasper Park Lodge (tel 780/852-3301; toll-free 800/554-1811; $$$).

# Day 7

**Morning** Drop in at the interesting Jasper Information Centre in **6 Jasper National Park** (► 63–64), then take the Jasper Tramway up **Whistlers Mountain** for a refreshing hike to the summit.
**Lunch** Eat in the restaurant at the top of Whistlers Mountain.
**Afternoon/evening** Drive to **Maligne Lake**, stroll the lakeshore and rent a boat to paddle over to Spirit Island. Later find a place with a westerly view and stick around to see the sun set over the mountains.

# ❶ Victoria

The provincial capital of British Columbia is incredibly pretty, with a wealth of historic buildings, a lovely harborfront and all the main attractions within a few city blocks. Known as "Canada's Garden City," it has colorful floral displays everywhere you turn, and though it is a sophisticated city, Victoria is proud to maintain a "village" atmosphere.

More than a touch of British influence lingers on – double-decker buses, red telephone booths, cricket games in Beacon Hill Park, and English-style shopping streets lined with stores selling crafts and souvenirs. Market Square has a great atmosphere, and Fan Tan Alley in Chinatown is Canada's narrowest street, with lots of tiny stores.

Victoria has one of the finest natural harbors in the world and was once the regional headquarters of the Hudson's Bay Company and a major port for the British Navy's Pacific Fleet. Now the **Inner Harbour**, overlooked by the imposing, copper-domed Parliament Buildings and the grand Empress Hotel, is the focal point of the city, full of pleasure craft, ferries, sightseeing and whale-watching boats, and flightseeing floatplanes. This is the atmospheric heart of Victoria, bustling with crews from the boats, day-trippers and street entertainers.

Close to the Parliament Buildings is the excellent **Royal British Columbia Museum**, which should not be missed. Highlights include a series of superb natural history dioramas portraying various BC environments and the wonderful First Nations galleries, with reconstructions of dwellings, totem poles and Haida carvings. The modern history galleries feature a fascinating old town street exhibit, a cannery and a replica of HMS *Discovery*. The museum also houses the National Geographic IMAX theater. Just behind the museum, **Thunderbird Park** has the best collection of totem poles in the world.

At the **Maritime Museum of British Columbia** you can learn all about explorers such as George Vancouver, James Cook and Sir Francis Drake, whalers and fishermen, merchants and military vessels. Also on display is the *Tilikum*,

➕ 202 B1

**Tourism Victoria**
✉ 4th Floor, 31 Bastion Square ☎ 250/414-6999, www.tourismvictoria.com; also Visitor Centre at 812 Wharf Street ☎ 250/953-2033

**Royal British Columbia Museum**
✉ 675 Belleville Street ☎ 250/356-7226 or 888/447-7977 ⏰ Daily 9–5, closed Dec 25 and Jan 1 💰 Expensive ℹ Gift shop

**Maritime Museum of British Columbia**
✉ 28 Bastion Square ☎ 250/385-4222 ext 102, www.mmbc.bc.ca
⏰ Daily 9:30–4:30 (to 5:30 mid-Jun to mid-Sep). Closed Dec 25
💰 Moderate

an 11.5-m (38-ft) native dugout canoe that went round the world at the turn of the 20th century. Across from the museum, Bastion Square is the site of Fort Victoria, the original settlement here.

**Oak Bay** is one of the most attractive suburbs of the city – and one of the most English. Its stately avenues are lined by large homes with colorful gardens, and you'll see the best architecture along Marine Drive on the rocky coastline. The oak trees that gave the settlement its name are Garry oaks, which are native to the island and have become quite rare.

**Opposite: Thunderbird Park has some splendid totums**

### TAKING A BREAK

Go to the **Fairmont Empress Hotel** (➤ 67) for afternoon tea or call in at the **Sticky Wicket Pub** on Douglas Street – two Victoria institutions that reflect the British heritage.

**Victoria's busy Inner Harbour is the focus of the city**

## VICTORIA: INSIDE INFO

**Top tips** If you plan to take a **whale-watching trips** from Victoria, make sure the one you select is a member of the Whale Watch Operators Association, which regulates the industry to ensure the safety of the passengers and the whales.
• There are lots of **sightseeing boats** moored up at the Inner Harbour, but you can't do better than the one operated by the Victoria Harbour Ferry. Quaint vessels, carrying a maximum of 12 passengers, tour the Inner and Outer harbors and continue out to Gorge Park, north of the city, all for $12.

**Hidden gem** The diminutive **Abkhazi Garden** on Fairfield Road was originally laid out in 1946 by Georgian Prince and Princess Abkhazi, and is a delightful half-hectare (1 acre), with mature trees and flowering shrubs. It was saved from the developers shovel in 1999 by the Land Conservancy of British Columbia, who are still struggling to cover the mortgage repayments.

# 2 Vancouver Island

Stretching about 500km (300 miles) from tip to tip, Vancouver Island is separated from the mainland by a narrow stretch of water that sets it apart in more ways than one. Though it's home to the provincial capital, there's a particular tranquility and a more laid-back atmosphere here. With its temperate climate, the island has a burgeoning wine industry, year-round golf and a permanent population of orcas offshore.

**Windswept Long Beach, in the Pacific Rim National Park, is great for beachcombing**

Heading north out of Victoria, the first big attraction is the famous **Butchart Gardens**, which began as a project to pretty-up a worked out quarry and developed into one of Canada's most glorious gardens. Farther north, **Duncan** is famous for its totem poles – more than 80 of them – each of which depicts a First Nations legend or a real family history. There's a strong Cowichan presence in the area, and their superb **Quw'utsun Cultural and Conference Centre** offers an insight into their history and lifestyle. It includes the world's largest carving house, where in summer you can watch craftsmen in action. The center also organizes three-course salmon barbecues (Jul–Sep, Thu–Sat at noon; $35, child $26), which feature traditional songs and dancing. To the west, Lake Cowichan is at the heart of the island's principal wine region.

A little way north is **Nanaimo**, with a fine natural harbor that's home to a working fishing fleet as well as the many pleasure craft. Main attractions are the tiny, white-painted **Bastion**, built by the Hudson's Bay Company in 1853, and the **Nanaimo District Museum**, which has good displays on local First Nations and the coal-mining industry.

Beyond Nanaimo, at Parksville, Highway 4 heads west to **Port Alberni**, the main center for the **Pacific Rim National Park**. The park protects 400sq km (193sq miles) of some of the most diverse and abundant ecosystems in North America, including virgin temperate rain forest, superb beaches (notably **Long Beach**) and remote islands. It's also on the migration routes of many whale species. Summer sunsets here are as magnificent as the winter storms. Bounded on the west by the Pacific Ocean and on the east by the aptly named Insular Mountains, there remains a tangible sense of being cut off from the world. The park also protects more than 290 native archeological sites. **Tofino**, at the northern extremity, offers various excursions, and there's a boardwalk through the forest to **Hotsprings Cove**, where naturally hot water flows into rock pools where you can bathe overlooking the ocean.

The northern tip of the island is capped by the **Cape Scott Provincial Park**, a forested wilderness that's home to black bears, cougars, wolves and deer. It has a spectacular coastline where sea lions and seals bask on the rocks and offshore islands.

## TAKING A BREAK

The restaurant at the **Wickaninnish Inn** (near Tofino, tel: 250/723-3100) has a wonderful location on a rocky headland and great seafood.

---

🕂 202 B2

**Tourism Vancouver Island**
✉ 203–335 Wesley Street, Nanaimo
☎ 250/754-3500; www.islands.bc.ca

**Butchart Gardens**
✉ 800 Benvenuto Avenue, Brentwood Bay
☎ 250/652-4422 or 866/652-4422,
www.butchartgardens .com 🕓 Daily 9–5, Apr;
9–6, May; 9–7, early Jun; 9 am–10:30 pm, mid-
Jun–Aug; 9–9, early Sep; 9–5, late Sep; 9–4:30,
early Oct; 9–4, late Oct; 9–3:30, Nov; 9–9, early
Dec;  9 am–10 pm, mid-Dec–early Jan; 9–3:30,
mid-Jan–Feb; 9–4, Mar 🎟 Expensive

**Quw'utsun' Cultural and Conference Centre**
✉ 200 Cowichan Way, Duncan ☎ 250/746-
8119, www.quwutsun.ca ✉ Daily 9–6,
May–Sep;  10–5 rest of year 🎟 Expensive

**Nanaimo District Museum and Bastion**
✉ 100 Cameron Road, Nanaimo ☎ 250/753-
1821, www. nanimo.museum.bc.ca 🕓 Daily
10–5. Closed Sun–Mon in winter (Bastion
summer only) 🎟 Inexpensive

**Wickaninnish Interpretive Centre**
✉ Long Beach 🕓 Daily 10:30–6 mid-May to
mid-Sep

---

## VANCOUVER ISLAND: INSIDE INFO

**Top tips** A great way to get from the southern part of the island to points north is via the **ferry** (for vehicles and passengers) that runs from Brentwood Bay to Mill Bay. It's not only a short-cut, it's a wonderfully scenic route.
• To walk the **West Coast Trail** you'll need to obtain a permit from the national park authority and attend an orientation session.

**Hidden gem** The **North Island Wildlife Recovery Centre** in Errington, near Parksville (open daily 10–4 Apr–Oct; all year for animal drop-off), cares for sick, injured or orphaned wildlife, with a view to releasing as many as possible back into the wild. In addition to its nature museum and any animals that happen to have been brought in, you'll see permanent resident Brian the Eagle. After his beak was damaged in a shooting incident he was provided with a prosthetic version that was devised and fitted by a local dentist.

# Vancouver

Vancouver is constantly at the top of the "Best Places in the World to Live" list, and with good reason. A glittering downtown sits astride the Fraser River estuary, encircled by the waters of the Burrard Inlet, English Bay and False Creek; to the north is the magnificent backdrop of the snow-capped Coast Mountains, while the foreground includes the distinctive Canada Place and the leafy expanse of Stanley Park. It's also a supremely cosmopolitan city with lots to see and do.

**Vancouver ferry rides are as good as sightseeing trips**

A good place to start is in the oldest part of town, **Gastown**. It takes its name from "Gassy" Jack Leighton, who opened a bar here in 1859 to serve workers in the local lumber industry, and the community that soon developed was incorporated in 1869 and named Granville. Today, its cobblestoned alley-

## VANCOUVER: INSIDE INFO

**Top tips** The **Vancouver City Passport** offers discounts of up to 50 percent at around 35 of the city's attractions, restaurants and museums. Call 604/694-2489 or 877/694-2489 or order online at www.vancouverattractions.ca.
• Even getting around this lively city is fun, with **Aquabus**, **Seabus** and **ferry services** linking waterfront areas, the **Skytrain** whisking you around on land, largely on elevated sections with wonderful views, and the **Downtown Historic Railway** making short tours on an old interurban tram.

**Hidden gem** Dwarfed by the surrounding skyscrapers, the tiny **Christ Church Cathedral** (tel: 604/682-3849) is one of very few 19th-century buildings still standing in the downtown area, and has wonderful Douglas fir roof timbers and some pretty stained-glass windows, including three by William Morris in the vestibule at the office entrance.

ways and courtyards are lined with restored brick buildings
housing boutiques, antiques stores, art galleries and restau-
rants that can occupy a pleasant couple of hours wandering.
Look for the famous Steam Clock, the world's first, on the
corner of Water and Cambie streets (performances on the
quarter-hour) and the statue of Gassy Jack on Maple Tree
Square. Gastown's newest attraction, opened in 2004, is the
massive **Storyeum**, where live storytellers and performers use
imaginative sets and technological devices to tell the tale of
the West Coast and its people. History repeats itself here
every half-hour in summer, hourly in winter.

At Cambie Street, you can pick up the Silk Road walking
route (identified with colored banners), which leads to the
**Millennium Gate** entrance to **Chinatown** and beyond, incor-
porating all of the attractions in this exotic neighborhood.
After San Francisco, Vancouver has the largest Chinese
community in North America, and is full of stores selling all
kinds of Oriental goods. Go to the **Chinese Cultural Centre**
to discover why Vancouver has such a large Chinese popula-
tion and how they have contributed to city and national
culture. They lead guided walking tours through Chinatown
in summer. There's a wonderful night market, too, in summer.
The restaurants offer superb authentic cuisine and attractions

Stanley Park is a great place for recreation within the city

include the beautiful **Dr. Sun Yat-Sen Classical Chinese Garden**. Replicating a 14th-century Ming scholar's garden, it reflects the subtle balance between yin and yang, with gardens, courtyards, pavilions, bridges and covered galleries. It was constructed by Chinese workers, and no nails, screws or power tools were used.

A reminder, in Stanley Park, of BC's strong First Nations heritage

Vancouver has a number of fine museums, but if you have time for only one of them, make sure it's the **Museum of Anthropology** at the University of British Columbia. Its vast, 15-m (49-ft) high entrance hall contains towering totems and massive sculptures from West Coast First Nations tribes. Leading on from here are galleries of ethnographic materials from many parts of the world, including some 6,000 objects relating to the local First Nations. The highlight of the entire collection is the enormous *The Raven and the First Men*, by Bill Reid (▶ 31), displayed in the Rotunda. Real museum buffs can also visit the **Vancouver Museum**, **Science World**, and a clutch of specialist museums covering subjects from minerals to maritime matters to model trains – and there's the **BC Sports Hall of Fame**, too.

It is absolutely obligatory to spend some time on **Granville Island**, with its atmospheric narrow streets, high-quality artists' and artisans' workshops and galleries, and street entertainers. This is also home to some of the city's hottest restaurants and nightspots, innovative theater companies and comedy clubs. The **Public Market** has a wonderful array of fresh foods, crafts, flowers and coffee shops, and there are some unusual and quirky items in the island's stores.

Bringing the countryside right into the city, **Stanley Park** is a huge green oasis jutting out into the Burrard Inlet, 400ha (1,000 acres) that incorporates unspoiled natural woodland, parkland, beaches, playgrounds and all kinds of recreational facilities. It's a haven for wildlife as well as Vancouverites. In addition to the tennis courts, lawn bowling and swimming pools, you can cycle or rollerblade around the Seawall that encircles the park. For kids there's a farmyard, miniature railway, waterpark and swimming pool, as well as the superb **Vancouver Aquarium Marine Science Centre**. It's the largest in Canada, and among the 60,000-plus creatures here, you can get up close to beluga whales, sharks, sea lions, sea otters and dolphins.

The **North Shore** has some of the best outdoor attractions, including 1,250-m (4,100-ft) **Grouse Mountain**, where the Skyride gondola will whisk you up to the top for a panoramic vista. There's a First Nations feast house and cultural center up here, and the **Refuge for Endangered Wildlife**, where you can see orphaned grizzly bears, cared for until they can be returned to the wild. All of this is within a few minutes of downtown, as is the **Capilano Regional Park**, which protects an area of first-growth temperate rain forest with some huge Douglas firs. Those with a head for heights can cross the very strong, but disconcertingly pliable **Capilano Suspension Bridge**, spanning the gorge high above the Capilano River.

The splendid ship's figurehead of the *Empress of Japan* can be found in Stanley Park

In contrast to the sights, it's worth while just soaking up the atmosphere of the various neighborhoods – upscale Yaletown, with its designer stores, hip pubs and galleries; cosmopolitan Kitsilano, full of trendy cafés and clothes; and Commercial Drive, Vancouver's "Little Italy."

## TAKING A BREAK

The **Granville Island Coffee House** (tel: 604/682-7865; $), behind the Arts Club Theatre, has good snacks and light lunches, plus 30 minutes' free internet/email access for customers.

---

✚ 202 C2

**Vancouver Tourist Information Centre**
✉ Waterfront Centre, 200 Burrard Street
☎ 604/683-2000, www.vancouvertourism.com

**Storyeum**
✉ 142 Water Street, Gastown ☎ 604/687-8142, www.storyeum.com ⏰ Daily 9–7, Jul–Oct; 10–6, Nov–Apr 💷 Expensive

**Dr. Sun Yat-Sen Classical Chinese Garden**
✉ 578 Carrall Street ☎ 604/662-3207 or 604/689-7133, www.vancouverchinesegarden.com ⏰ Daily 10–6, May to mid-Jun and Sep; 9:30–7, mid-Jun to Aug; 10–4:30 Oct–Apr. Closed Dec 25 and Jan 1 💷 Moderate

**Museum of Anthropology**
✉ 6393 Marine Drive NW ☎ 604/822-5087 ⏰ Daily 10–5 (also 5–9pm Tue), mid-May to Aug; Tue 11–9, Wed–Sun 11–5, rest of year. Closed Dec 25 💷 Moderate

**Science World**
✉ 1455 Québec Street ☎ 604/443-7440 ⏰ Mon–Fri 10–5, Sat–Sun 10–6 💷 Expensive

**Vancouver Museum**
✉ 1100 Chestnut Street, Vannier Park ☎ 604/736-4431 ⏰ Daily 10–5 (also 5–9 Thu) 💷 Expensive

**Vancouver Aquarium**
✉ 845 Avison Way ☎ 604/659-3474, www.vanaqua.org ⏰ Daily 9:30–7, Jul–Aug; 10–5:30 rest of year 💷 Expensive

**Grouse Mountain**
✉ 6400 Nancy Greene Way, North Vancouver ☎ 604/980-9311, www.grousemountain.com ⏰ Daily 9 am–10 pm 💷 Expensive

# 4 Sea to Sky Highway and Whistler

There's romance in the name of the Sea to Sky Highway, but it's far surpassed by the scenery. Craggy mountains, cloaked in rain forest and cut through with foaming white waterfalls, tower above the blue water of Howe Sound. Inland are lake-studded valleys, alpine meadows, extinct volcanoes and glaciers. And it's all within a two-hour drive from Vancouver.

*An atmospheric mist rises over beautiful Howe Sound*

The starting point of the Sea to Sky Highway, more prosaically Highway 99, is at the pretty little town of **Horseshoe Bay**, on the tip of West Vancouver. Its painted clapboard houses cluster on the steep hillside above a bay dotted with sailboats from the marina. The harbor is also a terminal for ferries

## SEA TO SKY HIGHWAY AND WHISTLER: INSIDE INFO

**Top tips** Bring something **warm to wear** if you're going underground at the BC Museum of Mining. The temperature down there is 12°C (54°F) year-round.
• If you want to see **bald eagles** in large numbers, visit between November and March, when they arrive in their thousands to feast on salmon.

**Hidden gem** One-Mile Lake in Pemberton is a wonderfully peaceful haven to get away from the bustle of Whistler. It has a boardwalk across its northern marshes and is great for spotting birds, particularly during the migrations.

heading north or across to Vancouver Island. From here, the highway heads north along Howe Sound to the seaside and artisan town of Lions Bay (the "lions" are twin mountain peaks above the town), with a sand beach, boating and hiking trails into the mountains.

Beyond here, you soon reach **Britannia Beach** and the **BC Museum of Mining.** A working mine until 1974, and at one time the British Commonwealth's largest copper producer, it is now a National Historic Site offering underground tours, mining demonstrations, gold panning and interesting exhibits.

At about the midway point you reach **Squamish**, at the head of Howe Sound, surrounded by spectacular mountain scenery, renowned as one of the world's premier mountain-biking locations. It's also home to the **West Coast Railway Heritage Park**, with a fine collection of rolling stock, tracks, buildings and equipment, and evolving streets of historic buildings. There are eight provincial parks nearby, and the area around Brackendale, to the north, has the largest concentrations of wintering bald eagles in the world, which come to feed on the plentiful salmon. Leaving the coast now, the route heads northeast through the Garibaldi Provincial Park to **Whistler**, an upscale, year-round resort and one of the best winter sports destinations in the world, with a huge range of summer activities too. Man-made and traffic free, the "village" is full of luxury hotels, restaurants, designer boutiques and craft galleries, but prices here are not as high as you might expect and, in true Canadian style, it is friendly, relaxed and welcoming.

Whistler is among the finest winter sports resorts in the world

## TAKING A BREAK

A good place to break the journey is at the **Howe Sound Inn and Brewing Company** (tel: 604/892-2603 or 800/919-2537; $$) in Squamish.

## Winter Olympics

Since Vancouver and Whistler were chosen to co-host the Winter Olympics in 2010, a major improvement scheme is being carried out on the Sea to Sky Highway so that it will be more able to cope with all the additional traffic. In the interim, be prepared to encounter construction along the way.

➕ 202 C2

**Tourism Whistler**
✉ 4010 Whistler Way, Whister ☎ 604/938-2769 or 877/991-9988; www.mywhistler.com or www.tourismwhistler.com

**BC Museum of Mining**
✉ PO Box 188, Britannia Beach ☎ 800/896-

4044 ext.227; www.bcmuseumofmining.org
🕐 Daily 9–4:30, early May to mid-Oct; Mon–Fri 9–4:30, rest of year 💰 Summer: expensive; winter: moderate (prices include gold panning)

**West Coast Railway Heritage Park**
✉ Squamish ☎ 604/898-9336; www.wcra.org
🕐 Daily 10–5 💰 Expensive

# 5 Banff and Yoho National Parks

Banff National Park was the first of Canada's 40 national parks to be established (1885), and enjoys enduring popularity with its spectacular and accessible mountain scenery. Neighboring Yoho (Cree for "awesome") lives up to its name.

**Banff** town makes a good base for exploring both parks, with a good selection of places to stay, restaurants, upscale shopping and some interesting places to visit. It is located on the Bow River and almost encircled by mountain peaks.

This is where the whole national park concept took shape, when railroad engineers discovered hot springs southeast of the town and started a tourist boom. Visitors can no longer soak in those waters, now the **Cave and Basin National Historic Site**, but you can go into the cave, see the pool and smell the sulfur. An exhibition tells the history of the spring, sacred to the Stoney First Nations, and local ecology. You *can* soak in the **Banff Upper Hot Springs** close by, where the water temperature averages 38°C (100°F). There's a modern spa here, with

✚ 203 E2

**Banff and Lake Louise Tourism**
✉ PO Box 1298, Banff ☎ 403/762-8421;
www.banfflakelouise.com, www.pc.gc.ca

**Yoho Visitor Centre**
✉ Field ☎ 250/343-6783 🕐 Daily 9–7, May–early Sep
(to 5 late Sep); 9–4 rest of year 🎟 Day pass: moderate

**Cave and Basin National Historic Site**
✉ Cave Avenue, Banff ☎ 403/762-1566 🕐 Daily 9–6,
mid-May to Sep; Mon–Fri 11–4, Sat–Sun 9:30–5 rest of year
🎟 Inexpensive

**Banff Upper Hot Springs**
✉ Mountain Avenue, Banff ☎ 403/726-1515; www.pc.gc.ca 🕐 Daily 9 am–
11 pm, Jun to mid-Sep; Sun–Thu 10–10, Fri–Sat 10 am–11 pm rest of year
🎟 Moderate

**Sulphur Mountain Gondola**
✉ Mountain Avenue, Banff ☎ 403/762-2523; www.banffgondola.com 🕐 Daily
8:30–6, Apr–May; 7:30 am–9 pm, Jun–Aug; 8:30–6:30, Sep to mid-Oct; 8:30–4:30,
mid-Oct–Nov; 10–4, Dec–Jan; 10–5, Feb–Mar. Closed Dec 25 🎟 Expensive

## A few facts
Banff National Park, weighing in at 6,641sq km (2,565sq miles), is now part of the UNESCO Canadian Rockies World Heritage Site, as is Yoho, smaller but still perfectly formed at 1,310sq km (505sq miles).

many amenities, but a mid-winter dip in the big outdoor pool when the snow is falling is still the best experience. Next to the Hot Springs, the glass-enclosed **Sulphur Mountain Gondola** climbs Sulphur Mountain for views that can extend as far as 145km (90 miles). At the top there are restaurants, viewing platforms and walking trails.

Head out of town on the scenic **Bow Valley Parkway** to **Lake Louise**, one of the most beautiful spots in the Rockies. The lake, set in a bowl and backed by snow-capped mountains, was discovered in the late 19th century; in 1890 work began on the luxury **Château Lake Louise Hotel**, and visitors have been flocking here ever since. The amazing color of the water, caused by microscopic particles reflecting only the blue-green element of the spectrum, looks even better from above, and many trails head up into the mountains for superb views (the Lake Louise Gondola is an easy alternative).

Going north along the **Icefields Parkway** (➤ 180–181) you'll see some of the most stunning scenery in the Rockies, with a series of views of vertiginous peaks, dazzling blue lakes and sparkling waterfalls – and, of course, glaciers.

Opposite: Banff shopping mall is prettily illuminated

Bottom: visitors throng the promenade at Lake Louise Inset: solitude above Lake O'Hara in Yoho National Park

From Lake Louise, cross the border into British Columbia to **Yoho National Park**, which has a great deal for the casual drive-through visitor, but can also offer more seclusion than Banff National Park for serious outdoor types. It has 400km (248 miles) of hiking trails, many of them day-long, and the most spectacular is the 26-km (16-mile) round trip to **Lake O'Hara**, a jewel surrounded by alpine meadows. Other popular attractions are pretty **Emerald Lake** and the **Wapta** and **Takakkaw falls**, the latter with a freefall of 254m (833ft).

Renting a canoe at Lake Louise is one way to escape the crowds

### TAKING A BREAK

The **Château Lake Louise Hotel** (tel: 403/522-3511) is the obvious choice, or hike up to the famous **Teahouse** (call Château Lake Louise Hotel for information) at Lake Agnes.

## BANFF AND YOHO NATIONAL PARKS: INSIDE INFO

**Top tips** If you don't want to hike to **Lake O'Hara**, there's also a bus shuttle from the Visitor Centre. However, numbers are strictly limited to preserve the delicate ecology, and you need to book your seat as much as three months in advance (tel: 250/343-6433).

• **Never venture out on to glaciers on your own.** There are areas of thin ice and holes covered by a thin layer of snow that are quite literally death traps – if the fall doesn't kill you, the cold will. Make sure you take one of the excellent tours from the Icefields Centre.

• If you see **grizzly or black bears or any other wildlife** on the highway, stop at a safe distance (the national parks authority recommend 30m/100ft from elk and 100m/330ft from bears) and view them from *inside* your vehicle. Keep windows closed and never throw out food for the animals. Unless the wildlife is blocking your way, you should not park on the side of the highway – only in designated parking areas.

• To see the **waterfalls at their best**, visit between late June and the end of July, when the meltwater is at its peak and rainfall adds to the volume in the rivers

**Hidden gem** It's worth taking the steep 1.6-km (1-mile) trail from the **Hoodoo Creek Campground** in the western section of the park to take a look at the **hoodoos**, glacial debris that has been carved by the weather into strangely shaped pillars.

# 6 Jasper National Park

Away from the Icefields Parkway, this park isn't as crowded as Banff and even short hiking trails offer a real sense of solitude and a glimpse of exciting wildlife, following in the footsteps of bison herds, First Nations and the early explorers.

Jasper is the most northerly park in the UNESCO Canadian Rockies World Heritage Site, 10,878sq km (4,200sq miles) of magnificent mountain scenery. Its main town is **Jasper**, with the gritty character of a working town, one of the earliest places settled by Europeans. Prosperity was assured by the arrival of the railroad in 1908 and the town still benefits from being on two of Via Rail's famous scenic routes – the **Rocky Mountaineer**, which crosses the mountains en route from Vancouver to Edmonton, and the **Skeena**, linking Edmonton with Prince Rupert up on the far northwestern coast.

South from Jasper after 5km (3 miles) is the **Jasper Tramway**, the longest and highest tramway in Canada,

**Maligne Lake presents the quintessential face of the Canadian Rockies**

ascending to 2,500m (8,200ft) on Whistlers Mountain. There's another viewpoint on **Mount Edith Cavell**.

On Highway 16 toward Edmonton, take a right turn on to Maligne Lake Road. Stop for a 3.5-km (2-mile) hike through **Maligne Canyon**, then follow the river to **Maligne Lake**, the largest glacial lake in North America. Toward the far end, little **Spirit Island** is an icon of the Rockies, and of Canada.

## TAKING A BREAK

Try the Ukrainian, Greek and North American cuisine at **Kontos Family Restaurant** (tel: 780/852-3444; $$) in Jasper.

Some forms of transportation have changed little in the Rockies

➕ 203 D3

Jasper National Park Information Centre
✉ 500 Connaught Drive ☎ 780/852-6176 🕐 Daily 9–7, mid-June to Aug; 9–6, Sep; 9–5, Oct to mid-Jun

## JASPER NATIONAL PARK: INSIDE INFO

**Top tips** For any hikes in the national park, you should carry at least a liter (nearly 2 pints) of **drinking water** – more for day-long trips – and never scoop it up from the park's waterways, no matter how sparkling and clear they appear. Surface water is often contaminated with Giardia, an intestinal parasite.
• It's tempting to **get up close to the foot of the glaciers**, but beware – chunks of ice as big as a house sometimes break off and come crashing down. Keep to designated trails, or employ a local guide.
• The park still has populations of **creatures that once roamed free** and undisturbed all over the continent – coyotes, elk, cougars, wolves, wolverines and bears to name just a few – but the balance is delicate, even in this protected environment. The woodland caribou is in decline here, and numbers are being carefully monitored. If you see caribou, or signs that they are in the area, take particular care not to disturb them.

# At Your Leisure

## 7 Okanagan Valley

This lush and fertile region of British Columbia offers a striking contrast to the majestic Rockies. It's an area of vast rolling grasslands, rivers that offer some of the best rafting in the country, lakes for sailing, fruit orchards, and more than 40 wineries producing top-quality wines. Many offer tours and tastings.

**Kelowna**, on the eastern shore of Okanagan Lake, is a vibrant city, with a full calendar of events, and plenty of activities. At the southern end of the valley is the remarkable **Nk'Mip Desert**, 20ha (50 acres) of arid sage grass and ponderosa pine.

➕ 203 D2

**Thompson Okanagan Tourism Association**
✉ 1332 Water Street, Kelowna
☎ 604/435-5622 or 800/567-2275;
www.thompsonokanagan.com

**Nk'Mip Desert & Heritage Centre**
✉ 1000 Rancher Creek Road, Osoyoos
☎ 250/495-7901 or 888 495-8555;
www.nkmipdesert.com ⏰ Daily 10–4,
May–Jun and Sep–Oct; 9–7, Jul–Aug.
Evening programs Tue and Thu
6:30–8:30 🅿 Moderate

## 8 Wells Gray Provincial Park

In the foothills of the Cariboo and Columbia mountains, Wells Gray is the best of British Columbia's provincial parks, covering 5,000sq km (1,931sq miles) of volcanic landscapes, alpine meadows with colorful wild flowers, rain forests, lakes and waterfalls. **Helmcken Falls** is the best – more than twice the height of Niagara, at 137m (450ft). Wildlife includes black and grizzly bears and a large herd of moose.

**Visitor Information Centre**
➕ 203 D3 ✉ 425 East Yellowhead
Highway, Clearwater ☎ 250/674-2646;
www.wellsgray.ca

## 9 Glacier and Mount Revelstoke National Parks

On the British Columbia side of the Rockies, these parks protect widely differing landscapes in the Columbia and Selkirk mountains. They are not as accessible as some other parks, particularly Glacier, since its main role is to protect its 400 remote glaciers. Revelstoke is an area of meadowland with high trails that are swathed in wild flowers in summer.

Lake Osoyoos, in the lush Okanagan Valley

➕ 203 D2

**Glacier Park HQ**
✉ Rogers Pass Discovery Centre
☎ 250/837-7500; www.pc.gc.ca/np-pn/
bc/glacier ⏰ Daily 9–5, Apr–Oct (8–7
mid-Jun to Aug); Thu–Mon 9–5, Nov;
Thu–Mon 7–5, Dec–Mar 🅿 Moderate

**Mount Revelstoke Park HQ**
➕ 203 D2 ✉ 301-B 3rd Street West,
Revelstoke ☎ 250/837-7500;
www.pc.gc.ca/revelstoke

# Farther Afield

## 10 Skeena Valley

In BC's remote northwest, the Skeena River flows down from its source near the Continental Divide to empty into the Pacific at Prince Rupert. It's very scenic, but the land route to reach it is not especially interesting and it's better to come by sea (see Inside Passage Cruise, ➤ 178–179). **Prince Rupert** has a busy deep-water harbor serving commercial and passenger vessels. The **Museum of Northern British Columbia** covers the heritage of the Tsimshian First Nations.

Waterton Lakes National Park is home to a herd of buffalo

The valley includes waterfalls, tiny islands and forested slopes backed by the snow-capped Coast Mountains. Highlights include **Terrace**, a logging center with beautiful forests, and New Hazelton's **'Ksan Historical Village** representing the lifestyle and heritage of the Gitxsan people.

➕ 202 B4

**Prince Rupert Visitor Centre**
✉ Cow Bay, Prince Rupert ☎ 250/624
5637 or 800/667-1994; www.tourism-princerupert.com

**Museum of Northern BC**
✉ 100 First Avenue West, Prince Rupert ☎ 250/624-3207; www.museumofnorthernbc.com 🕐 Mon–Sat 9–5, (to 8pm Jun–Aug; also Sun 9–5, Jun–Aug) 🎟 Moderate

**'Ksan Historical Village**
✉ Box 326, Hazelton ☎ 250/842-5544 or 877/842-5518; www.ksan.org 🕐 Daily 9–5, Apr–Sep; Mon–Fri 9:30–4:30, rest of year 🎟 Inexpensive, guided tours expensive

## 11 Waterton Lakes National Park

Four ecosystems – mountains, lakes, prairies and alpine meadows – are preserved in this 325 sq km (125 sq mile) national park, right up against the US border, adjacent to Montana's Glacier National Park. Together they form the **Waterton-Glacier International Peace Park**, the first of its kind when it was inaugurated in 1932. Rugged mountain peaks rise steeply and dramatically from the flat land and the vegetation of the scree slopes attracts foraging bears.

**Waterton Lakes National Park**
➕ 203 E1 ☎ 403/859-2224; www.pc.gc.ca/waterton or www.watertonchamber.com

## For Kids

Kids love creatures, whether it's the creepy-crawlies at **Victoria Bug Zoo** (✉ 1107 Wharf Street ☎ 250/384-2847, www.bug zoo.bc.ca 🕐 daily 🎟 moderate), the cute domestic animals at the **Children's Farmyard and Miniature Railway** (☎ 604/257-8531 🎟 moderate) in Stanley Park, Vancouver, or the white beluga whales that feature in an exciting sleepover beside their tank at the **Vancouver Aquarium** (☎ 604/659-3504 for information).

# Where to... Stay

**Prices**
High season room only rates, based on two sharing a double room, excluding taxes
**$** under $120    **$$** $121–$260    **$$$** more than $260

## VICTORIA

### Abigail's $$–$$$

This is a Tudor-style hotel with English gardens, close to the Inner Harbour. The 23 bedrooms are furnished with antiques, and most have wood-burning fireplaces. All have ensuite bathrooms, some with Jacuzzi, and the breakfasts are outstanding.

➕ 202 B1 ⌂ 906 McClure Street
☎ 250/388-5363, 800/561-6565; fax: 250/388-7787; www.abigailshotel.com

### Fairmont Empress $$$

A historic icon of the city, located right on the Inner Harbour, the Empress is undoubtedly the best place to stay in the city, the choice of visiting royalty, dignitaries and celebrities. It's pure luxury throughout, with gleaming wood floors and traditional-style furnishings. It has a superb indoor pool and luxury spa, and it has several fine restaurants. Elegant afternoon teas are a famous institution here.

➕ 202 B1 ⌂ 721 Government Street
☎ 250/348-8111; fax: 250/381-4334;
www.fairmont.com

### Robin Hood Motel $

Rolf and Brigitte Ullrich offer a friendly welcome at this two-story, family-run motel just 2km (1.2 miles) from the Inner Harbour, on the city bus route. It's peacefully set back from the road and rooms all have coffee-makers and cable TV. There's plenty of parking, an on-site laundry and a recreation room.

➕ 202 B1 ⌂ 136 Gorge Road East
☎ 250/388-4302; fax: 250/383-4399;
www.robinhoodmotel.com

## VANCOUVER

### Granville Island Hotel $$

This is a great place for soaking up the atmosphere of vibrant Granville Island, and it has wonderful views across the water to the city and mountains. Luxurious penthouse suites have the best views, but all rooms have big windows for good reason. The Dockside Restaurant has an open kitchen, the pub serves beer brewed on the premises, and there's a superb waterside patio. There's a fee for parking ($6 a day).

➕ 202 C2 ⌂ 1253 Johnston Street
☎ 604/683-7373; fax: 604/683-3061;
www.granvilleislandhotel.com

### Grouse Inn $–$$

This low-rise inn has a central court-yard with parking, gardens and a swimming pool and it's conveniently located for North Shore attractions. It's one of the best in its category in Vancouver, and offers a range of rooms up to two-bedroom suites, some with kitchens. Continental breakfast is included in the price; the restaurant also serves lunch.

➕ 202 C2 ⌂ 1633 Capilano Road,
North Vancouver ☎ 604/988-7101;
fax: 604/988-7102

### Pan Pacific $$$

The ultimate luxury place to stay in Vancouver, right on the harbor, with spectacular views across the water to the mountains. More than 500 rooms and suites, have stylish modern furnishings, cable TV, high-speed internet connection, control-lable air-conditioning and marble bathrooms.

➕ 202 C2 ⌂ 300–999 Canada Place
☎ 604/662-8111; fax: 604/685-8690;
http://vancouver.panpacific.com

# Where to...
## Eat and Drink

## WHISTLER

### Durlacher Hof Alpine Inn $$–$$$

A terrific alternative to the Whistler resort, this lovely flower-decked alpine chalet offers comfortable accommodations, with goose-down comforters and hand-carved pine furniture, and a family welcome. To preserve the peace and quiet there's no TV or in-room telephones. Austrian breakfasts are gargantuan.

✚ 202 C2 ⊠ 7055 Nesters Road
☎ 604/932-1924; fax: 604/938-1980;
www.durlacherhof.com

## BANFF

### Brewster's Mountain Lodge $$–$$$

The Brewster family have been pioneers, cowboys and outfitters for generations, always based in the Rockie Mountains. Today, they run this hotel in the style of a grand mountain lodge with Western-style decor and log furniture. The rooms and suites have rich color schemes; some have a private balcony.

✚ 203 E2 ⊠ 208 Caribou Street
☎ 403/762-2900 or 888/762-2900;
fax: 403/762-2970;
www.brewsteradventures.com

## ICEFIELDS PARKWAY

### Columbia Icefield Chalet $$

Occupying the third floor of the Icefield Centre, with visitor information on the first floor, and the restaurants on the second, this is the perfect place to stop along the Icefields Parkway (▶ 180–181). The lovely stone building is set amid some of the most magnificent mountain and glacier scenery in Canada, and most of the 32 rooms have two queen-size beds and a loft. It's good value for families.

✚ 203 E2 ⊠ PO Box 1140, Banff;
50km (30 miles) N of Saskatchewan
River Crossing ☎ 780/852-6550; fax:
877/766-7433; www.brewster.ca
⊘ Closed Oct–Apr

features strongly, but there are also such dishes as prosciutto-wrapped pork tenderloin and braised lamb. Lunch fare includes salads and sandwiches, and there's a sushi bar.

✚ 202 B1 ⊠ 1327 Beach Drive
☎ 250/598-8555; www.marinarestaurant.com ⊘ Mon–Sat 11:30–2:30,
5–10 (to 11 Fri–Sat; from 10 am Sun)

## VANCOUVER

### Da Pasta Bar on Robson $–$$

Vancouver's favorite pasta place, this is a casual eatery with seriously good food. You can sit at the pasta

## VICTORIA

### Blethering Place $–$$

Set in that most English of Victoria's suburbs, Oak Bay, this tearoom serves crustless sandwiches, scones with jam and cream, and traditional meals like roast beef and Yorkshire pudding or fish and chips.

✚ 202 B1 ⊠ 2250 Oak Bay Avenue
☎ 250/598-1413 or 888/598-1413;
www.thebletheringplace.com ⊘ Daily
8 am–9 pm

### Marina $$

Food with a view is on offer at this waterside restaurant. Seafood

First Nations people. It's rewarding to browse the little places around **Fan Tan Alley** in Chinatown and the **Fort Street** antiques area.

## VANCOUVER

Vancouver is by far the biggest and best place to shop, and **Robson Street** is the main drag, full of designer labels, chic boutiques and gourmet coffee shops. **Gastown** has been revitalized and though some may think it's been over-prettified, it does have some interesting individual stores, art galleries and craft stores in its converted 19th-century buildings. Ever-trendy **Granville Island** is renowned for its wonderful public market and its art and craft workshops, and is the place to make for if you want something unusual. **Crafthouse** (1386 Cartwright Street, tel: 604/ 687-7270) is a non-profit gallery run by the Crafts Association of British Columbia, showcasing the work of around 150 artisans. Book-hounds

There's excellent main-stream and specialty shop-ping in British Columbia, with everything from European designer fashions to the wonderful arts and crafts of the Haida and other west coast First Nations.

## VICTORIA

Victoria's main shopping street is **Government Street**, but it's stores tend to concentrate on British-made goods rather than Canadian items, though the **Cowichan Trading Company** (1328 Government Street, tel: 250/383-0321) is a noteworthy exception, with jewelry and clothing made by the Cowichan

# Where to...
## Shop

## BANFF

### ▼▼▼ Ticino Swiss-Italian Restaurant $$

With big rustic timbers supporting the ceiling and crisp blue-and-white tablecloths, there's a distinctly European feel to this well-established restaurant in the Banff Avenue hotel zone north of downtown. You can start the day here with a great-value Swiss breakfast buffet and end it with southern Swiss and Italian specialties, such as veal scaloppini, medallions of venison with glazed pear or a traditional fondue.

🚹 202 E2 ⊠ High Country Inn, 415 Banff Avenue ☎ 403/762-3848; www.ticinorestaurant.com 🕜 Daily 7–10:30 am, 5:30–10 pm

Decadence" for dessert. Zev's has a great patio for summer dining.

🚹 202 C2 ⊠ 1906 Haro Street ☎ 604/408-4783; www.zevs.ca 🕜 Tue–Sun 5:30–11, also Sun brunch 10–2 in summer

bar and watch the chefs at work, or get a table and relax over a gourmet pizza or a pasta, chicken or steak.

🚹 202 C2 ⊠ 1232 Robson Street ☎ 604/688-1288; www.dapastabar.com 🕜 Daily 11:30–10

### ▼▼▼ Five Sails $$–$$$

Vancouver's highest-rated restaurant, with superb food, exemplary service and a spectacular harbor view. Menus are largely inspired by the sea – spiced hazelnut-crusted halibut and lobster in a black truffle emulsion. Reservations advised.

🚹 202 C2 ⊠ Pan Pacific Hotel, 300–999 Canada Place ☎ 604/662-8111; www.dinepanpacific.com 🕜 Daily from 6 pm

### Zev's $$

This stylish restaurant serves delicious and interesting food – grilled salmon comes wrapped in a banana leaf with a Thai ginger and coconut sauce; pan-seared chicken has a pomegranate demi-glace. Order the unforgettable "Wet Chocolate

# Where to...
# Be Entertained

## VICTORIA

The provincial capital has some fine theaters, including the **Royal** (805 Broughton Street, tel: 250/386-6121 or 888/717-6121), the **MacPherson** (3 Centennial Square, tel: 250/386-6121), the **Port** (125 Front Street, tel: 250/754-8550) and the **Belfry** (1291 Gladstone Avenue, tel: 250/385-6815).

### OKANAGAN VALLEY

Among the specialties to look out for here are wines from the Okanagan wineries. One that is particularly interesting to visit is **Summerhill Estate Winery** (4870 Chute Lake Road, Kelowna, tel: 250/764-8000 or 800/667-3538), which matures its wines in a huge pyramid. You can buy unique jewelry from **Okanagan Opal** (7879 Highway 97, Vernon, tel: 250/542-1103), or even visit the mine and dig for your own opal. This is also a major fruit-growing area, so look for stands and cabins selling fresh fruit at the roadside.

### BANFF AND JASPER

Of these two mountain communities, Banff is the most tourist-oriented and consequently the prices are somewhat higher here, but quality and choice are excellent. **Banff Avenue** is the main street, lined with stores selling all kinds of arts, crafts and clothing. Jasper, a working town populated by mountain people, includes the **Totem Ski Shop** (408 Connaught Drive, tel: 780/852-3078), a good place to get kitted out for mountain sports.

## VANCOUVER

This is the place where you'll find the biggest venues and the biggest choice of entertainment, covering everything from big stadium rock concerts to intimate jazz clubs. Major venues include the **Queen Elizabeth Theatre Complex** (600 Hamilton Street, tel: 604/665-3050);

the **Orpheum** (Smithe Street, tel: 604/665-3050); **BC Place Stadium** (777 Pacific Boulevard, tel: 604/589-7627); and **General Motors Place** (800 Griffiths Way, tel: 604/899-7550).

On a more intimate level, there's theater at the **Granville Island Stage** (1585 Johnston Street, tel: 604/687-1644), and for live music the **Backstage Lounge** (1585 Johnston Street, tel: 604/687-1354) and **Richards on Richards** (1036 Richards Street, tel: 604/688-1099), while jazz fans should head for **The Cellar** (3611 West Broadway, tel: 604/738-1959). The best gay clubs, at the time of going to press, are **Odyssey** (1251 Howe Street, tel: 604/689-5256) and the long-established **Dufferin** (900 Seymour Street, tel: 604/683-4251).

should head for **Pender Street**, which has a concentration of secondhand bookstores; for new books, **Bolllums** (650 West Georgia Street, tel: 604/687-0083) is huge, stays open late, and stocks something like 100,000 titles, plus international newspapers. The list of shopping malls is headed by **Metrotown** (604-4720 Kingsway, tel: 604/438-4700) in the suburb of **Burnaby**, the second-largest shopping mall in the world (after West Edmonton Mall in Alberta); others include the sparkling **Pacific Centre** (700 West Georgia Street, tel: 604/688-7236) and **Lonsdale Quay** (Lonsdale Avenue, North Vancouver, tel: 604/985-6261), in a spectacular harborfront location, with an indoor market area.

# The Prairies

# Getting Your Bearings

Don't let anyone tell you – and many will try –
that the Prairies are just flat and boring. Sure,
there are vast and featureless wheatfields and
cattle ranges, but there are real gems to be
found in among them. Several features punc-
ture the sky, notably the lovely Cypress
Hills – the highest land between
The Rockies and Labrador –
and the five major cities:
Calgary, Edmonton, Winnipeg,
Regina and Saskatoon.

**The Horseshoe Canyon viewpoint
in Cypress Hills Provincial Park**

You can see these cities a long time
before you reach them, their sparkling
high-rise office blocks standing proud
amid the surrounding plains, and the
anticipation this creates is well rewarded.
Each is a modern, vibrant city with world-
class entertainment and festivals, historic
attractions, fine museums and good shopping –
Edmonton has the largest shopping mall in the
world. Their top restaurants feature international cuisines and
employ innovative chefs to shake off the steak-and-ribs image that
continues to stick like barbecue sauce on small-town menus.

The landscapes are cut through with great rivers and dotted with sparkling
lakes, which makes this a great destination for fishing, canoeing and white-
water-rafting. There are huge forests, gently sloping wooded hillsides, and
meadows full of wild flowers, with some terrific hiking and cycling trails. In
stark contrast, there is the dusty moonscape of the Badlands of Alberta, the
Great Sand Hills of Saskatchewan, and the Arctic tundra of the far north.

The Prairies have an interesting cultural mix, too, including a very strong
First Nations heritage, a French-speaking community in Winnipeg, and immi-
grants from all over the globe who are keeping their colorful traditions alive.

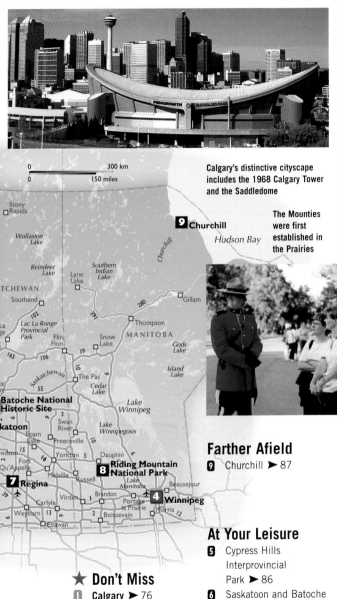

Calgary's distinctive cityscape includes the 1968 Calgary Tower and the Saddledome

The Mounties were first established in the Prairies

## Farther Afield

## At Your Leisure

## ★ Don't Miss

Page 71:
The nation's top rodeo stars compete at the Calgary Stampede

Explore the history in the Prairies, from the world's best Dinosaur graveyard to reminders of pioneer days, and enjoy some unique modern cities too.

# The Prairies in Five Days

## Day One

**Morning** In ❶ Calgary (➤ 76–77), rain or shine, head straight for the **Glenbow Museum** (below) to see the amazing First Nations galleries. Afterward wander down to the river for a stroll around Eau Claire Market.

**Lunch** There are plenty of options in the market area for lunch

**Afternoon** Choose between the **Heritage Park Historic Village** and **Calgary Zoo**, depending on your personal preference.

**Evening** Watch the sun go down from the top of the **Calgary Tower**, then take in some western-style food and entertainment.

## Day Two

**Morning** Drive out to Drumheller (right) and spend the rest of the morning at the **Royal Tyrrell Museum** (➤ 80).

**Lunch** at the museum restaurant; if it's nice out sit on the terrace overlooking the ❷ Badlands (➤ 78–80).

**Afternoon** Set out to drive the 48-km (29-mile) Dinosaur Trail and visit the Royal Tyrrell Museum's Field Station in the ❷ Dinosaur Provincial Park (➤ 78–80)

**Evening** Drive up to ❸ Edmonton (➤ 81–82) and spend the night there.

# Day Three

**Morning** Take the Historic Streetcar down to the **Old Strathcona District** and explore its historic streets.

**Lunch** Strathcona has lots of good pubs and restaurants for lunch

**Afternoon** Head out to **West Edmonton Mall** (right) for a retail experience and maybe some thrill rides at Galaxyland.

**Evening** Stay at the mall for dinner and a movie.

# Day Four

**Morning** Explore the **River Valley Parks** and the Muttart Conservatory (left).

**Lunch** Picnic in the park.

**Afternoon** Spend the afternoon at **Fort Edmonton Park**.

**Evening** Get an evening flight over to 4 Winnipeg (➤ 83–85).

# Day Five

**Morning** Go down to **The Forks** and explore the National Historic Site and the Market (or the Children's Museum if you have youngsters with you). Take the Splash Dash Water Bus tour.

**Lunch** Have lunch in one of the Forks Market restaurants

**Afternoon** Take the Riverwalk along to the **Manitoba Legislature** (right), then catch the free shuttle bus up to the Exchange District to view the fine architecture and visit the **Manitoba Museum**.

**Evening** Head for the **French Quarter**, sample some French cuisine and maybe chill at a jazz club.

# Calgary

With the snow-capped peaks of the Rocky Mountains on the western horizon, and vast swaths of prairie stretching away to the east, Calgary, on the banks of the Bow River, draws its character from both sides. It has the grit of a hardy mountain community and just a touch of prairie cowboy culture; it has the buzz of a modern city tempered by a well-defined sense of its own history. This is a city of gleaming high-rise towers that bear witness to its economic prosperity, resulting largely from the discovery of oil in Alberta. Though Edmonton is the provincial capital, this is Alberta's commercial hub.

Even though much of the long-range view is now blocked by taller buildings, it's worth going up the 190-m (623-ft) **Calgary Tower**, a city icon built in 1968 and refurbished in 2002. Back on the ground, it's easy to get around this compact, flat city and its excellent light-rail transit system is free downtown.

Sooner or later, you'll wind up on the river, where **Eau Claire Market** is a bustling area of fresh produce stands, specialty stores and entertainment venues. On an artificial island in the river, **Prince's Island** is a wonderful oasis of formal gardens, lawns and woodland that's home to raccoons, coyotes and other wild urban creatures.

*Opposite: Eau Claire Market is a colorful part of the city*

In the heart of downtown, the **Glenbow Museum** is one of the most important museums in North America, with renowned First Nations exhibits, tracing the history and culture of those who lived here before the Europeans arrived. The other 19 galleries cover pioneers, the Métis uprising, military history, world ethnography and more.

*The Calgary Stampede recalls the land-grabs of pioneer days*

There's living history at the **Heritage Park Historic Village**, south of the city, with more than 150 buildings re-creating life here in the early 20th century. On the eastern side of the city is the superb 32-ha (79-acre) **Calgary Zoo**, with an excellent record for wildlife conservation.

### Calgary Stampede

Many people visit Calgary for one reason alone, and that is to attend the Calgary Stampede (tel: 403/261-0101 or 800/661-1260; www.calgarystampede.com) in July. The world-famous event recalls the days when land was up for grabs to the first settler to stake a claim. The Stampede is a week of rodeo events, Western entertainment and wagon races, with a frontier town, Indian Village and gambling hall on the Stampede Grounds, and a great party atmosphere throughout the city.

## TAKING A BREAK

Try the "cowboy cuisine" at **Buzzards** on 10 Avenue (tel: 403/264-6959; $$)
or **The Ranchman** on McLeod Trail South (tel: 403/253-1100; $$$); the latter
has a museum of rodeo memorabilia to add to the atmosphere.

---

✚ 203 E2

**Tourism Calgary**
✉ 200, 238–11 Avenue SE ☎ 403/750-2361
or 800/661-1678; www.tourismcalgary.com

**Calgary Tower**
✉ 101 9 Avenue; 403/266-7171;
www.calgarytower.com ⏰ Daily 7:30 am–
midnight, mid-May to Sep; 8 am–11 pm rest of
year 💰 Moderate

**Eau Claire Market**
✉ 202, 200 Barclay Parade SW ☎ 403/264-
6450; www.eauclairemarket.com ⏰ Mon–Sat
10–9, Sun and holidays noon–5

**Glenbow Museum**
✉ 130 9th Avenue SE ☎ 403/268-4100, 24-
hour information 403/777-5506; www.glen-
bow.org ⏰ Daily 9–5 (also 5–9 pm Thu)
💰 Expensive

**Heritage Park Historic Village**
✉ 1900 Heritage Drive SW ☎ 403/268-
8500; www.heritagepark.ab.ca ⏰ Daily 9–5,
early May–early Sep; weekends only, mid-Sep
to mid-Oct 💰 Expensive

**Calgary Zoo**
✉ 1300 Zoo Road North East; ☎ 403/232-
9300; www.calgaryzoo.ab.ca ⏰ Daily 9–5
💰 Expensive

---

### CALGARY: INSIDE INFO

**Top tips** Make reservations a long way in advance if you're visiting during or
for the **Calgary Stampede**. The city fills up very quickly.
• If you are visiting Calgary as a prelude to a vacation in the Rockies, buy your
**mountain clothing and footwear** here – it's much less expensive than in Banff.
• Calgary has more than 300km (180 miles) of **pathways** linking major down-
town sights and outlying areas, and you can rent bicycles and rollerblades to
explore them. Maps are available from the tourist offices and bicycle shops.

# 2 Badlands and the Dinosaur Provincial Park

Amid the lush prairies, the Badlands are a startling, desolate area almost devoid of vegetation, where the bedrock has been eroded into strange shapes and the land is cut through by deep, twisting canyons. Small wonder that it was considered "bad" by just about everyone from the First Nations to the early settlers. Everyone, that is, except for paleontologists.

In 1883 J. B. Tyrrell stumbled quite by chance across some dinosaur bones here and subsequent excavations, particularly in Dead Lodge Canyon, revealed this to be one of the richest sources of dinosaur fossils in the world. More than 300 complete skeletons have been uncovered here, and the land is still giving up its hoard of treasures.

In 1955 the 73sq km (28sq mile) **Dinosaur Provincial Park** was created to protect the area from the attentions of unauthorized fossil hunters and in 1980 it was declared a UNESCO World Heritage Site. The **Field Station**, an outpost of the Royal Tyrrell Museum (➤ 80) within the park, is the summer base for paleontologists, and though it is impractical for visitors to be present at the actual excavation site, you can view their meticulous work on new finds in their laboratory. The station has an information point and bookstore, good interpretive displays and a program of summer lectures. The bus tours of the Badlands are highly recommended, offering an excellent view of the landscape, together with explanations of the geological formations.

Opposite: the Royal Tyrrell Museum has superb displays of dinosaur skeletons from the Badlands

---

➕ 203 F2

**Drumheller Regional Chamber of Development and Tourism**
✉ 60 First Avenue West, Drumheller
☎ 403/823-8100

**Field Station Visitor Centre**
☎ 403/378-4342  🕐 Daily 8:15 am–9 pm, mid-May to Aug; 8:15–4:30, Sep–early Oct; Mon–Fri 8:15–4:30, early Oct to mid-May  🛒 Shop
🍴 Café May–Oct  🎟 Free; display gallery inexpensive

**Atlas Coal Mine National Historic Site**
✉ East Coulee  ☎ 403/822-2220; www.atlas-coalmine.ab.ca  🕐 Daily 9:30–5:30, mid-May to late Jun; 9:30–8:30, late Jun–Aug; spring and Sep hours vary  🎟 Moderate

**Royal Tyrrell Museum**
✉ Drumheller  ☎ 403/823-7707, 403/310-0000 (toll-free in Alberta only) or 888/440-4240 (toll-free throughout North America); www.tyrrellmuseum.com  🕐 Daily 9–9, late May–early Sep; Tue–Sun 10–5, rest of year
🎟 Expensive

**Centrosaurus**

*Centrosaurus was a powerful ceratopsian with a single long horn on its nose. It may have used its horns for protection, often however probably only to scare animals away.*

Aside from the bus tours, the easiest way to see the park is on the 48-km (29-mile) **Dinosaur Trail**, a circular route from Drumheller that passes a number of attractions, including the the **Atlas Coal Mine National Historic Site**, a relic of the mining history of the area, and **Horsethief Canyon**, where 19th-century rustlers hid stolen horses. The canyon offers spectacular views, and paths lead to petrified oyster beds, from the days when these rocks were beneath the ocean. The shorter **Hoodoo Trail** along Highway 10 explores the other-worldly rock stacks known as hoodoos, with their multicolored strata and mushroom-shaped caps.

No tour of the Badlands is complete without a visit to the **Royal Tyrrell Museum** at Drumheller. This superlative institution, in a sleek modern building, contains the best dinosaur and fossil collection in the world, with almost 40 complete skeletons. Other displays include re-creations of the marine world that once covered Alberta and BC, a Burgess Shale exhibit, with models of some of the weirdest creatures you could imagine, and a Cretaceous Garden.

Hoodoos add an otherworldly appearance to the Badlands

### TAKING A BREAK

There's a large cafeteria at the **Royal Tyrrell Museum**, with a terrace overlooking the Badlands.

## BADLANDS AND DINOSAUR PROVINCIAL PARK: INSIDE INFO

**Top tips** You'll need sturdy **footwear** for walking the park's rough terrain.
• If you don't have a **tour reservation**, tickets are issued on a first come, first served basis at the Field Station at 8:30 each morning. Tours are always over-subscribed at peak times, and a reservation limit of one tour per day and four tickets per credit card booking is imposed. However, it's always worth checking at the Field Station to see if there are any spare places available.
• It's against the law to **remove fossils** from the park.
• Don't visit the Badlands at all if the **weather** is, or has recently been wet – the heavy clay turns into a quagmire underfoot.

# 3 Edmonton

Seen from a distance, the high-rise buildings of downtown Edmonton emerge from a sea of green formed by the largest series of urban parks in North America. Close up you will discover century-old buildings and historic neighborhoods, excellent museums and a lively cultural scene. In addition, the provincial capital of Alberta is most famous for two things – shopping and festivals.

Begin your exploration of Edmonton with a ride on the **Historic Streetcar**, dating from 1920, which travels south from the 1912 Alberta Legislature building across the North Saskatchewan River to the **Old Strathcona District**. Originally a First Nations settlement, Strathcona became home to European settlers in the late 19th century and flourished during the Klondike Gold Rush. In 1912, it was incor-

**West Edmonton Mall offers many diversions besides shopping**

porated into the city of Edmonton, but has retained its historic atmosphere, and has lots of antiques shops, specialty stores, a farmers' market, and good pubs and restaurants.

Edmonton's history is portrayed at **Fort Edmonton Park**, the largest living history park in Canada, with original and reconstructed buildings on streets that represent four different eras of the city's history from a First Nations camp to the 1920s. In addition to buildings populated by costumed interpreters, there are steam train, streetcar and carriage rides.

One of the glasshouses of the climate-controlled Muttart Conservatory

Down on the river are the lush River Valley Parks, extending for 28km (17 miles) along both banks. Here, the four dramatic glass pyramids of the **Muttart Conservatory** replicate four different ecological environments, with spectacular displays of the relevant plants.

Sooner or later all visitors to Edmonton wind up at **West Edmonton Mall**, 9km (5.5 miles) west of downtown. Not only is this the world's biggest shopping mall, with more than 800 stores it includes a number of superlative leisure facilities and attractions, including the world's largest indoor amusement park; the huge World Waterpark, with thrill rides, waterslides and wave pool; the Deep Sea Adventure, featuring real submarines, coral reefs and marine life; and Dolphin Lagoon and Sea Life Caverns. There's also an NHL-size skating rink and countless other activities and entertainments.

### TAKING A BREAK

Stop in at the **Café La Gare** (tel: 780/439-2969) on Whyte Avenue in Strathcona for the ambience of a European-style

---

✚ 203 F3

**Edmonton Tourism**
✉ 9797 Jasper Avenue ☎ 780/426-4715 or 800/463-4667 www.tourism.ede.org; also at: ✉ 2404 Gateway Boulevard, at entrance to the city, north of Edmonton Airport ☎ 780/496-8400

**Historic Streetcar**
✉ PO Box 45040, Lansdowne PO ☎ 780/496-1464; www.edmonton-radial-railway.ab.ca 🕐 Daily 11–4, Victoria Day weekend–Labour Day weekend (11–10 during the Edmonton Fringe Festival, usually mid-Aug); Fri–Sun and holidays 10–4, Labour Day weekend–Thanksgiving 💵 Inexpensive

**Fort Edmonton Park**
✉ Fox Drive and Whitemud Drive ☎ 780/496-8787; www.gov.edmonton.ab.ca/fort 🕐 Mon–Fri 10–4, Sat–Sun and holidays 10–6, late May–late Jun; daily 10–6, late Jun–Aug; Sun 10–6, Sep–early Oct 💵 Moderate

**Muttart Conservatory**
✉ 9626-96A Street ☎ 780/496-8755; www.edmonton.ca/muttart 🕐 Mon–Fri 9–5:30, Sat, Sun 11–5:30 💵 Moderate

**West Edmonton Mall**
✉ 2472, 8882-170 Street ☎ 780/444-5200 or 800/661-8890; www.westedmontonmall.com 🕐 Stores: Mon–Fri 10–9, Sat 10–6, Sun noon–6. Hours vary for other attractions

---

## EDMONTON: INSIDE INFO

**Top tips** West Edmonton Mall has the **largest parking lot** in the world, with 20,000 spaces. Make a note of your lot and entrance number as you enter the mall so you can find your car at the end of the day.
• If you are planning to use the **LRT system** to get around, the $6 day pass is excellent value. It can be purchased from vending machines in stations.

**In more depth** If you would like to **discover more about Edmonton's history**, guided tours for small groups (up to seven people) organized by Peter's Edmonton Tours (tel: 780/469-2641) provide a personal approach. Alternatively, you can take the creepy after-dark Edmonton Ghost Tour around Old Strathcona and hear stories of unearthly events (available Jun–Aug and Oct; tel: 780/469-3187).

# 4 Winnipeg

At the geographic center of Canada, Winnipeg, on the Red and Assiniboine rivers, has a cosmopolitan atmosphere and a great cultural mix. It is home to the largest French Canadian community west of Québec, has some splendid architecture, including a fine cathedral, and is economically prosperous, culturally stimulating, historically fascinating and very attractive.

Where the Red and Assiniboine rivers meet you will find **The Forks National Historic Site**, a historic First Nations meeting place where people still congregate. The 5-ha (13-acre) park includes a preserved Aboriginal settlement that's thousands of years old and has many displays and memorials charting historical events. It is also home to the **Forks Market**, housing specialty food stores, craft shops and restaurants. Open-air concerts and street theater take place on the Market Plaza and Festival Park. The Manitoba Children's Museum, with lots of hands-on fun, and the Manitoba Theatre for Young People are also at The Forks.

From The Forks, you can get a guided tour on the Splash Dash Water Bus, or take a stroll along the Riverwalk beside the Assiniboine River to the west. This leads to the **Manitoba Legislature Building**, topped by the city's much-loved icon, the "Golden Boy" statue. Head north up Memorial Boulevard

*The dignified Manitoba Legislature is topped by the "Golden Boy"*

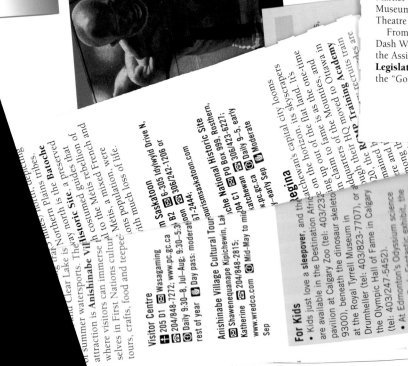

north, depicting
Plains tribes.
Northern the **Batoche**
way north is the a preserved
**Historic Site**, a preserved guides that
costumed French and
the Métis French and
First Nations cultur Métis, a mixed
food and teepee population of life.
ith much loss of life.

**Visitor Centre**
205 D1 Wasagaming
204/848-7272; www.pc.gc.ca
Daily 9.30–8, Jul–Aug; 9.30–5.30
rest of year Day pass: moderate

Anishinabe Village Cultural Tour
Shawenequanape Kipichewin, Lak
Katherine 204/848-2815;
www.wredco.com Mid-May to mic
Sep

m Saskatoon
B2 6-305 Idylwyld Drive N.
306/242-1206 or
306/242-2444;
67-2444; tourismsaskatoon.com

che National Historic Site
sthern. PO Box 999, Rosthern.
204 C1 306/423-6221;
katchewan Daily 9–5, early
n.pc.gc.ca Moderate
early Sep

egina
atchewan's capital city looms
on the horizon, its skyscrapers
Africa on out of the flat land. It's
403/23 g up out of fame is as the one-time
Zoo (tel: claim to the Mounties, and
dinosaur skeleton adquarters of the Mounties. In
Museum in ugh their HQ moved to Ottawa in
403/823-7707), or 20, ROMP Training Academy
Hall of Fame in Calgary ained t their recruits train
247-5452). re and des are
mong th
rill vis
main at
Centr
parks
ums

**For Kids**
• Kids just love a **sleepover**, and the
are available in the Destination
pavilion at Calgary Zoo (tel: 403/23
9300), beneath the dinosaur skeleto
at the Royal Tyrrell Museum in
Drumheller (tel: 403/823-7707), or
the Olympic Hall of Fame in Calgary
(tel: 403/247-5452).
• At Edmonton's Odyssium science
centre's Body Fantastic exhibit, the
**Gallery of Gross** is a perennial favorite
with kids (tel: 780/452-9100).
• The Provincial Museum of Alberta in
Edmonton (tel: 780/453-9100) has a
**Bug Room**, filled with creepy-crawlies
of all sizes.

from here and you'll reach the **Winnipeg Art Gallery**, an artistic lifeforce. The Gallery promotes art in all its forms, and has a lively program of international exhibitions to complement its extensive permanent collection. It contains the largest public collection of Inuit art in the world and has more than 22,500 items in its possession, from a 5th-century Roman bust to 20th-century video art.

The **Exchange District** is a National Historic Site, the early 20th-century heart of the city and its modern commercial hub, where magnificent terra-cotta architecture blends with modern office towers. Here you will find the main theaters and concert halls and the excellent **Manitoba Museum**. Its galleries provide a fascinating walk-through experience of the province's history, from the southern prairies to the frozen north. A star attraction is the replica of the 17th-century ketch, *Nonsuch*, which opened up the trading route to Hudson's Bay. There's also a science gallery with more than 100 interactive exhibits and a planetarium show. Winnipeg's multicultural heritage is also in evidence in the Exchange District, in the Ukrainian Cultural Centre, the Scots Memorial and the Dynasty Building at the heart of the Chinese community.

*The Museum of Manitoba has some good dioramas, here featuring a York boat*

*Opposite: This mural in the Exchange District is part of an anti-graffiti campaign that has brightened the city streets with art works*

Across the Red River from The Forks, the **French Quarter** comes complete with French street names, Parisian-style cafés and jazz clubs. At its heart i͏ **Boniface Cathedral**, built in 1968 to replace the original remain. Its cemetery contain Francophone citizens, inclu by Manitobans as the found **Boniface Museum** close by Métis (people of mixed Fre

### TAKING A BREAK

Head up to the **Bridgepor** Gallery; in summer the ro panoramic view over the the eclectic range of eater

# Where to...
# Be Entertained

The Prairies are more than the country music capital of Canada, and cultural institutions include the Calgary Opera, Opera Saskatchewan and the Alberta Ballet, the Edmonton, Regina and Winnipeg symphony orchestras and the Manitoba Theatre for Young People. In the world of sport, try to get to a rodeo (Canadian Cowboys' Association, tel: 306/931-2700 for information). There are *Where* magazines for Edmonton, Calgary and Winnipeg, and Calgary's *Straight* is a weekly paper with listings.

### CALGARY

This is a lively town, with plenty of entertainment and nightlife. Its magnificent **Epcor Centre for the Performing Arts** (205 8th Avenue SE, tel: 403/294-7455) incorporates a 2,000-seat concert hall and four theaters, and there's the **Southern Alberta Jubilee Auditorium** (1415 14th Avenue NW, tel: 403/297-8000), home to the Alberta Ballet and Calgary Opera. For live rock and blues go to the **King Edward Hotel** (438 9th Avenue SE, tel: 403/262-1680), **Woody's Taphouse** (225 - 4307 103 Avenue SE, tel: 403/257-1666), and the **Back Alley Nightclub** tel (403/287-2500).

The **Calgary Flames** are the NHL hockey team, or you can catch some football with the **Calgary**

**Stampeders**. Don't look for them at **Stampede Park** though, because this is the race track (2300 Stampede Trail SE, tel: 403/261-0214).

### EDMONTON

Edmonton's **Francis Winspea Centre for Music** (4 Sir Wi͏ Churchill Square, tel: 780/42 or 800/563-5081) is a world concert hall, home of the Symphony, and the big **N** **Alberta Jubilee Auditor** (11455 87 Avenue NW, 2760), has a full and va͏ One of Canada's forem͏ ties, the **Citadel The** 101A Avenue, tel: 78 comprises five theat͏ school. Jazz fans sh͏ **Yardbird Suite** (1 Way, tel: 780/432 For sport, check **Oilers** hockey baseball team **Eskimos** foot͏

# ④ **Winnipeg**

At the geographic center of Canada, Winnipeg, on the Red and Assiniboine rivers, has a cosmopolitan atmosphere and a great cultural mix. It is home to the largest French Canadian community west of Québec, has some splendid architecture, including a fine cathedral, and is economically prosperous, culturally stimulating, historically fascinating and very attractive.

Where the Red and Assiniboine rivers meet you will find **The Forks National Historic Site**, a historic First Nations meeting place where people still congregate. The 5-ha (13-acre) park includes a preserved Aboriginal settlement that's thousands of years old and has many displays and memorials charting historical events. It is also home to the **Forks Market**, housing specialty food stores, craft shops and restaurants. Open-air concerts and street theater take place on the Market Plaza and Festival Park. The Manitoba Children's Museum, with lots of hands-on fun, and the Manitoba Theatre for Young People are also at The Forks.

From The Forks, you can get a guided tour on the Splash Dash Water Bus, or take a stroll along the Riverwalk beside the Assiniboine River to the west. This leads to the **Manitoba Legislature Building**, topped by the city's much-loved icon, the "Golden Boy" statue. Head north up Memorial Boulevard

The dignified Manitoba Legislature is topped by the "Golden Boy" from here and you'll reach the **Winnipeg Art Gallery**, an artistic lifeforce. The Gallery promotes art in all its forms, and has a lively program of international exhibitions to complement its extensive permanent collection. It contains the largest public collection of Inuit art in the world and has more than 22,500 items in its possession, from a 5th-century Roman bust to 20th-century video art.

The **Exchange District** is a National Historic Site, the early 20th-century heart of the city and its modern commercial hub, where magnificent terra-cotta architecture blends with modern office towers. Here you will find the main theaters and concert halls and the excellent **Manitoba Museum**. Its galleries provide a fascinating walk-through experience of the province's history, from the southern prairies to the frozen north. A star attraction is the replica of the 17th-century ketch, *Nonsuch*, which opened up the trading route to Hudson's Bay. There's also a science gallery with more than 100 interactive exhibits and a planetarium show. Winnipeg's multicultural heritage is also in evidence in the Exchange District, in the Ukrainian Cultural Centre, the Scots Memorial and the Dynasty Building at the heart of the Chinese community.

The Museum of Manitoba has some good dioramas, here featuring a York boat

Across the Red River from The Forks, the **French Quarter** comes complete with French street names, Parisian-style cafés and jazz clubs. At its heart is **St.-Boniface Cathedral**, built in 1968 to replace the original Gothic structure, of which traces remain. Its cemetery contains the graves of many important Francophone citizens, including Louis Riel (1844–85), seen by Manitobans as the founder of the province. The **St.-Boniface Museum** close by tells the story of the rise of the Métis (people of mixed French and First Nations blood).

Opposite: This mural in the Exchange District is part of an anti-graffiti campaign that has brightened the city streets with art works

## TAKING A BREAK

Head up to the **Bridgeport Restaurant** at the Winnipeg Art Gallery; in summer the rooftop terrace is open for a panoramic view over the city and live jazz. Or choose from the eclectic range of eateries at the **Forks Market**.

🔶 205 E1

**Tourism Winnipeg**
✉ 279 Portage Avenue ✉ 204/943-1970
or 1-800-665-0204 (toll-free in North
America; www.tourism.winnipeg.mb.ca
🕐 Mon–Fri 8.30–4.30

**Winnipeg Art Gallery**
✉ 300 Memorial Boulevard ☎ 204/786-
6641; www.wag.mb.ca 🕐 Tue–Sun 11–5
(also 5–9 pm Wed) 💵 Moderate

**Manitoba Museum**
✉ 190 Rupert Avenue ☎ 204/956-2830;
www.manitobamuseum.ca 🕐 Daily 10–5
💵 Moderate; additional charge for
Science Gallery and Planetarium: both
moderate

**St.-Boniface Cathedral**
✉ 190 Avenue de la Cathédral ☎ 204/233-
7304; www.franco-maitobain.org
🕐 Mon–Fri 9–5, Sun noon–4, late Mar to
mid-May; Mon–Fri 9–5, mid-May to Sep
💵 Free

**St.-Boniface Museum**
✉ 494 Avenue Tache ☎ 204/237-4500;
www.franco-maitobain.org 🕐 Mon–Fri 9–5,
Sun noon–4, late Mar to mid-May; Mon–Fri
9–5, Sat 10–4, Sun and holidays 10–8, mid-
May to Sep; Mon–Fri 9–5, Sun noon–4, Oct to
mid-Nov; Mon–Fri 9–5, mid-Nov to mid-Mar
💵 Inexpensive

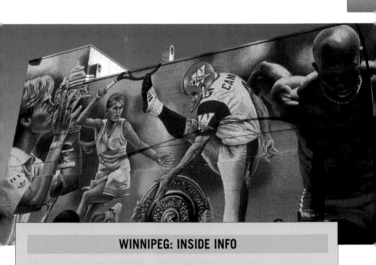

## WINNIPEG: INSIDE INFO

**Top tips** Winnipeg's **Downtown Watch ambassadors,** in red and black uniforms,
are there to offer assistance to visitors; just stop one of them on the street.
• Downtown Spirit is a **free shuttle bus** that takes a circular route around the
city's core and links all of the major attractions except the French Quarter.

**Hidden gem** As you walk around Winnipeg, look for the **100 or so murals** that
have been created as part of an anti-graffiti, clean city campaign.

**In more depth** To learn more about the history of the French community, you
could attend the unusual **Theatre in the Cemetery,** (Wed–Fri 2, 4 and 7pm,
Jul–Aug), featuring actors as characters from the past. Call 204/233-8343 or
866/808-8338 for information.

# At Your Leisure

Old-style harvest re-created in Saskatoon

## 5 Cypress Hills Interprovincial Park

Rising some 600m (1,970ft) from the surrounding prairie, the Cypress Hills form the highest landmass between the Rockies and Labrador. Canada's only interprovincial park, spanning the Alberta-Saskatchewan boundary, it covers 18,400ha (45,450 acres) of lush forests, open grassland and an alpine environment that is home to rare wild flowers. A herd of elk is being reestablished here. The **Fort Walsh National Historic Site**, the restored birthplace of the Royal Canadian Mounted Police, founded during the 19th century to stamp out whiskey smuggling, is populated with costumed guides. The still unpaved **Gap Road**, much as it was when the original Mounties use it, is one of the park's main attractions.

**Tourist information**
🚩 203 F1 ✉ Elkwater, Alberta
☎ 403/893-3833; Loch Leven, Saskatchewan; 306/662-5411;
www.cypresshills.com

**Fort Walsh National Historic Site**
✉ Maple Creek, Saskatchewan
☎ 306/662-3590; www.cypresshills.com or www.pc.gc.ca ⏰ Daily 9:30–5:30, mid-May to Sep (tel: 306/622-2645 for winter schedule) 💵 Moderate

## 6 Saskatoon and Batoche National Historic Site

Saskatoon, amid the vast prairies, is a small, friendly city with a low-key atmosphere and a lively arts scene. Its riverbanks are lined by pleasant gardens and woodland populated in summer by pelicans. The city's museums mainly focus on local history, and there's a good art gallery. More interesting is **Wanuskewin Heritage Park**, 5km (3 miles) north, depicting the lives of Northern Plains tribes.

A little way north is the **Batoche National Historic Site**, a preserved village with costumed guides that was central to the Métis rebellion of 1885. The Métis, a mixed French and First Nations population, were quelled with much loss of life.

**Tourism Saskatoon**
🚩 204 B2 ✉ 6-305 Idylwyld Drive N, Saskatoon ☎ 306/242-1206 or 800/567-2444;
www.tourismsaskatoon.com

**Batoche National Historic Site**
🚩 204 C1 ✉ PO Box 999, Rosthern, Saskatchewan ☎ 306/423-6227;
www.pc.gc.ca ⏰ Daily 9–5, early May–early Sep 💵 Moderate

## 7 Regina

Saskatchewan's capital city looms large on the horizon, its skyscrapers jutting up out of the flat land. It's main claim to fame is as the one-time headquarters of the Mounties, and though their HQ moved to Ottawa in 1920, the **RCMP Training Academy** remained here. All new recruits train here and their graduation parades are among the colorful ceremonies that thrill visitors. Most of Regina's other main attractions are at the **Wascana Centre**, one of Canada's largest urban parks and home to its major museums and an art gallery.
🚩 204 C1

**Tourism Regina**
✉ Highway 1, at eastern entrance to the city ☎ 306/789-5099 or 800/661-5099
🕐 Mon–Fri 8–7, Sat–Sun and holidays 10–6, Victoria Day–Labour Day ; Mon–Fri 8:30–4:30 rest of year

### 8 Riding Mountain National Park

This is an area of rolling hills rather than spectacular peaks, with huge meadows of fescue grassland merging into forest, supporting a wide range of animals and 733 species of plants. It contains some of the best hiking trails in the province, and Clear Lake is the focus of summer watersports. The main attraction is **Anishinabe Village**, where visitors can immerse themselves in First Nations culture, with tours, crafts, food and teepee stays.

**Visitor Centre**
🏠 205 D1 ✉ Wasagaming
☎ 204/848-7272; www.pc.gc.ca
🕐 Daily 9:30–8, Jul–Aug; 9:30–5:30 rest of year 🎫 Day pass: moderate

**Anishinabe Village Cultural Tours**
✉ Shawenequanape Kipichewin, Lake Katherine ☎ 204/848-2815; www.wredco.com 🕐 Mid-May to mid-Sep

The RCMP Musical Ride, based in Ottawa, is often performed in Regina too, and at other events across Canada

# Farther Afield

### 9 Churchill

The little town of Churchill, in the far north of Manitoba, has a population of just 3,000 and is surrounded by tundra, and if it were not for one thing, no tourist would ever make the long journey here. The thing that draws visitors is the chance to see polar bears in the only place where they exist side by side with humans. The bears congregate here in summer, but the best time to see them is in October and November when the ice starts to form on Hudson's Bay, giving them access to water and food. "Tundra buggy" tours offer safe, close-up views.

In addition to the polar bears, there are opportunities for viewing beluga whales and seals, for birding, and for seeing the great herds of caribou that migrate through the region twice a year. The Wapusk National Park stretches away to the southeast, protecting important polar bear denning areas and waterfowl migration environments.
🏠 205 E4

**Parks Canada Visitor Reception Centre**
✉ PO Box 127, Churchill ☎ 204/675-8863; www.pc.gc.ca 🕐 Mon–Fri 8:30–4:30 (also 4:30–8:30 Oct–Nov)

---

**For Kids**
• Kids just love a **sleepover**, and these are available in the Destination Africa pavilion at Calgary Zoo (tel: 403/232-9300), beneath the dinosaur skeletons at the Royal Tyrrell Museum in Drumheller (tel: 403/823-7707), or at the Olympic Hall of Fame in Calgary (tel: 403/247-5452).
• At Edmonton's Odyssium science centre's Body Fantastic exhibit, the **Gallery of Gross** is a perennial favorite with kids (tel: 780/452-9100).
• The Provincial Museum of Alberta in Edmonton (tel: 780/453-9100) has a **Bug Room**, filled with creepy-crawlies of all sizes.

# Where to... Stay

## CALGARY

### Calgary Westways $-$$

A historic home with cozy accommodations and a Victorian theme, plus modern amenities like free internet access and private bathrooms with jetted tubs.

+ 203 E2  216 25th Avenue
403/229-1758, 866/846-7038; fax:
403/228-6265; www.westways.ab.ca

## DRUMHELLER

### Inn at Heartwood Manor $-$$

Minutes away from the Royal Tyrrell Museum, this is a lovely

1920s building with many original features, including carvings and turrets. Each room has individual color schemes, antique pine furniture and superb bathrooms, most with whirlpool tub. There's also a spa offering a range of treatments.

+ 203 F2  320 North Railway
Avenue East  403/823-6495,
888/823-6495; fax: 403/823-4935;
email: heartinn@telusplanet.net;
www.innsatheartwood.com

## EDMONTON

### Fantasyland $$-$$$

This West Ed Mall hotel offers a unique combination of luxury and

fun. Though most of its 355 rooms are standard hotel style, there are unrestrained theme rooms depicting Ancient Rome, the African Jungle, Polynesia, the Wild West and more. Comfort is not compromised, even when your bed is in a stagecoach, a simulated igloo or a pick-up truck.

+ 203 F1  17700 87th Avenue
780/444-3000, 800/737-3783; fax:
780/444-3294; www.fantasylandhotel.com

### Union Bank Inn $$$

A 1911 bank building imaginatively converted into a chic boutique hotel. Stylish rooms have goose-down comforters and some bathrooms have jet tubs. Extras include Reece bathrobes, and complimentary cheese and wine (with homemade cookie) are delivered to the room each evening. The restaurant serves renowned regional cuisine.

+ 203 F1  10053 Jasper Avenue
780/423-3600, 888/423-3601; fax:
780/423-4623; email: info@union-bankinn.com; www.unionbankinn.com

## WINNIPEG

### Place Louis Riel $-$$

Winnipeg's only all-suite hotel offers spacious accommodations, each unit with separate kitchen, bathroom, cable TV, internet access, video games and voice mail. Standard suites include a sitting area, and there are one- and two-bedroom options too, culminating in the ultimate "Cloud Nine" suites. Original works by First Nations artists adorn the walls. There's a restaurant, convenience store and gym. Small charge for parking.

+ 205 E1  190 Smith Street
204/947-6961, 800/665-0569; fax:
204/947-3029; www.placelouisriel.com

## DAUPHIN

### Canway Inn and Suites $

Handy for Riding Mountain National Park, this modern low-rise hotel is a good budget option, offering standard or deluxe rooms and suites. All have queen-size beds, air-

## Where to...
## Eat and Drink

**Prices**

Based on the cost of a three-course dinner, excluding drinks and service

$ under $25    $$ $26–$50    $$$ more than $50

## CALGARY

### ⊚⊚ La Dolce Vita $$–$$$

In typical Italian style, this restaurant caters to the whole family. Upstairs is an informal place where you can take the children, while the downstairs restaurant provides a more formal setting for a romantic dinner for two. The decor is chic and continental, with Italian paintings, and the menu features fresh pasta, veal and seafood prepared to traditional Italian recipes.

🚼 203 E2 ◻ 916 1st Avenue Northeast; ☎ 403/263-3445
🕑 Mon–Fri 11:30–2, 5:30–10.30, Sat 5:30–11. Closed Sun

### ⊚⊚ Brewsters Brewing Company $$–$$$

With 11 locations in Alberta and Saskatchewan, this is Canada's largest brewpub chain, but every site has its own onsite brewery turning out up to 12 hand-crafted ales. This one is a huge brick building, with tables out on the sidewalk in summer. There's a long menu of pub favorites, including "hand-crafted" burgers, thin-crust pizza, steaks and more exotic choices, such as Thai green curry.

🚼 203 E2 ◻ 101 Barclay Parade SW
☎ 403/233-2739; email: eauclaire@brewstersbrewingco.com 🕑 Daily 11am–midnight (to 2am Thu–Sat)

### ⊚ Nellie's Kitchen $

Fabulous home-cooked breakfasts, available throughout the day, are a highlight of this bustling diner, which is particularly popular on weekends. The selections include omelets, french toast and pancakes and there are good lunch options on the menu, too. It's worth a detour just to sample their delicious home-made banana bread.

🚼 203 E2 ◻ 738B 17th Avenue SW
☎ 403/244-4616 🕑 Daily 7:30 am–3:30 pm (from 8:30 am Sat & Sun)

## EDMONTON

### ⊚ Da-De-O New Orleans Diner & Bar $–$$

In the trendy Whyte Avenue district, this diner offers an authentic taste of the Deep South. Retro decor includes booths with individual jukeboxes and the food is pure Cajun, including hearty jambalaya.

🚼 203 F3 ◻ 105–48A 82nd Avenue
☎ 780/433-0930 🕑 Mon–Sat 11:30–11 (midnight Fri & Sat) Sun 10–10

---

conditioning, TV, coffee-maker and voice mail, and the best rooms have a Jacuzzi. There's a superb indoor swimming pool, with hot-tub and sauna.

🚼 205 D2 ◻ 1601 Main Street
☎ 204/638-5102, 888/325-3335; fax: 204/638-7475; www.canwayinn.com

## CHURCHILL

### ⊚⊚ Polar Inn & Suites $–$$

Located on Churchill's main street, the Polar Inn is a comfortable and convenient base for your polar bear and tundra experience. Spacious rooms and suites have individual climate control, cable TV, hair dryers and complimentary tea and coffee, and units with kitchens are also available. There's a gift shop on site, with cold-weather clothing and souvenirs.

🚼 205 E4 ◻ 153 Kelsey Boulevard
☎ 204/675-8878, 877/POLAR-33; fax: 204/675-2647; www.churchillmb.net ~polarinn

### La Ronde $$–$$$

Perched on the top floor of the Château Lacombe hotel, this is Alberta's first revolving restaurant, with a spectacular view over the city and a menu of creative regional Canadian dishes. You might start with bison consommé with hempseed dumplings or maple-smoked Atlantic salmon, followed by organic rabbit and smoked wild boar bacon ragout or roasted Arctic char with a lemon caper butter sauce. All of the ingredients used in the restaurant are sourced locally from family farms.

⊞ 203 F3 ⊠ 10111 Bellamy Hill
☎ 780/428-6611, 800/661-8801;
www.chateaulacombe.com ⊙ Daily
5:30–10:30, Sun also 10:30 am–2 pm

### The Creperie $–$$

You get an idea of what to expect here from the name, but you may not be prepared for the interesting combinations of crêpe fillings, such as chicken, shrimp and fruit cocktail in a curry cream sauce. There are dishes other than crêpes on the menu, including seafood, filet mignon and chicken à la Florentina. It's worth holding back a little to save room for the heavenly chocolate fondue dessert.

⊞ 203 F3 ⊠ 10220 103rd Street
☎ tel: 780/420-6656; www.the-creperie.com ⊙ Mon–Thu 11:30–10, Fri 11:30–11, Sat 11:30–10, Sun 5–9

## WINNIPEG

### Amici $$–$$$

This classy, low-lit modern restaurant is a special occasion place, with comfortable upholstered chairs and crisp white linen. Tuscan specialties feature on the daily-changing menu (favorites such as roast quail, linguini with salmon and breast of duck), alongside more exotic choices such as wild boar and bison.

⊞ 205 E1 ⊠ 326 Broadway
☎ 204/943-4997;
www.amiciwpg.com ⊙ Mon–Fri
11:30–2, 5–10, Sat 5–10. Closed Sun

### Medicine Rock Café $$

It's well worth taking the short trip out of Winnipeg to this beautiful rustic log home in rural surroundings on the bank of an oxbow of the Assiniboine River. Antique artifacts decorate the walls and there's a fine stone fireplace. The menu features Canadian regional cuisine, using fresh walleye or pickerel, salmon and Manitoba lamb. Specialties include local game, including bison, elk, musk ox and wild boar.

⊞ 205 E1 ⊠ 990 Highway 26, St.
Françoise-Xavier ☎ 204/864-2451;
www.medicinerockcafe.com
⊙ Mon–Sat 11–10, Sun 10–9

## SASKATOON

### Saskatoon Station Place $$

Great for railroad enthusiasts as well as those who enjoy tender ribs and succulent steaks, this restaurant consists of the old station building and two Pullman railcars, all done out in gleaming Victorian style. In addition to the ribs and steaks, there's a long menu that includes pastas, salads, chicken dishes and Greek specialties.

⊞ 204 B2 ⊠ 221 South Idylwyld
Drive ☎ 306/244-7777; www.stn-biz.dom/saskatoonrestaurant
⊙ Mon–Sat 10:30am–midnight,
Sun 10–10

## REGINA

### Mediterranean Bistro $$

Big and boisterous, this upscale bistro on the eastern edge of town (just off the TransCanada Highway) has a cool decor in shades of blue, gray and terra-cotta and a long menu of classic European favorites – escargots, coq au vin, linguini carbonara, medallions of beef – with some exotic touches in the use of wasabi, coconut curry and chili flavorings.

⊞ 204 C1 ⊠ 2589 Quance Street
East ☎ 306/757-1666;
www.mbistro.sk.ca ⊙ Mon–Sat 11–3,
5–11, Sun 5–11

# Where to... Shop

Though there are vast areas of this region that have little in them bar cattle ranges and wheat fields, the cities offer some great shopping opportunities. Oil-rich Alberta levies no Provincial Sales Tax, so not only is there a fantastic range of goods available, it's also a bargain-hunter's paradise.

## CALGARY

With its strong cowboy culture, this is a great place to buy cowboy boots. There are plenty of retailers, but **Alberta Boot** (614 10th Avenue SW, tel: 403/263-4605) is the only manufacturer in the province, with 12,000 pairs always in stock, along with Western-style clothing. You can get a Stetson to top off the outfit at **Smithbilt Hats** (1235 10th Avenue, tel: 403/244-9131). Another highlight of Calgary shopping is **Eau Claire Market** (200 Barclay Parade, tel: 403/264-6450), a huge complex that is central to the Calgary experience. Aside from this, the hub of downtown shopping is on Stephen Avenue, where there's a big shopping complex. The **Mission District** has a concentration of upscale stores and **Inglewood** is good for antiques.

## EDMONTON

Shopping takes on a whole new dimension in Edmonton, for this is home of the world's biggest shopping mall – **West Edmonton Mall** (▶82). The main downtown mall is called **Edmonton City Centre** (2000 10025-102A Avenue, tel: 780/426-8444), which has more than 160 stores, but historic **Strathcona District** is the place for individual boutiques. For locally produced crafts, go to the **Alberta Craft Council** (10186 106 Street, tel: 780/488-6611 or 800/362-7238). Antiques-hunters will find more antiques shops here than in any other Canadian city; the largest complex in the country is the **Strathcona Antique Mall** (7614 103 Street, tel: 780/433-0398), with more than 200 vendors.

## WINNIPEG

Shopping here centers on the **Forks Market** (201 One Forks Market Road, tel: 204/942-6302), with a wonderful array of food stands and local arts and crafts. Good areas to look for individual stores include **Corydon Avenue** and **Osborne Village**, while **Academy Road** has a concentration of designer fashions and gourmet food stores. For art and crafts, check out the **Bayat Gallery** (163 Stafford Street, tel: 204/475-5873), one of Canada's largest and finest galleries for Inuit works from the Arctic regions.

## SASKATOON

The main downtown mall here is **Midtown Plaza** (1st Avenue and 21st Street, tel: 306/653-8844), with more than 130 stores, or visit the **Broadway District**, with its independent storekeepers and specialty stores. First Nations items are available at the **Wanuskewin Heritage Park Gift Shop** (Wanuskewin Road and Highway 11, tel: 306/931-6767) or **The Trading Post** (226 2nd Avenue South, tel: 306/653-1769). **Riverhouse Gallery** (308 Spadina Crescent West, tel: 306/933-2399) has artists in residence.

## REGINA

The heart of Regina's downtown shopping is located around **Market Square** and **Albert Street**, and there are box stores (superstores) out in **Victoria East**, alongside the TransCanada, but for more interesting retail experience, wander round **Cathedral Village** to the west, with its individual types of store.

# Where to...
# Be Entertained

The Prairies are more than the country music capital of Canada, and cultural institutions include the Calgary Opera, Opera Saskatchewan and the Alberta Ballet, the Edmonton, Regina and Winnipeg symphony orchestras and the Manitoba Theatre for Young People. In the world of sport, try to get to a rodeo (Canadian Cowboys' Association, tel: 306/931-2700 for information). There are *Where* magazines for Edmonton, Calgary and Winnipeg, and Calgary's *Straight* is a weekly paper with listings.

## CALGARY

This is a lively town, with plenty of entertainment and nightlife. Its magnificent **Epcor Centre for the Performing Arts** (205 8th Avenue SE, tel: 403/294-7455) incorporates a 2,000-seat concert hall and four theaters, and there's the **Southern Alberta Jubilee Auditorium** (1415 14th Avenue NW, tel: 403/297-8000), home to the Alberta Ballet and Calgary Opera. For live rock and blues go to the **King Edward Hotel** (438 9th Avenue SE, tel: 403/262-1680). **Woody's Taphouse** (225 – 4307 103 Avenue SE, tel: 403/257-1666), and the **Back Alley Nightclub** tel (403/287-2500).

The **Calgary Flames** are the NHL hockey team, or you can catch some football with the **Calgary**

**Stampeders**. Don't look for them at **Stampede Park** though, because this is the race track (2300 Stampede Trail SE, tel: 403/261-0214).

## EDMONTON

Edmonton's **Francis Winspear Centre for Music** (4 Sir Winston Churchill Square, tel: 780/428-1414 or 800/563-5081) is a world-class concert hall, home of the Edmonton Symphony, and the big **Northern Alberta Jubilee Auditorium** (11455 87 Avenue NW, tel: 780/427-2760), has a full and varied program. One of Canada's foremost arts facilities, the **Citadel Theatre** (9828 101A Avenue, tel: 780/425-1820), comprises five theaters and a theater school. Jazz fans should head for the **Yardbird Suite** (11 Tommy Banks Way, tel: 780/432-0428).

For sport, check out the **Edmonton Oilers** hockey team, the **Trappers** baseball team and the **Edmonton Eskimos** football team.

## WINNIPEG

There are a remarkable number of first-class entertainment facilities in this cultured city, including the **Canwest Global Performing Arts Centre** (The Forks, tel: 204/942-8898 or 877/871-6897) and the **Centennial Concert Hall** (555 Main Street, tel: 204/956-2792). Theaters include the historic **Burton Cummings Theatre** (364 Smith Street, tel: 204/956-5656), the **Manitoba Theatre Centre** (174 Market Avenue, tel: 204/942-6537 or 877/446-4500), the lavish **Pantages Playhouse** (180 Market Avenue, tel: 204/989-2889) and **Winnipeg Jewish Theatre** (123 Doncaster Boulevard, tel: 204/477-7478). An open-air **Shakespeare** season is imaginatively staged on a vast downtown rooftop (tel: 204/957-1753).

For sport seek out the **Manitoba Moose** for hockey, the **Winnipeg Blue Bombers** for football and **Assiniboia Downs** race track.

# Ontario

# Getting Your Bearings

Ontario stretches for 1,600km (1,000 miles) from the tundra around Hudson's Bay in the north to the vineyards of the south, and the landscapes in between are enormously varied. Water plays a great part – the province borders on all but one of the Great Lakes and there are countless smaller bodies of water. The Ottawa River forms part of the border with Québec and the mighty St. Lawrence links Lake Ontario with the open sea far away to the east.

**A blazing sun goes down over the Thousand Islands**

Most of the population clusters in the south, where there are two capital cities – the national capital, Ottawa, and the provincial capital, Toronto. Unusually, it is the national capital that gets overshadowed. Toronto is not only much bigger (Canada's largest city, in fact), but it's the financial, entertainment and shopping capital of the country and an exciting place to visit. Ottawa is altogether more cozy, but the government buildings by the wide Ottawa River give it more than a touch of grandeur, the National Gallery of Art is a magnificent institution, and the compact, low-rise downtown is a delight.

Ontario also has the most famous waterfall in the world (Niagara) and the only theme park in Canada that comes anywhere near to Disney (Canada's Wonderland). But the province is not all brash tourist attractions. It has some beautiful scenery, notably the Thousand Islands, Georgian Bay and the Algonquin Provincial Park, and there are many charming and interesting rural towns in its heartland.

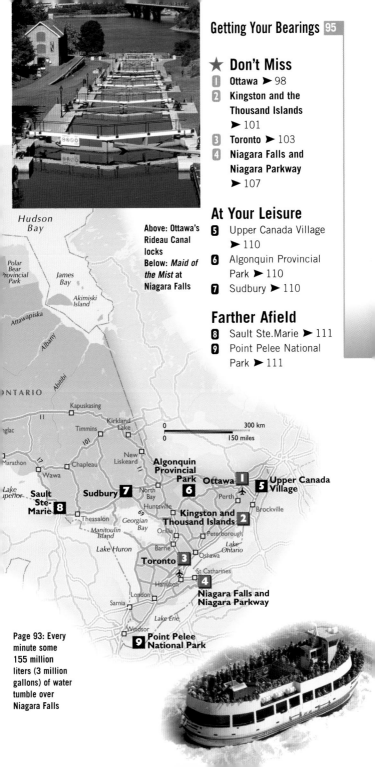

Above: Ottawa's Rideau Canal locks
Below: *Maid of the Mist* at Niagara Falls

Page 93: Every minute some 155 million liters (3 million gallons) of water tumble over Niagara Falls

From the national capital to the provincial capital, via the beautiful Thousand Islands, then on to Canada's most famous natural attraction – Niagara Falls.

# Ontario in Five Days

## Day One

**Morning** Start in **❶** Ontario (➤ 98–100). Take a walk around the **Canadian Parliament Buildings** on your way to the **National Gallery of Canada**. Get a cup of coffee at the Cafétéria des Beaux-Arts, with a great river view, then stroll across town to explore **Byward Market** (left).

**Lunch** The Fish Market Restaurant on York Street (tel: 613/241-3474, $$) is a Byward Market institution.

**Afternoon** Spend the whole afternoon at the **Canadian Museum of Civilization**, across the river in Gatineau, Québec.

**Evening** Catch a performance of the **sound-and-light show** that is projected onto the central façade of the Parliament Buildings (check which time your preferred language – French or Engligh – is featured).

## Day Two

**Morning** Drive south from Ottawa on Highway 416 to the junction with Highway 401. Turn west on the 401, following the St. Lawrence River, to Gananoque. Take a cruise (right) around the beautiful **❷ Thousand Islands** (➤ 101–102; Gananoque Boat Lines, tel: 613/382-2146).

**Lunch** Have lunch at Muskie Jakes Tap and Grill at the waterside Gananoque Inn (tel: 613/382-2165, $$).

**Afternoon** Continue west to **❸ Kingston** (➤ 101–102) and take the **Confederation Trolley tour** (tel: 613/548-4453 or 888/855-4555) for a 50-minute overview of this lovely lakeside city. After that, visit **Fort Henry** for a living history experience.

**Evening** Catch a show at the historic Grand Theatre (tel: 613/546-4465) or take to the water for a dinner cruise (tel: 613/549-5544 or 800/848-0108).

# Day Three

**Morning** Continue west on Highway 401 to
3 Toronto (► 103–106). Abandon your car
and do all your city travel by metro and
streetcar. Explore the stores and galleries
of the **Harbourfront Centre** and **Queen's Quay
Terminal** (left).

**Lunch** Have lunch at one of the restaurants
in Queen's Quay Terminal, overlooking the lake.

**Afternoon** Head north to Dundas Street West to visit the wonderful **Art
Gallery of Ontario**, then walk down to Nathan Phillips Square and City Hall
before continuing to the **Eaton Centre**.

**Evening** Have an early dinner (of the famous ribs) at the Baton Rouge (tel:
416/593-9667, $$$) in the Eaton Centre, then catch a show in the
nearby Theatre District.

# Day Four

**Morning** Still in Toronto, get to the **CN Tower** early and spend an hour up
at the top of the world's tallest free-standing structure. Back on the
ground, get the ferry to the **Toronto Islands** for magnificent city views.

**Lunch** Have a picnic in the park on Centre Island.

**Afternoon** Return to the mainland and visit the **Royal Ontario Museum**.

**Evening** Experience more of Toronto's nightlife – perhaps a concert, or a
comedy show at the famous Second City.

# Day Five

**Morning** Take Queen Elizabeth Way west from Toronto to Niagara-on-the-
Lake, then follow the 4 **Niagara Parkway** to 4 **Niagara Falls** (► 107–109).

**Lunch** Have lunch at the Victoria Park Restaurant (tel: 905/356-2217,
$$) for good-value food and spectacular views of the falls.

**Afternoon** View the
**Horseshoe Falls** from above
on Table Rock, then take
the **Journey Behind the Falls**.
After this, get in line for the
*Maid of the Mist*.

**Evening** Treat yourself to
dinner at the Sheraton
Fallsview (► 113) and see
the falls illuminated (right).

# Ottawa

Canada's capital city is also one of its loveliest, its downtown area a compact mixture of grand government buildings, superlative museums and galleries, and intimate shopping areas that are full of character. The wide Ottawa River and the Rideau Canal enhance the scene, with pleasure and tour boats in summer and skating in winter.

**First Nations mask at the Canadian Museum of Civilization**

The **Canadian Parliament Buildings**, commonly referred to as "Parliament Hill," form a High Victorian Gothic set-piece with their turrets, towers and copper roofs. They stand in spacious lawns on a bluff high above the Ottawa River and are at their most impressive when seen from the water. Tours are available, and at the end you can climb the Peace Tower for a splendid view across the city (by law no city building can be higher than this tower). The colorful Changing of the Guard ceremony is a daily event in summer, as are the evening sound-and-light shows.

A short distance from Parliament Hill is the architectural masterpiece of the **National Gallery of Canada**, with its gleaming glass walls and glittering prisms allowing natural light to stream in. Not surprisingly, the gallery contains the world's largest collection of Canadian art – over 1,500 works on permanent display – including Inuit and First Nations art, the Group of Seven (► 43), religious art of "New France," and naïve murals from Nova Scotia. There are also European and American works, notably Barnett Newman's enormous *Voice of Fire* (1967), simply featuring three huge stripes. Its $11 million price tag is still the cause of some controversy among Canadian tax-payers. At the heart of the gallery is the Rideau Street Chapel, a dramatic presentation of French Canadian religious art, removed here to save it from demolition.

The magnificent **Canadian Museum of Civilization** is not in Ottawa – nor Ontario for that matter – but lies just across the river in **Gatineau**, Québec. The extraordinary building borrows from First Nations traditions in that it has no straight lines and no corners; it also represents the geology of the nation, with fossil-rich Manitoba limestone cladding its façade. Inside, the Grand Hall is the centerpiece, with floor-to-ceiling windows rising 112m (365ft) high. It houses a fine collection of totems, displays about traditional culture, and six Pacific Coast First Nations houses set against a forest backdrop. The entire hall is overlooked by Bill Reid's magnificent *Spirit of Haida Gwaii* sculpture. The Canada Hall uses actual-size buildings to reveal the nation's history, sometimes aided by costumed actors. It includes a Maritimes shipyard, a whaling station, a Prairies church and a French Canadian town square, complete with authentic artifacts and furniture.

**Opposite: Totems tower over visitors in the Canadian Museum of Civilization**

The federal
government
buildings sit
high above the
Ottawa River on
Parliament Hill

To experience the atmosphere of the city, visit the **Byward Market** area –
several historic streets are lined with stands selling fresh fruit and vegetables,
crafts and clothing, and interesting little stores. There are plenty of good
restaurants, cafés and pubs here too.

Throughout the city there are lovely river- and canal-side paths for walking,
cycling and rollerblading, and on summer weekends some roads are closed to
traffic to allow cyclists even greater freedom.

### TAKING A BREAK

The **Café du Musée** at the Canadian Museum of Civilization (tel: 819/776-
7009, $) has wonderful views across the river toward Parliament Hill and in
summer you can eat on the terrace.

---

## OTTAWA: INSIDE INFO

**Top tips** The **Parliament Buildings tours** are very popular, so it's wise to arrive
early and reserve your time slot. For Canadians, these tours are a sort of neces-
sary pilgrimage, but others might be happy just to stroll around the exterior.

**Hidden gem** In the **National Gallery of Canada**'s Inuit collection, seek out the
remarkable *When Days are Long and the Sun Shines into the Night* (1966–69)
by Jessie Oonark. It is the largest Inuit artwork ever completed, and gives a view
of life in the North, incorporating such traditional themes as hunting, fishing
and celebration.

**In more depth** Visit **Canada and the World Pavilion** on Sussex Drive (tel:
613/239-5000 or 800/622-6232; open Wed–Mon 9:30–5, early May–mid-Oct;
daily 9:30–6 late Jun–early Sep) to learn about the Canadians who have distin-
guished themselves on the world stage. It's a real eye-opener.

---

✚ 207 F3

**National Capital Commission
Infocentre**
✚ 217 B1 ✉ 90 Wellington Street
☎ 613/239-5000 or 800/465-1867;
www.canadascapital.gc.ca

**Parliament Buildings**
✚ 217 B1 ✉ Wellington Street;
☎ 800/622-6232; www.parliamenthill.gc.ca
🕐 Daily mid-May–early Sep; closed Jul 1
📖 Call for information

**National Gallery of Canada**
✚ 217 B2 ✉ 380 Sussex Drive
☎ 613/990-1985 or 800/319-2787;
www.national.gallery.ca 🕐 Daily,
May–Sep; Wed–Sun rest of year (open to
8pm Thu year-round)

**Canadian Museum of Civilization**
✚ 217 A2 ✉ 100 Laurier Street, Gatineau,
Québec ☎ 819/776-7000 or 800/555-5621;
www.civilization.ca 🕐 Daily 9–6 (also
6–9pm Thu) 📖 Expensive

# **2** Kingston and the Thousand Islands

Kingston, in a beautiful location on Lake Ontario, once had aspirations to become the capital of Canada, and though it ultimately lost out to Ottawa, the city has a legacy of fine limestone buildings and stately tree-lined streets that sets it apart from many cities of similar size. Right on the doorstep is one of southern Ontario's loveliest regions – the Thousand Islands – where the wide St. Lawrence River is scenically littered with wooded islands.

Kingston started out as a fur-trading settlement, later became a British military base and dockyard, and a temporary seat of government between 1841 and 1843. The waterfront is still full of interest, with its busy marina, sightseeing boats and the **Marine Museum of the Great Lakes**. Outside you can board the icebreaker, **Alexander Henry** (offering unique bed-and-breakfast accommodations in summer), and nearby is the **Pump House Steam Museum**, with working engines.

The city is still dominated by **Fort Henry**, built between 1832 and 1836 to protect the naval dockyard and the entrance to the Rideau Canal. The fort, staffed by costumed guides, has been magnificently restored to provide a vision of military life

*At least* a thousand islands dot this lovely stretch of the St. Lawrence

# Ontario

in the mid-19th century, and there are wonderful river views.

Close to Kingston, Wolfe Island marks the start of the **Thousand Islands** area, which stretches downstream to Brockville Narrows. No one can agree about the true number of islands here – many of them are little more than a rock – but there is absolutely no dispute regarding its beauty, with pinkish rocks contrasting with the sparkling blue water and deep green of the foliage. Boating is, naturally, the main activity here, and sightseeing trips leave from Kingston, Gananoque, Ivy Lea and Rockport. Take your passport with you as the U.S. border runs along the St. Lawrence in mid-stream, so many of the islands are U.S. territory, including the fairy-tale **Boldt Castle**, with a real-life story that is equally as heartbreaking as any fictional tale.

Boldt Castle is as romantic as the tragic story of its past

## TAKING A BREAK

In Kingston, call in at the **Delightfully Different Tea House** (tel: 613/546-0236, $) on Wellington Street; in the Thousand Islands, **Pecks Marina Restaurant** (Lansdowne, tel: 613/659-3185 or 800/951-7325, $$) has a waterfront patio.

---

## KINGSTON AND THE THOUSAND ISLANDS: INSIDE INFO

**Top tips** Kingston's picturesque **Confederation Trolley** departs hourly from Confederation Park, across from City Hall, for a 50-minute sightseeing tour of the city's historic highlights (daily 10–6, mid-May to Oct).

**Hidden gem** Bellevue House on Kingston's Centre Street (tel: 613/545-8666; open daily 9–6, Jun–Labour Day; 10–5 Apr–May and Labour Day–Oct) is a delightful Italian villa and former home of Canada's first prime minister, Sir John A. Macdonald. Costumed guides present the house as it was in 1848.

---

➕ 207 F2

**Kingston Tourist Information**
✉ 209 Ontario Street, Kingston
☎ 613/548-4415 or 888/855-4555;
www.kingstoncanada.com

**1000 Islands Gananoque Chamber of Commerce**
✉ 10 King Street East, Gananoque
☎ 613/382-3250; www.1000islands-gananoque.com

**Marine Museum of the Great Lakes**
✉ 55 Ontario Street, Kingston
☎ 613/542-2261; www.marmus.ca

🕐 Daily 10–5, May–Oct; Mon–Fri 10–4, rest of year; *Alexander Henry* and Pump House: mid-May to Sep only 💵 Moderate

**Fort Henry**
✉ PO Box 213, Kingston ☎ 613/542-7388 or 800/437-2233; www.forthenry.com
🕐 Daily 10–5, mid-May to early Oct
💵 Expensive

**Boldt Castle**
✉ Heart Island, New York, USA
☎ 315/482-9724; www.boldtcastle.com
🕐 Daily 10–6:30, mid-May to mid-Oct (to 7:30 Jul–Aug) 💵 Moderate (Canadian currency accepted)

# ❸ Toronto

Big, beautiful, supremely confident, Toronto is the epicenter of Canada's entertainment, commercial and financial worlds. It is set on the shores of Lake Ontario, and the view from offshore of its skyscrapers, the slender CN Tower, and the big white SkyDome is quite breathtaking. It is ultramodern and innovative, but there is a lot of history between the highrises.

As the entertainment capital of Canada, Toronto has a huge number of first-rate concert halls, theaters, live music venues and nightclubs. It's also a movie capital, with dozens of location shoots taking place on any day of the year – it is often used as a stand-in for New York – and you may see the movie stars hanging round upscale Yorkville on their days off.

Baseball at the SkyDome, with its retractable roof open to the summer sky

Highlights of Toronto's modern architecture include the striking **BCE Place** (1993), north of Front Street between Yonge and Bay, and the twin curved towers of **City Hall** (1965) that dominate spacious Nathan Phillips Square, but towering above them all, in every respect, is the **CN Tower**, a city icon since 1976. The tallest free-standing structure in the world, it was originally built to improve TV reception, but the inspired addition of the observation levels quickly made it a top tourist attraction. A glass-fronted elevator whisks you at a stomach-churning speed up to the Look Out at 346m (1,136ft) and its outdoor observatory (with a glass floor).

From here an internal elevator climbs another 447m (1,465ft) to the SkyPod, the highest man-made observatory in the world, for views that extend to more than 160km (100 miles) on a clear day.

A big downtown attraction is the **Eaton Centre**, a spectacular atrium of arched glass and steel soaring above three floors of stores, restaurants and services. It is linked to the extensive PATH underground walkway system, its 12km (7 miles) of corridors lined by stores and food outlets.

The oldest site in Toronto is **Fort York**, where the city was founded in 1793. Today it's so peaceful that it is hard to imagine the bitter fighting that took place when an American army attacked the fort on April 27, 1813. In the face of defeat, the Canadians ignited the remaining gunpowder and blew up the fort, but it was rebuilt immediately, and still retains a number of structures from that time. Guides wear period uniform, and military drills are enacted in summer, complete with musket fire and drums.

*History is regularly re-created for visitors to Fort York*

In the north end of the city, the **Black Creek Pioneer Village** provides a splendid counterpoint to the modernity of downtown. Original farm buildings and reconstructions form a complete village, all inhabited by costumed guides carrying out the crafts and chores of everyday life.

Of the handful of historic homes that are open to the public in Toronto, the most remarkable is **Casa Loma**, a conspicuous edifice of turrets, towers, Elizabethan chimneys and machicolations that has been described as a mixture of 17th-century Scottish baronial and 20th-century Fox. Sir Henry Pellatt spent a fortune to build and provide his home with every conceivable luxury and fanciful feature, but his finances took a severe downturn and he had to auction it all off. Now restored and re-furnished, it's fun to explore.

*Opposite: hot lakefront property, backed by the CN Tower Inset: Toronto by night, from the observation deck of the CN Tower*

Toronto has a number of fine museums, headed by the **Royal Ontario Museum** (ROM). The largest in Canada, it contains a wonderful collection of Chinese art and the only Ming tomb in the Western world; European galleries span the

---

## TORONTO: INSIDE INFO

**Top tips** The **Toronto City Pass** gives access to six of the top attractions: the AGO, CN Tower, Casa Loma, Ontario Science Centre, ROM and Toronto Zoo, and provides great savings. Buy it at any of the attractions listed, or online at www.citypass.com.
• **Lines** for the CN Tower can be long at peak times, so plan to arrive early.
• Don't drive into downtown because traffic is heavy and parking expensive.
**Public transportation** is excellent and you can transfer between the subway, streetcars and buses for one fare on a one-way trip with no stopovers. If you are paying cash for your ticket, you'll need the exact change. Day passes are available in all subway stations (Toronto Transit Commission; 416/393-4636).

Middle Ages to the 20th century, and there's Canadiana aplenty. Children will want to head straight for the superb dinosaur displays and Bat Cave. At the time of writing the ROM was in the throes of a major expansion and redevelopment.

Of the city's art galleries, the **Art Gallery of Ontario** (AGO) stands supreme, one of the most highly regarded galleries on the continent. Its has a superb European collection, and the Canadian Wing houses works by Lucius O'Brien, Paul Peel, and the Group of Seven (► 43), while the Henry Moore Sculpture Centre houses the world's largest collection of Moore's works. In 2002, the massive Thomson Collection was donated to the AGO, and with his gift Lord Thomson provided $50 million for the necessary expansion, due to be completed in 2007.

Away from downtown, you can relax on the lake shore – stroll around the stores and galleries at **Queen's Quay Terminal**, catch a performance at the **Harbourfront Centre**,

The ROM has some splendid dinosaur displays

take the kids to Ontario Place, or take the ferry across to the **Toronto Islands**. Don't miss a visit to **Toronto Zoo**, a superb collection of the wildlife of the world, kept in spacious, near-natural habitats.

## TAKING A BREAK

For a meal with a view, you can't beat the revolving **360 Restaurant at the CN Tower** (► 114), or one of the restaurants overlooking the lake at Queen's Quay Terminal.

---

🞖 207 E2

**Toronto Tourism**
🞖 221 D1 ✉ 207 Queen's Quay West
☎ 416/203-2600 or 800/499-2514;
www.TorontoTourism.com

**CN Tower**
🞖 220 C2 ✉ 301 Front Street
☎ 416/868-6937; www.cntower.ca
🕓 Daily: hours vary seasonally, so call for information 🖐 Expensive

**Fort York**
🞖 220 A2 ✉ 100 Garrison Road
☎ 416/392-6907 www.fortyork,ca 🕓 Daily 10–5; may close earlier Sep to mid-May. Closed mid-Dec to Jan 2 🖐 Moderate

**Black Creek Pioneer Village**
🞖 221, off D4 ✉ 1000 Murray Ross Parkway ☎ 416/736-1733 or 888/872-2344 ext 5400; www.blackcreek.ca
🕓 Mon–Fri 9:30–4, Sat–Sun 11–5, May–Jun

and Labour Day–Dec; Mon–Fri 10–5, Sat–Sun 11–5, Jul–early Sep 🖐 Expensive

**Casa Loma**
🞖 220, off B5 ✉ 1 Austin Terrace
☎ 416/923-1171; www.casaloma.org
🕓 Daily 9:30–5 🖐 Expensive

**Royal Ontario Museum**
🞖 221, off D5 ✉ 100 Queen's Park
☎ 416/586-5549 or 8000; www.rom.on.ca
🕓 Daily 10–6 (also 6–9:30 Fri) 🖐 Expensive

**Art Gallery of Ontario**
🞖 220 C4 ✉ 317 Dundas Street West
☎ 416/979-6648; www.ago.net 🕓 Tue–Fri 11–6 (also 6–8:30 Wed) Sat–Sun 10–5:30
🖐 Expensive; free Wed 6–8:30 pm

**Toronto Zoo**
🞖 221 off F2 ✉ Meadowvale Road, Scarborough ☎ 416/392-5900 www.torontozoo.com 🕓 Daily 9–7:30; closes earlier in winter 🖐 Expensive

# 4 Niagara Falls and Niagara Parkway

One of the most famous sights in the world, Niagara Falls is spectacular, and the sight of 155 million liters (3 million US gallons) per minute of water crashing down onto the rocks below is truly awesome. The name comes from the local First Nations word for "thundering water" and it's no misnomer. If you're expecting a let-down after the big build-up, prepare to be stunned by the reality.

There are two waterfalls at Niagara – the Horseshoe (or Canadian) Falls and the American Falls across the border – which runs midstream all the way along the Niagara River. Tiny Goat Island, also American soil, separates the two cascades. Only 10 percent of the river winds up in the **American Falls**, which are 300m (1,000ft) wide and 54m (176ft) high. These dimensions would be impressive enough if the falls stood alone, but alongside the wide curve of the **Horseshoe Falls**, 800m (2,600ft) wide and about 51m (167ft) high, they are dwarfed.

To many, the most impressive sight of the Horseshoe Falls is at the top, at **Table Rock**, where the deep, dark green water slips silently over the edge. It's a compelling sight. From here, you can take the **Journey Behind the Falls**. You descend by

The *Maid of the Mist* sails close into the thundering waters of the Horseshoe Falls elevator to a short tunnel leading to a rock platform behind the falls (disposable, biodegradable waterproofs are provided).

Just about the most popular thing to do, though, is to take a trip on the **Maid of the Mist**, a little craft that chugs just a little farther than you would think advisable into the turbulent water at the bottom of the falls. Again, waterproofs are provided for the thrilling experience.

The highway that runs alongside the falls is the **Niagara Parkway**, which follows the the river for 53 kilometers (33 miles) and makes for an interesting scenic drive (► 182–184). Taking the Parkway in the same direction as the flow of the river, you begin at **Old Fort Erie**, where the Peace Bridge forms the border crossing to the city of Buffalo, New York. The British fort that

**Nothing can prepare you for the sheer power of the falls**

stood here during the War of 1812 (destroyed by the Americans in 1814) has been reconstructed as a living history exhibit, with costumed guides.

Beyond the falls, the river continues over boiling rapids, and you can descend to the riverbank for the thrilling **White Water Walk**. Next along the Parkway is the Whirlpool Bridge, another border crossing to the US and the historic **Whirlpool Aero Car**, which has been making the trip over the famous vortex in the river here since 1916.

**Queenston Heights**, 11km (7 miles) downstream from Niagara Falls, was the original site of the falls before erosion pushed them upstream. Queenston was the home of Canadian heroine of the War of 1812, Laura Secord, who journeyed on foot to warn the British of an imminent attack by the Americans after they ransacked her home. The charming **Laura Secord Homestead** is open to the public. The Niagara Parkway ends at **Niagara-on-the-Lake**, one of the most charming towns in Ontario, with gracious 19th-century homes and wide, tree-lined streets. At the entrance to the town the restored **Fort George National Historic Park** played an important role in the War of 1812. Beyond the town is the Niagara wine area, where several wineries welcome visitors.

## NIAGARA FALLS AND NIAGARA PARKWAY: INSIDE INFO

**Top tips** The falls are equally impressive in **winter**, when they are partially frozen, but beware – the spray freezes in the air and can drop onto you as ice pellets.
• The **Niagara Falls Great Gorge Adventure Pass** gives admission to the Journey Behind the Falls, White Water Walk, *Maid of the Mist*, Butterfly Conservatory, Falls Incline Railway and a day's travel on the People Mover, plus discounts on the Whirlpool Aero Car, Niagara Parks Heritage sites. It costs $34.95 (child 6–12 $21.95) and is available at www.niagaraparks.com.
• **Information centers** are located in the Table Rock Complex, Rapids View Parking Lot, Queen Victoria Park, Murray Street and in the Maid of the Mist Plaza. They are open year-round, but hours vary seasonally.

**Hidden gem** A short way north of Niagara Falls on the Niagara Parkway, you'll reach the delightful **Butterfly Conservatory**, full of exotic, colorful butterflies fluttering free in a tropical rain-forest setting, alighting every so often on the lush plants. It's a great place to warm up on a winter visit, too.

## TAKING A BREAK

Take an hour to lunch in the **Skylon Tower's** revolving restaurant (tel: 905/356-2651, $$$) – that's how long it takes to do the full circuit, including a superb view of the falls.

---

✛ 207 F1

**Niagara Parks Commission**
✉ 7400 Portage Road South, PO Box 150, Oak Hall Administrative Building, Niagara Falls ☎ 905/356-2241; www.niagara-parks.com

**Niagara-on-the-Lake Chamber of Commerce**
✉ 26 Queen Street, PO Box 1043, Niagara-on-the-Lake ☎ 905/468-1950; www.niagaraonthelake.com

**Journey Behind the Falls**
✉ 6650 Niagara Parkway ☎ 905/356-2241; www.niagaraparks.com ◷ Mon–Thu 9–8, Fri–Sun 9 am–9.30 pm 🎫 Expensive

*Maid of the Mist*
✉ 5920 Niagara Parkway ☎ 905/358-0311 (recorded information) ◷ May to mid-Oct (depending on weather) daily 9:45–4:45 🎫 Expensive

**Old Fort Erie**
✉ 350 Lakeshore Road, Fort Erie ☎ 905/356-2241; www.niagaraparks.com

◷ Late May–late Sep daily 10–4 🎫 Moderate

**White Water Walk**
✉ 4330 Niagara Parkway ☎ 905/356-2241; www.niagaraparks.com ◷ Mid-Apr to Oct daily 10–5 🎫 Moderate

**Whirlpool Aero Car**
✉ 3850 Niagara Parkway ☎ 905/356-2241 ◷ Mid-Mar to late Nov Mon–Fri 10–5, Sat–Sun 9–5 🎫 Expensive

**Laura Secord Homestead**
✉ 29 Queenston Street, Queenston ☎ 905/356-2241; www.niagaraparks.com ◷ Mon–Fri 9:30–3:30, Sat–Sun 11–5, late May–late Jun 🎫 Inexpensive

**Fort George National Historic Park**
✉ Queen's Parade, Niagara-on-the-Lake ☎ 905/468-6614; www.pc.gc.ca ◷ Daily 10–5, Apr–Oct 🎫 Moderate

**Butterfly Conservatory**
✉ 2405 Niagara Parkway ☎ 905/356-2241 www.niagaraparks.com ◷ Daily 9–6 (last admission 5:30) 🎫 Expensive

# At Your Leisure

## 5 Upper Canada Village

When the St. Lawrence Seaway was constructed in the 1950s, the Long Sault rapids were dammed to form Lake St. Lawrence and in the process eight villages, 200 farms and thousands of homes were submerged. But not all was lost – 30 historic buildings were carefully removed and reconstructed to form Upper Canada Village. Today, the "village" looks as if it has always been here, and there is constant activity from the costumed guides, who represent all the trades and professions that a village such as this would need.

➕ 207 F2 ✉ Rural Route 1, Morrisburg ☎ 613/543-3704; www.uppercanadavillage.com
🕐 Mid-May to early Oct daily
💷 Expensive

## 6 Algonquin Provincial Park

Algonquin Park is the very essence of the wilderness, with maple-clad hills, sparkling lakes, rivers and marshes. It is Ontario's best-known provincial park, and provides a haven for wildlife that includes bear, deer and the wolves that are often heard but rarely seen. Three attractions are right on Highway 60: the **Algonquin Gallery**, with wildlife art; the **Visitor Centre**, with exhibits about the nature and human history of the park; and the **Algonquin Logging Museum**, a re-creation of a logging camp.

### Algonquin Visitor Centre
➕ 207 E2 ✉ Highway 60, 43km (27 miles from west gate) 🕐 Daily in summer, weekends only off season

## 7 Sudbury

Up in northern Ontario, Sudbury is a mining town on top of the largest known source of copper and nickel in the world. It's not pretty, and it's most prominent landmark is a 380m (1,250ft) smokestack, but tourists flock to Sudbury. Why? To visit the outstanding **Science North**, with its exceptional hands-on displays and superb underground auditorium, and for **Dynamic Earth**, which takes visitors deep underground in a glass elevator (while watching a spectacular multimedia show) for an imaginative geological experience.
➕ 207 D2

### Sudbury Tourism
☎ 705/674-4455 or 877/304-8222

### Science North
✉ 100 Ramsey Lake Road
☎ 705/522-3700 or 800/461-4898; http://sciencenorth.ca 🕐 Daily: May–late Jun 9–5; late Jun–early Sep 9–6; early Sep–Apr 10–4 💷 Expensive

### Dynamic Earth
✉ 122 Big Nickel Road ☎ 705/522-3701 or 705/522-3700; http://dynamicearth.ca 🕐 Same as Science North (above) 💷 Expensive

The "Big Nickel," a famous landmark in the nickel-mining town of Sudbury

# Farther Afield

## 8 Sault Ste. Marie

"Sault" is the French word for rapids, and Sault Ste. Marie (familiarly "the Soo"), has a turbulent mile on which the St. Mary's River drops more than 6m (21ft). The river connects lakes Superior and Huron and forms the border between Ontario and the US state of Michigan. To bypass the rapids on the American side, four side-by-side locks were built, the last of 16 between the Atlantic Ocean and Lake Superior, and they are among the busiest (and longest) in the world. By contrast, the Canadian side has one small lock that's used for pleasure craft and a **cruise** that gets up close to the seagoing freighters.

Another trip from Sault Ste. Marie goes north on the **Agawa Canyon Train**, a 184km (114 mile) route crossing high trestle bridges, and passing pristine lakes, forest and granite rock formations. A two-hour stop is made in the canyon, which is as much as 175m (574ft) deep.

➕ 206 C2

**City of Sault Ste. Marie**
✉ 99 Foster Drive, Sault Ste. Marie
☎ 705/759-2500; www.city.sault-ste-marie.on.ca

**Lock Tours Canada Boat Cruises**
✉ Roberta Bondar Park, PO Box 325
☎ 705/253-9850 or 877/226-3665; www.locktours.com 🕐 Daily 12:30 and 3, mid-May to mid-Oct (also 10 and 6 early Jun–early Sep) 💷 Expensive

**Algoma Central Railway**
✉ 129 Bay Street (PO Box 130), Sault Ste. Marie ☎ 705/946-7300 or 800/242-9287; www.agawacanyontourtrain.com 🕐 Tours daily 8 am, early Jun to mid-Oct 💷 Expensive

## 9 Point Pelee National Park

On the same latitude as Rome and northern California, Point Pelee is the southernmost tip of Canada, and the 20-sq km (8-sq mile) national park is a triangular oasis jutting into

The boardwalk at Point Pelee opens up an otherwise inaccessible marshland

Lake Erie. It is a lush area of marsh and woodland, with plant and animal life that is unique in Canada. Each spring and fall, nearly half a million birdwatchers come to the park to view the annual migrations of thousands of birds – more than 350 species have been recorded. This is also a stopping-off point for hoards of Monarch butterflies on their autumn migration to Mexico.

At any time of year, the **Marsh Boardwalk** shouldn't be missed, a 1.5-km (1-mile) walk through a sea of cattails, with observation towers at both ends.

➕ 207 E1 ✉ 407 Monarch Lane, RR1, Leamington ☎ 519/322-2365; www.pc.gc.ca 🕐 Daily; bus to the Tip Apr–Oct (access for visitors' vehicles Nov–Mar) 💷 Inexpensive

### For Kids

For thrill-rides and water-based fun take them to **Canada's Wonderland** (905/832-8131; www.canadas-wonderland.com; open daily late May–early Sep, weekends May and Sep–Oct, expensive) or **Ontario Place** on Toronto's lakeshore. For animals, you can't beat **African Lion Safari** (Safari Road, RR1; tel: 519/623-2620 or 800/461-WILD; www.lionsafari.com; open daily late Apr to mid-Oct; expensive), or **MarineLand** at Niagara Falls.

# Where to... Stay

## Prices
High season room only rates, based on two sharing a double room, excluding taxes
$ under $120    $$ $121–$260    $$$ more than $260

## OTTAWA

### ☞☞☞ Albert House Inn $–$$

Built in 1875, this is a lovely downtown inn with old-style furniture and period décor, offering distinctive accommodations with private bathrooms, some with whirlpool tubs. It's famous for its breakfasts (included in the price), featuring a both traditional and unusual items.

✚ 207 F3 ☒ 478 Albert Street
☎ 613/236-4479, 800/267-1982; fax: 613/237-9079; www.albertinn.com

### ☞☞☞ Arc the Hotel $$

Just four blocks from Parliament Hill and close to the National Arts Centre, this is the city's only designer boutique hotel and is pure minimalist chic. Bedrooms are stylishly elegant and include fresh orchids, a bowl of apples, Bulgari toiletries and deep bathtubs.

✚ 207 F3 ☒ 140 Slater Street
☎ 613/238-2888, 800/699-2516; fax: 613/238-0053; www.arcthehotel.com

### ☞☞☞ Fairmont Château Laurier $$$

This is the grandest hotel in Ottawa, truly château-like with its sturdy limestone walls topped by turrets. It mirrors the dignified government buildings across the canal. Inside the rooms and suites leave nothing to chance in the way of comfort.

✚ 207 F3 ☒ 1 Rideau Street
☎ 613/241-1414; fax: 613/562-7030; www.fairmont.com

## KINGSTON

### ☞☞☞ Hotel Belvedere $–$$

Down on Kingston's waterfront, near to City Hall, this is a fine restored mansion dating to the 1880s and preserving many original features. It's furnished in keeping with its age, with antique Canadian pieces, and modern comforts include down comforters (and whirlpool tubs in a couple of the suites).

✚ 207 F2 ☒ 141 King Street East
☎ 613/548-1565, 800/559-0584; fax: 613/546-4692; www.hotelbelvedere.com

## TORONTO

### ☞☞☞ Cambridge Suites Hotel $$

This is a hotel that offers the best of both worlds – it's on the corner of Yonge Street, at the heart of the entertainment district, yet is surprisingly peaceful. It has a cool, classy décor, and rooms on the top floors have high-speed internet, CD players, VCR... and great views. The on-site parking is a bonus, though there is a charge.

✚ 207 E2 ☒ 15 Richmond Street East ☎ 416/368-1990, 800/463-1990; fax: 416/601-3750; www.cambridgesuiteshotel.com

### ☞☞☞ Fairmont Royal York $$–$$$

The stately grande-dame of Toronto hotels, the Royal York has been hosting visiting royalty and celebrities since 1929 and its distinguished exterior is a city landmark, right opposite Union Station. Its the ultimate luxury, with original features such as hand-painted ceilings, travertine pillars and glittering chandeliers, and every modern convenience has been added, including a pool, spa and fitness center.

✚ 207 E2 ☒ 100 Front Street
☎ 416/368-2511, 800/441-1414; fax: 416/368-9040; www.fairmont.com

# Where to...
## Eat and Drink

**Prices**
Based on the cost of a three-course dinner, excluding drinks and service.
$ under $25  $$ $26–$50  $$$ more than $50

## OTTAWA

### ⬩⬩ Fish Market Restaurant $$–$$$

A Byward Market institution, at the heart of this lively part of the city. It has a nautical theme and tanks of live lobsters and trout. Choose from a menu of seafood that is brought in from all over the world. There are some interesting recipes, including coconut curry shrimp and cajun and creole dishes, plus a few non-fish items.

➕ 207 F3 ⬛ 54 York Street
📞 613/241-FISH (3474); www.fish-market.ca 🕐 Mon–Sat 11:30–2, 5–10 (11 Fri–Sat), Sun 11:30–3, 5–10

### ⬩⬩⬩ Merlot $$$

This is Ottawa's revolving restaurant, on the 29th floor of the Marriott Hotel, with wonderful views across the city and the Ottawa River. Don't be in a hurry, the full circuit takes two hours. The service is formal and the menu has fairly standard international dishes.

➕ 207 F3 ⬛ 100 Kent Street
📞 613/783-4212 🕐 Mon–Sat 5:30–10:30, Sun 10:30 am–2:30 pm

## KINGSTON

### ⬩⬩⬩ Chez Piggy $$

The *Chez Piggy Cookbook* is a Canadian bestseller and if you eat

### ⬩⬩⬩ Palmerston Inn B&B $$

In a beautiful historic building, with a stately verandah, this elegant property is on a tree-lined street close to downtown. Rooms are individually styled, some with antiques, and though not all have private bathrooms, they do have bathrobes and complimentary sherry.

➕ 207 E2 ⬛ 322 Palmerston Boulevard 📞 416/920-7842; fax: 416/960-9529; email: palmerston inn@sympatico.ca

### ⬩⬩⬩ Westin Harbour Castle $$

This has got to be the best location in the city – right on the lakeshore, with superlative views, and close to the major attractions and theater district. Rooms feature "Heavenly Beds" with pillow-top mattresses, and there are casual and formal restaurants offering gourmet cuisine and a long list of leisure amenities.

➕ 207 E2 ⬛ 1 Harbour Square 📞 tel: 416/869-1600; fax: 416/869-0573; www.westin.com/harbourcastle

## NIAGARA FALLS

### ⬩⬩⬩ Sheraton Fallsview $$–$$$

Overlooking the Horseshoe and American falls, this is a superb modern high-rise hotel. There is a variety of room types, the best of which have nice reproduction furniture and, of course, the view.

➕ 207 E1 ⬛ 6755 Fallsview Boulevard 📞 905/374-1077, 800/267-8439; fax: 905/374-6224; www.fallsview.com

## NIAGARA-ON-THE-LAKE

### ⬩⬩⬩ Pillar and Post Inn $$

In an 1890 building, this is one of Canada's loveliest inns, with an exceptional range of services and a spa. Rooms, each with a Victorian fireplace, are superb and have big-screen TV, Playstation and robes.

➕ 207 E1 ⬛ 48 John Street 📞 905/468-2123, 888/669-5566; fax: 905/468-3551; www.vintageinns.com

here you'll see why. It serves up brilliantly executed home-cooking from several countries, including Turkey and Vietnam, and the staff are particularly cheerful and friendly. It's a favorite with academics, business people, the Kingston artsy set…just about everyone.

➕ 207 F2 ⊠ 68R Princess Street
☎ 613/549-7673 ⏰ Daily
11:30–midnight

## GANANOQUE

### 🍷🍷🍷 Gananoque Inn $$–$$$

At the heart of the Thousand Islands area, this historic inn sits beside the St. Lawrence. Its sophisticated dining room serves continental cuisine – grilled chicken with guacamole and spinach salad, for example. The pub, with a patio deck, serves pasta and burgers.

➕ 207 F2 ⊠ 550 Stone Street S
☎ 613/382-2165; www.gananoque inn.com ⏰ Daily 7–10 am, 11:30–2, 5:30–10, May–Nov; Fri–Sun 5:30–10, Apr and Dec. Closed Jan–Mar

## TORONTO

### 🍷🍷 Golden Thai $–$$

There are a lot of Thai restaurants in Toronto, but this one is up there with the best. The pad Thai here is a real triumph. The menu is huge (though portions are small), service is speedy, and the decor is warm and restful.

➕ 207 E2 ⊠ 105 Church Street
☎ 416/868-6668 ⏰ Mon–Fri
11:30–10, Sat–Sun 5–10

### 🍷🍷 Sassafraz $$–$$$

Soak up the atmosphere of upscale Yorkville at this trendy restaurant where, for a price, you'll dine among celebrities on imaginative French and California cuisine with an Oriental influence. Signature dishes include an intricate assiette of Australian lamb, Asian-influenced steak Miss Saigon, and a daily seafood creation.

➕ 207 E2 ⊠ 100 Cumberland Street
☎ 416/964-2222; www.sassafraz.ca
⏰ Daily 11 am–2 am

### 🍷🍷🍷 360 Restaurant at the CN Tower $$–$$$

This is the ultimate revolving restaurant, the highest in the world, and the quality of the food and service is equally lofty. Canadian specialties feature on the menu, including Ontario rainbow trout, Atlantic Salmon, Alberta beef and a delicious maple syrup cheesecake. There's an excellent wine list (from the highest "cellar" in the world). Surrounded by picture windows, you are guaranteed a spectacular view and you'll see it all in 72 minutes. The admission charge to the tower is refunded to diners.

➕ 207 E2 ⊠ CN Tower, 301 Front Street West ☎ 416/362-5411; www.cntower.ca/restaurants/360
⏰ Daily 11–2, 4:30–10:30, Sun 10:30 am–2 pm. Closed lunch Jan–May

## NIAGARA FALLS

### 🍷🍷 Mick & Angelo's Eatery and Bar $–$$

There are plenty of upscale Niagara restaurants with views of the falls,

but if you want to get away from all that for a good simple meal, this is the place. With typical Italian decor and hospitality, it's a fun place that serves great pizza, pasta, meatballs and other Italian favorites. There's a lovely patio for summer dining.

➕ 207 E1 ⊠ 7600 Lundy's Lane, at corner of Montrose ☎ 905/357-6543
⏰ Daily 11 am–12:30 am

## NIAGARA-ON-THE-LAKE

### Terroir La Cachette $$$

If you are touring the Niagara wine region, aim to be at the Strewn Winery when you get hungry. Their superb restaurant uses top-quality Niagara produce in such dishes as Provençal tart with braised onions and roasted peppers, or fennel seed-crusted Atlantic salmon. The wine list is exclusively from Ontario wineries. There's also informal eating at the wine bar and patio.

➕ 207 E1 ⊠ 1339 Lakeshore Road
☎ 905/468-1222; www.lacachette. com ⏰ Daily

# Where to... Shop

You won't be disappointed in the shopping opportunities in Ontario. Toronto is home to a large number of flagship stores, Ottawa is renowned for quality and Niagara Falls for tourist kitsch, but throughout Ontario there are hidden gems to be found – individual crafts at workshops and local galleries, and boutiques with unique fashions.

## OTTAWA

This is a national capital with a small-town feel, but the stores are excellent, with a good range of quality items. The busy hub of the city is around **Rideau Street**, where you'll find the **Rideau Centre** (50 Rideau Street, tel: 613/236-6565), with about 200 stores. Traffic-free **Sparks Street**, one block back from Parliament Hill, is a famous thoroughfare lined with individual stores and craft galleries. Another great attraction is **Byward Market** (▶ 100), where stands spill out of the undercover market into the surrounding streets; nearby stores are interesting too, such as the artist-run **Inuit Artists' Shop** (2081 Merivale Road, tel: 613/224-8189).

## TORONTO

Toronto is heaven for shoppers, with a huge number of downtown and suburban malls and every kind of specialty store. The **Eaton Centre** (220 Yonge Street, tel: 416/598-8700), a world leader when it opened in the 1980s, is still a major tourist attraction, with around 300 stores beneath a beautiful glass roof. Another superb mall is **Queen's Quay Terminal**, on the lakeshore, an imaginative conversion of an old warehouse that is full of upscale stores and galleries. At the other end of the scale, just for the fun of it, check out **Dr. Flea's** (8 Westmore Drive, tel: 416/745-3532), an undercover flea market, and **Honest Ed's** (581 Bloor Street West, tel: 416/537-1574), a glittering temple to the great bargain.

Toronto's neighborhoods open up a treasure trove of individual stores. **Bloor-Yorkville** is the best area for upscale shopping, with a village atmosphere and leafy streets lined with fashion boutiques, antiques shops, galleries and specialty stores. There's great people-watching and celebrity-spotting in its sidewalk cafés. **St. Lawrence Market** (Front and Jarvis, tel: 416/392-7120) and **Kensington Market** (Dundas and College) are worth exploring too for their unique atmosphere, eclectic array of vendors and street entertainers.

## NIAGARA FALLS

**Niagara Falls** is not noted as a shopping destination, though there is a factory outlet mall, **Canada One** (7500 Lundy's Lane, tel: 905/356-8989) with around 40 stores offering huge discounts on Ralph Lauren, Tommy Hilfiger, Reebok, Villeroy and Bosch and other designer labels.

**Niagara-on-the-Lake** has better opportunities, with some nice craft galleries and antiques shops, including **Europa Antiques** (1523 Niagara Stone Road, tel: 905/468-3130), a converted old church building full of furniture and household bits and pieces. There's also the **French Perfume Factory** (393 York Road, tel: 905/685-6666) where you can see big-name fragrances being made, and then buy them. In the surrounding area you can shop for wine at the many wineries that welcome visitors and buy delicious fresh fruit direct from the orchards or their roadside stands.

# Where to...
## Be Entertained

Ontario is extremely rich in entertainment. Toronto is the entertainment capital of Canada, practically on a par with New York and London; Ottawa has the National Arts Centre and several theaters; Niagara-on-the-Lake offers the summer Shaw Festival; Stratford has its Shakespeare Festival, and www.summertheatre.org is a good source for what's on in Ontario's theater world.

## OTTAWA

Ottawa's **National Arts Centre** (53 Elgin Street, tel: 613/947-7000) is one of the largest and most comprehensive performance centers in the world. City theaters include the **Great Canadian Theatre Company** (910 Gladstone Avenue, tel: 613/236-5196), **Ottawa Little Theatre** (400 King Edward Street, tel: 613/233-8948) and the **Centrepoint Theatre** (101 Centrepoint Drive, Nepean tel: 613/580-2700). Big-name touring acts also play at the **Corel Centre** (tel: 613/599-0250).

The **Lynx** (baseball), **Renegades** (football), **Senators** (hockey) and **Rebels** (lacrosse) represent Ottawa's sporting scene, and there's horse racing at the Rideau Carleton track.

## TORONTO

There's just too much going on in Toronto to list it all here and you should check out the listings magazines *Where* and *Now* for the full picture. Toronto's Theatre District includes the **Royal Alexandra** (260 King Street W, tel: 416/593-4142), the **Princess of Wales** (300 King Street W, tel: 416/593-4142), the **Canon** (244 Victoria Street, tel: 416/872-1212) and the **Elgin & Winter Garden** (189 Yonge Street, tel: 416/314-2871). There's also **Canstage** (26 Berkeley Street, tel: 416/368-3110), Canada's largest contemporary theater company. Big concert venues include the **Hummingbird Centre** (1 Front Street East, tel: 416/393-7429), the **Air Canada Centre** (40 Bay Street, tel: 416/815-5500), the **Roy Thompson Hall** (60 Simcoe Street, tel: 416/872-4255), the **SkyDome** (1 Blue Jays Way, tel: 416/341-3000) and **Molson Amphitheatre** (Ontario Place, tel: 416/260-5600).

There are hundreds of live music clubs, including the **Horseshoe** (368 Queen Street W, tel: 416/598-4226), **Healey's** (178 Bathurst Street, tel: 416/703-5882), run by legendary guitarist Jeff Healey, **C'Est What?** (67 Front Street E, tel: 416/416/867-9499) and **Montréal Bistro and Jazz Club** (65 Sherbourne Street, tel: 416/363-0179).

Dance clubs jostle for position at the top; current favorites include **Baba'U** (tel: 416/515-0587), **The Government** (tel: 416/869-0045), and **Fly** (tel: 416/925-6222), which is primarily a gay club.

Comedy is big in Toronto (the likes of Mike Myers and Jim Carrey honed their skills here). **Second City** (tel: 416/343-0011) is the club that inspired "Saturday Night Live," and **Laugh Resort** tel: 416/598-5233) hosts top comedy stars.

Spectator sports include the **Blue Jays** (baseball), twice winners of the World Series, and the **Argonauts** (football), the **Maple Leafs** (hockey) and **Raptors** (basketball). The **Woodbine Race Track** (555 Rexdale Boulevard, tel: 416/675-1101) stages Canada's classic thoroughbred races.

# Québec

# Getting Your Bearings

The Maritimes have the Acadians, the Prairies have the Métis, and there's a smattering of Francophones in Ontario, but Québec is thoroughly French and immensely proud of its Gallic heritage. This gives any visit to the province an extra dimension, with signs in French, the French language ringing in your ears (though most Québecois are fluent in English too), a cosmopolitan sophistication in the cities, and a laid-back *joie-de-vivre* just about everywhere.

*Péninsule d'Ungava*

The province hugs both banks of the mighty St. Lawrence River as it flows east into the Gulf of St. Lawrence, and all the major cities are on or close to this busy waterway. Stretching to the north is a vast wilderness of lakes and tundra that is sparsely populated but very beautiful.

Some of the oldest settlements on the continent are here, notably the fabulous Québec City, with its intact city walls and mighty Citadelle fortress. Montréal is Canada's second city (after Toronto), a vibrant cultural and commercial center with ancient quarters and remarkably elegant modern architecture.

Out in the country, there's the vacation paradise of the Laurentian Mountains and Gaspésie, pretty rural areas of orchards and vineyards, cascading tributories flowing into the St. Lawrence, and the spectacular fall colors of the Gatineau Valley.

Chisasibi

Eastr

**Page 117: Québec City is split in two by a sheer escarpment that's dominated by the Château Frontenac hotel**

**Left: The Tremblant Resort is at the heart of the Laurentians**

# At Your Leisure

The rocky land-
scape of the
Saguenay Fjord

Kuujjuaq

Caniapiscau

Schefferville

Blanc
Sablon

Lac
Bienville

Lac
Caniapiscau

Fermont

Romaine

Réservoir
Manicouagan

Moisie

Havre-
Saint-Pierre

138

QUÉBEC

Manicouagan

Sept-Îles

Île Anticosti

Gulf of St
Lawrence

Lac
Mistassini

Baie-
Comeau

St Lawrence

Gaspé

Îles de la
Madeleine

▲1268

Mistassini

Forestville

Bonaventure

Matane

Chapais

167

**Saguenay Fjord** **4**

Chicoutimi

Rimouski

**Lac St-Jean** **9**

167

Clermont

Rivière-
du-Loup

Réservoir
Gouin

Parc Provincial
des Laurentides

**3** **Charlevoix Coast**

Ste-Thècle

**Québec City** **2** **7** **Île d'Orléans**

Beauceville

0          300 km

**Trois-
Rivières** **6**

0     150 miles

Réservoir
Cabonga

**Les**

Lac-Mégantic

117

**Laurentides** **8**

Drummondville

St-Jérôme

Granby

Sherbrooke

**Montréal** **1**

**5** **Cantons-de-l'Est**

Gatineau

## ★ Don't Miss

This tour takes in the nation's second-largest city and its oldest city, then heads out along the coast for some whale-watching and a magnificent fjord cruise.

# Quebec in Five days
## Day One

**Morning** Start your visit to ❶ **Montréal** (➤ 122–125) at place Jacques Cartier, take a horse-drawn calèche ride (➤ left), and explore the old city. Then make your way west along rue St.-Paul to place d'Armes.

**Lunch** Visit the **Basilique Nôtre-Dame** during its quietest period of the day, then find a place to eat from the many choices in Vieux Montréal.

**Afternoon** Take a look around the Vieux Port, then stop in at the Marché Bonsecour to browse the craft boutiques and have a coffee at Le Petit Paysan. Then head up to Mont-Royal to see the famous **Oratoire St.-Joseph**.

**Evening** Stay up on **Mont-Royal** to watch the sun go down and the lights of the city (and the Mont-Royal cross) go on. Make your way to the Latin Quarter for some French-style nightlife and cuisine.

## Day Two

**Morning** Still in **Montréal** start in the heart of downtown at place du Canada, visit the Cathédrale Marie-Reine-du-Monde, then go underground to explore the Ville Souterraine (➤ below).

**Lunch** Pick and choose from the delicious choices of food on offer at the Marché Mövenpick at place Ville-Marie in the underground city.

**Afternoon** Window-shop along rue Ste.-Catherine, then head northwest to visit the **Musée des beaux-arts** on rue Sherbrooke Ouest. Take a break in the museum café.

**Evening** Treat yourself to dinner at Nuances (➤ 137), at the Casino down on the water-front, one of the finest restaurants in North America. Stay on to catch a show at the Cabaret or play the tables and slots.

# Day Three

**Morning** Take Highway 40 northeast to ② **Québec City** (► 126–128) for a walk on Terrasse Dufferin (► left) and Promenade des Gouverneurs.

**Lunch** Reward yourself for all that walking, and have lunch in the city's oldest building at Aux Anciens Canadiens (► 137).

**Afternoon** Take the tour of the **Citadelle**, then have a quick look inside the **Basilique Notre-Dame de Québec** before taking the funicular down to the lower town. Visit the **Musée de la Civilisation**.

**Evening** Stay in the Basse-Ville for a stroll around its delightful narrow lanes and a meal at Terrasse d'Orsay (tel: 418/694-1582, $$$), either in the upstairs dining room or on the leafy terrace.

# Day Four

**Morning** Drive northeast out of Québec City along the ③ **Charlevoix Coast** (► 129–130), stopping at any little community that takes your fancy.

**Lunch** Aim to be in Baie St.-Paul around midday for lunch at Le Mouton Noir (tel: 418/240-3030, $$$) on rue St.-Anne.

**Afternoon** Continue along the coast, stopping at La Malbaie, Port-au-Persil and the viewpoint above Baie Ste.-Catherine. Take the ferry across to **Tadoussac** and visit the **Interpretation Centre for Marine Mammals**.

**Evening** Have a stroll around this charming little town and a meal in one of the restaurants at the Tadoussac Hotel.

# Day Five

**Morning** Get the earliest whale-watching trip you can, which will last about two hours. Then drive up the ④ **Saguenay Fjord** (► 131–132, right) to **Chicoutimi**.

**Lunch** Have lunch at La Bougresse (tel: 418/543-3178, $) in the town center.

**Afternoon** Take a cruise on the fjord from Chicoutimi's waterfront.

**Evening** Drive to lovely **Baie Éternité** for a stroll along its waterside path.

# Montréal

The capital of French-speaking Canada, Montréal is a beautiful and fascinating city, set on an island in the wide St. Lawrence River. It has a striking mixture of modern and historic buildings, some of the finest ecclesiastical architecture on the continent, and a vibrant, cosmopolitan atmosphere. It is Canada's second-largest city – after Toronto, with which there is a deal of rivalry – and the second-largest Francophone city in the world (after Paris).

**Mellow Montréal is one of the most beautiful cities in the world**

The first part of Montréal that many visitors see is the Dorchester Square/Place du Canada area, the commercial hub that is full of modern architecture and monuments. The real heart of the city, though, is up on **Mont-Royal** (Mount Royal), from which the city took its name. It rises 228m (750ft) above the downtown bustle, topped by a lovely park, and is a precious oasis for residents and a place where visitors can enjoy the wonderful panorama. The Chalet and Camilien Houde viewpoints have the best views of the St. Lawrence River. On the north slope is the famous **L'Oratoire St.-Joseph** (St. Joseph's Oratory), a city landmark, which has one of the largest domes in the world.

Montréal is fascinating to explore, with its striking contrasts. For instance, you can walk for many kilometers through the ultramodern **Ville Souterraine**, a vast underground network of corridors and sun-lit atriums that link stores, offices and the subway system, then emerge to stroll around **Vieux-Montréal** (Old Montréal). Founded by a little French mission in 1642, this area has been restored and revitalized and, though it is a great tourist attraction, it is also a working and residential area of enormous character. Touring it by horse-drawn calèche is one of the great Montréal experiences. Place Jacques Cartier is the hub, particularly lively on summer evenings with street performers, sidewalk cafés and flower-sellers.

One of the glories of Montréal is in the old city – the Roman Catholic **Basilique Nôtre-Dame de Montréal**. The twin towers, rising to more than 69m (226ft), are a city landmark and it has a stunning interior. Magnificent wood-carving and fine statuary adorns the huge, 68m (223ft) long nave, which is illuminated by three rose windows in the roof. Because of its excellent acoustics, the basilica is often used for concerts.

Over on rue Ste.-Catherine, its Anglican counterpart, **Christ Church** cathedral is squeezed between towering office blocks and underpinned by a large shopping center. It's a superb example of neo-Gothic architecture with flamboyant features on its façade. Inside, there are stained-glass windows from the studio of William Morris and a cross made from nails collected in the ruins of Coventry Cathedral in England after it was bombed in 1940.

Down on the river, the **Vieux-Port** (Old Port) was once the biggest grain port in North America, but was abandoned when the St. Lawrence Seaway opened in 1959. Rescued from dereliction in the late 1970s and converted for public use, it includes a waterfront park with superb views and a variety of leisure activities. It's also a venue for festivals and exhibitions. The Montréal Science Centre is here, too, with lots of hands-on activities for children, or

The interior of the Basilique Notre-Dame is breathtaking

Opposite: Paul Kane's *Mah-Min* in the Musée des beaux-arts

you can ferry them across to Île Ste.-Hélène for La Ronde, a huge amusement park, and the **Biosphère**. This huge geodesic dome, built as the US Pavilion for the 1967 World's Fair, tells the story of the St. Lawrence River, the Seaway and the Great Lakes, with interactive displays and multimedia presentations.

Montréal has some excellent museums and galleries, and a good place to start is the place des Arts complex. This is Canada's only cultural complex devoted to both the performing and visual arts, and is dominated by the elliptical façade of its concert hall. Here, too, is the **Musée d'art contemporain** (Contemporary Art Museum), the only gallery in Canada that is devoted solely to contemporary art.

The **Musée des beaux-arts de Montréal** (Montréal Museum of Fine Arts) occupies a number of buildings on rue Sherbrooke. It's one of Canada's oldest museums, with an encyclopedic collection of all kinds of art and a program of blockbuster exhibitions.

If the busy streets get too much, there's no better antidote than the wonderful **Jardin botanique de Montréal** (Montréal Botanical Gardens) over in the east end of the city. Extending to more than 73ha (180 acres), they are consid-

---

## MONTRÉAL: INSIDE INFO

**Top tips** Visit the **Basilique Nôtre-Dame** around lunchtime, when there are fewer tour groups. Alternatively, attend a Mass, which is the only time you can see the interior with all the lights on.
• Take advantage of the **mini-train** to get around the Botanical Gardens. It's free with admission and you can get on and off to explore different areas.
• An **STM Tourist Card** is excellent value, offering unlimited travel on Montréal's bus and métro network. For information call 514/280-5507.

**In more depth** The Old Fort on Île-Ste-Hélène houses the **Stewart Museum** (20 chemin Tour-de-l'Île, tel: 614/861-6701; www.stewart-museum.org; open year-round, closed Tue early Sep–early May; moderate) devoted to the history of European settlement in Québec. One of its best exhibits is a model of Montréal in 1760. For more local history, visit the **Château Ramezay** (280 rue Nôtre-Dame Est, tel: 514/861-3708; www.chateauramezay.qc.ca; open year-round, closed Mon Oct–May; moderate).

**Hidden gem** Tiny **rue St.-Amable**, close to rue St.-Paul, is known as the artists' street, and in summer it is lined with artists selling their canvases.

ered the finest of their kind in North America, with themed areas that include the First Nations Garden, a rose garden with more than 10,000 bushes, the serene Japanese Garden, a Chinese garden and 10 greenhouses.

Across the street is the **Parc olympique de Montréal**, built for the XXI Olympiad in 1976. Take the funicular elevator up its distinctive spine for spectacular views. The former velodrome is now the **Biodôme de Montréal**, a remarkable indoor zoo featuring four ecosystems of the Americas – tropical rain forest, Laurentian Forest, the marine environment of the St. Lawrence and the frigid Polar World.

### TAKING A BREAK

**Café des Beaux-Arts** (tel: 514/843-3233, $$) is an elegant bistro in the Musée des beaux-arts.

---

🚇 208 A1

### Centre Infotouriste
🚇 218 A1 ✉ 1001 Square Dorchester
☎ 514/873-2015 or 877/266-5687;
www.tourism-montreal.org

### Tourist Information Centre
🚇 219, off F5 ✉ 174 rue Notre-Dame Est, on corner of place Jacques Cartier
☎ 514/873-2015

### L'Oratoire St.-Joseph
🚇 218, off A4 ✉ 3800 chemin Queen Mary de Mont-Royal ☎ 514/733-8211; www.saint-joseph.org; call for times of Masses

### Basilique Nôtre-Dame
🚇 219 F3 ✉ 110 rue Nôtre-Dame Ouest
☎ 514/842-2925 or 866/842-2950,
🕐 Sound-and-light shows Tue–Sat evenings (times vary) 🖐 Inexpensive

### Christ Church
🚇 218 A3 ✉ 635 rue Ste.-Catherine Ouest ☎ 514/843-6577; www.montreal.anglican.org/cathedral

### Biosphère
🚇 219, off D1 ✉ 160 chemin Tour-de-l'Île, Île-Ste.-Hélène ☎ 514/283-5000; www.biosphere.ec.gc.ca 🕐 Daily 10–6, Jun–Sep; Mon & Wed–Fri noon–5, Sat–Sun 10–5, rest of year 🖐 Moderate

### Musée d'art contemporain
🚇 218 B4 ✉ 185 rue Ste.-Catherine Ouest ☎ 514/847-6226; www.macm.org
🕐 Tue–Sun 11–6 (also 6–9 Wed)
🖐 Moderate

### Musée des beaux-arts de Montréal
🚇 218, off A4 ✉ 1379–80 rue Sherbrooke Ouest ☎ 514/285-2000 or 800/899-6873; www.mmfa.qc.ca 🕐 Tue–Sun and holiday Mon (daily late Jun–early Sep) 🖐 Free (except temporary exhibitions)

### Jardin botanique de Montréal
🚇 218, off A5 ✉ 4101 rue Sherbrooke Est
☎ 514/872-1400;
www.ville.montreal.qc.ca/jardin 🕐 Daily Jun–Sep; Tue–Sun rest of year 🖐 May–Oct expensive; Nov–Apr moderate

### Parc olympique de Montréal
🚇 218, off A5 ✉ 4141 avenue Pierre-de-Coubertin ☎ 514/252-4141; www.rio.gouv.qc.ca 🕐 Daily 9–7, mid-Jun to early Sep; 9–5 rest of year 🖐 Ascent of tower: expensive

### Biodôme de Montréal
🚇 218, off A5 ✉ 4777 avenue Pierre-de-Coubertin ☎ 514/868-3000; www.ville.montreal.qc.ca/biodome
🕐 Daily, late Jun–early Sep; Tue–Sun rest of year 🖐 Expensive

# 2 Québec City

Canada's oldest, and one of its most beautiful cities, Québec City has the only intact city walls in North America and some wonderful French colonial architecture. It was declared a UNESCO World Heritage Site in 1985. The city is in two parts. The upper town sits proudly atop a huge rocky promontory; the lower town nestles below, linked by the aptly named Escalier Casse-Cou (Breakneck Stairs).

**Opposite: maple syrup for sale**

**Below: Château Frontenac**

The city sits on the north bank of the St. Lawrence at the narrowest point along this stretch (the Iroquois called it Kebec, meaning "place where the waters narrow"). It was for this reason, and for its commanding high point, that it was chosen as a defensive settlement when hostilities between the French and English (and Iroquois) were at their height.

Start in the **Haute-Ville** (Upper Town), on the place d'Armes, once a military parade ground but now the focal point of this part of the city. It is dominated by the **Château Frontenac** hotel, a monumental structure in the style of a

Loire Valley château, with green-roofed turrets and towers. Entertaining guided tours are led by staff in costume.

Adjoining place d'Armes is the **Terrasse Dufferin**, a wide boardwalk with magnificent views across the river. Stretching for 670m (2,200ft), it's a popular place for a stroll. It was built in 1834 to provide access over the ruins of the Château St. Louis, and became so popular that it was extended and improved. It runs into the **Promenade des Gouverneurs** (Governors' Walk), which clings to the cliff-side 90m (295ft) above the river alongside the Citadel.

## QUÉBEC CITY: INSIDE INFO

**Top tips** Even if you have paid to take the tour, the **restrooms at the Château Frontenac** are only accessible by key card to residents. Public facilities can be found at the Infotourist Centre on place d'Armes and in the cafés on the square.
• Don't venture down to the **Basse-Ville** before 11 am. Up to this time trucks are permitted to make deliveries to the restaurants, and the narrow streets can be congested.

**In more depth** Outside the city walls in the Haute-Ville, on the Plains of Abraham, the **Musée du Québec** (Parc des Champs-de-Bataille; tel: 418/643-2150 or 866/220-2150; www.mdq.org; open Jun–early Sep daily, early Sep–May Tue–Sun; free, except temporary exhibitions) has a permanent collection devoted primarily to works by Québec artists and in particular gives an insight into the importance of the Church in Québec society.

**Hidden gem** On **rue Nôtre-Dame**, between Place-Royal and Côte de la Montagne, there is a 420sq m (4,520sq ft) *trompe-l'oeil* mural representing Québec's 400 years of history.

Still a military post, home of the elite Royal 22e Régiment, the **Citadelle** (Citadel) can only be visited by joining a group tour, but it is well worth doing so. It is vast, occupying 15ha (37 acres), and was the most important fortification to be built in Canada under British rule. The tours, led by military personnel, begin on the enormous parade ground and include the small regimental museum. In summer visitors are treated to impressive traditional military ceremonies, in full dress uniform, complete with the Regimental Band and the mascot (a goat called Batisse). A word of warning: Don't be tempted to wander away from the rest of your tour group – the military frown on visitors with an independent spirit.

From here you can take a walk around all or part of the 4.5km (3 miles) of the **Fortifications**, the walls and gates that encircle the old part of the city. To learn about their construction and preservation, call in along the way at the Initiation Centre and the Esplanade Powder Magazine. Inside the northwest corner of the Fortifications is the **Artillery**

The gleaming interior of the church of Ste. Anne de Beaupré

**Park National Historic Site**, used by the French and English until it was taken over by Parks Canada. You can visit the Arsenal Foundry, now an interpretation center, and see the officers' quarters, a 19th-century kitchen and the officers' mess.

Return to the Terrasse Dufferin and take the Funicular down to the **Basse-Ville** (Lower Town), centered on cobblestoned Place-Royal. It's a lovely area to stroll as it is largely traffic-free and there are lots of interesting little stores. The Roman Catholic cathedral, **Cathédrale Nôtre-Dame de Québec** has an opulent interior culminating in the glowing gold-finished canopy over the altar. In summer there's an excellent sound-and-light show.

One modern building, close to the river, is the **Musée de la Civilisation.** With its copper roof pierced by stylized dormer windows, it blends nicely with the older architecture and contains diverse thematic displays devoted to civilization in the broadest sense.

### TAKING A BREAK

If you like savory or sweet crêpes, you'll love **Au Petit Coin Breton** (418/694-0758, $$) on rue St.-Jean. There are also branches on boulevard Laurier and Grande Allée.

---

�︎ 208 B1

**Québec City Tourism**
✉ 399 St.-Joseph Est (also an Infotourist office on place d'Armes) ☎ 418/641-6654

**Château Frontenac**
🚫 217 C4 ✉ 1 rue des Carrières
☎ 418/691-2166; www.fairmont.com/frontenac ⏱ Tours daily in summer, weekends in winter ⬛ Moderate

**Citadelle**
🚫 217 B3 ✉ Cote de la Citadelle, Haute Ville ☎ 418/694-2815;
www.lacitadelle.qc.ca ⏱ Daily, Apr–Oct by 1-hour guided tour only ⬛ Moderate

**Fortifications**
🚫 217 A3 ✉ 100 rue St.-Louis
☎ 418/648-7016 or 800/463-6769;
www.pc.gc.ca/lhn-nhs/qc/fortifications

⏱ Initiation Centre and Powder Magazine: daily 10–5, mid-May to mid-Oct; by appointment rest of year ⬛ Free; Initiation Centre and Powder Magazine: inexpensive

**Artillery Park National Historic Site**
🚫 217 A4 ✉ Corner rue St.-Jean and rue d'Auteuil ☎ 418/648-4205;
www.pc.gc.ca/artillerie ⏱ Daily 10–5, Apr to mid-Oct ⬛ Inexpensive

**Cathédrale Nôtre-Dame de Québec**
🚫 217 C4 ✉ rue Ste.-Famille
☎ 418/694-0665; www.patrimoine-religieux.com ⏱ Daily 7:30–4:30 ⬛ Free

**Musée de la Civilisation**
🚫 217 C5 ✉ 85 rue Dalhousie
☎ 418/643-2158 or 866/710-8031;
www.mcq.org ⏱ Daily 9:30–6:30, late Jun–early Sep; Tue–Sun 10–5 rest of year
⬛ Moderate

# ③ Charlevoix Coast

On the north shore of the wide St. Lawrence River, the
Charlevoix is one of Québec's most beautiful and varied
regions, with mountains sweeping down to the water's edge,
a mixture of wild and neat rural landscapes, and charming
villages nestling in the valleys. It stretches from Beaupré,
northeast of Québec City, to Tadoussac, at the confluence of
the Saguenay and St. Lawrence rivers, and for its unique
beauty, it is a UNESCO World Biosphere Reserve.

Every June a great flotilla of whales makes its way upstream to
feed in the deep waters off Tadoussac, at the mouth of the
Saguenay, and a great wave of visitors arrive to view them on
whale-watching boat trips. The most common species to visit
these rich waters are the minke and fin whale, but occasion-
ally a humpback will be sighted and if you're very lucky a
blue whale. There's also a resident population of belugas.

**Tadoussac's
boardwalk
overlooks the
pretty harbor**

    The mountains of the Charlevoix were not formed by
volcanic or glacial action, but by a 15-billion ton meteorite
that struck the earth 350 million years ago. The resulting
crater measures about 56km (35 miles), and is the largest of
its kind in the world.

    Heading northeast along the coast, **Baie-St.-Paul** is set
amid rolling hills on a bay where the Gouffre River flows into
the St. Lawrence, a site that has inspired many artists. As a
result, it has many galleries and a reputation as a cultural
center. Sheltering the bay is the delightfully rural **Île-aux-
Coudres**, 11km (7 miles) long and 5km (3 miles) across its
widest point, with exceptional views.

Baie-St.-Paul has a lovely little working harbor

Farther along the coast is **Les Éboulements**, perched 300m (980ft) above the river, with wonderful views. Later, the road sweeps down to river level, passing through **Ste.-Irénée**, host of a prestigious music festival, then continues to the popular resort of **La Malbaie**. It's said that it was named *malle baye* ("bad bay") by French explorer Samuel de Champlain in 1608 after his ship ran aground overnight.

**Baie-Ste.-Catherine** and **Tadoussac** face each other across the mouth of the Saguenay at the heart of the Saguenay-St. Lawrence Marine Park, and both provide whale-watching trips. Tadoussac has a fine site on the cliffs and sand dunes of the north shore, and swells with visitors when the whales are here. Near the marina, you can visit the **Interpretation Centre for Marine Mammals** (CIMM), with some fascinating interactive exhibits, models and photographs. You can test your lung capacity against that of a whale, and listen by hydrophone to the sounds they make out in the river.

### TAKING A BREAK

Stop where you see a big model sailboat on the signboard in Tadoussac for a meal on the deck of **Restaurant le Bateau** (tel: 418/235-4427, $$). Wonderful views and tasty Québecois specialties.

---

## CHARLEVOIX COAST: INSIDE INFO

**Top tips** You can **get a ferry** from St.-Siméon across the St. Lawrence River to Rivière-du-Loup on the opposite shore, with magnificent views in both directions during the entire voyage.

• For **whale-watching trips** you can choose between the standard, large boats that offer a good view from higher in the water, or the zippy little Zodiac inflatables that can get closer to the whales and provide a really exciting experience.

---

✚ 208 B2

**Tourisme Québec**
✉ Case postale 979, Montréal
☎ 514/873-2015 or 877/266-5687;
www.bonjourquebec.com

**Association Touristique Régionale de Charlevoix**

✉ 495 boulevard de Comporté, CP 275, La Malbaie ☎ 418/665-4454 or 800/667-2276; www.tourisme-charlevoix.com

**Interpretation Centre for Marine Mammals**
✉ Tadoussac ☎ 418/235-4701 🕐 Mid-May to Oct

# ④ Saguenay Fjord

Flowing through a great gash in the Precambrian rock, between the Laurentian Mountains and the wilderness of northern Québec, the Saguenay is not a long river, but it is incredibly dramatic, emptying into the St. Lawrence River between Baie-Ste.-Catherine and Tadoussac. In its upper reaches, it flows out of Lac-St.-Jean and drops about 90m (295ft) in wild and rocky rapids. Then, in its final 60km (37 miles) it transforms into a deep and majestic fjord, with sheer cliffs rising out of the water.

The best way to really appreciate the full grandeur of the Saguenay Fjord is from the water on one of the many cruises. A highlight of any cruise is the arrival at **Cap Trinité**, rising dramatically 500m (1,640ft) out of the dark waters. In its wild and rocky setting, it is an awesome sight. The name is derived from the three ledges that punctuate its face and on the first of these, about 180m (590ft) above the water, there is a statue of the Virgin. The statue was carved in 1881 for

**Much of the spectacular scenery of the fjord can only be truly appreciated from the water**

## Cruises

**Croisières La Marjolaine:** Boulevard Saguenay Est (CP 203), Port de Chicoutimi, tel: 418/543-7360 or 800/363-7248; www.quebecweb.com/marjo, open Jun–Sep, daily (reservations essential), expensive (under 6 free).

**Croisières AML:** From Tadoussac and Baie-Ste.-Catherine, tel: 418/692-1159 or 800/563-4643;, www.croisieresaml.com; open daily, Jul–early Sep.

**Famille Dufour Croisières:** From Tadoussec; www.groupedufour.com; open daily, June–Sep.

**These little craft get closer to the whales than conventional boats**

Charles-Napoléon Robitaille, whose life had been saved twice following appeals to the Virgin. Standing 9m (30ft) high, it was transported in three sections by boat then raised into position.

The cape is also accessible by land, on Route 170, about 65km (40 miles) east of Chicoutimi. Here, between Cap Trinité and Cap Éternité is the delightful little **Baie Éternité**, at the entrance to the **Parc du Saguenay**, which protects the edges of the fjord. The village has fine views and a waterside path. From here you can hike the 3km (2 miles) to the top of Cap Trinité, then descend to the statue (allow four hours).

**Chicoutimi** is the main center of population on the fjord and the starting point for many cruises. It was built and prospered on industry, with power generated from the rushing waters upstream, and its main tourist attraction today is the old pulp mill, **La Pulperie de Chicoutimi**. Set in a city park, it is now a museum and cultural center, with a trail through the old buildings and interesting displays. Unexpectedly, the site includes the house of artist Arthur Villeneuve, a remarkable building decorated with murals by the artist himself, which now houses exhibits on history and art.

### TAKING A BREAK

**La Bougresse** (tel: 418/543-3178, $$$) on the corner of rue Hotel Dieu and rue Riverin in Chicoutimi is a lively bistro serving wholesome Québecoise specialties.

## SAGUENAY FJORD: INSIDE INFO

**Top tips** Late afternoon provides the best light for taking **photographs** from Croix de Ste.-Anne, .
• Avoid hiking the trail to the top of Cap Trinité **in midsummer**, when it is plagued with mosquitoes.

---

✚ 208 B2

**Chicoutimi Tourism**
✉ 295 rue Racine Est (CP 1023), Chicoutimi ☎ 418/698-3167

**Parc du Saguenay**
✉ 91 Nôtre-Dame, Rivière-Éternité
☎ 418/272-1556 or 800/665-6527;

www.sepaq.com/saguenay 🕐 Daily, mid-May to mid-Oct 🎫 Moderate (per car)

**Pulperie de Chicoutimi**
✉ 300 Dubuc, Chicoutimi ☎ 418/698-3100; www.pulperie.com 🕐 Daily 9–6, late Jun–early Sep; museum only rest of year, 9 or 10–4 or 5. Closed most public holidays 🎫 Moderate

# At Your Leisure

**Gaspé Peninsula** ➤ 185–187

**Gatineau** ➤ 98

## 5 Cantons-de-l'Est (Eastern Townships)

A land of mountains, lakes and delightful villages, the Eastern Townships have a unique mix of Anglo-Saxon charm and Québécois *joie-de-vivre*. Here the rolling wooded slopes of the Appalachian Mountains rise to nearly 1,000m (about 3,000ft) and lakes fill the valleys.

Communities include **Knowlton**, a charming "Victorian" village brimming with craft shops, boutiques, art galleries and restaurants. Farther east, **Magog** has a wonderful location on Lake Memphremagog, beneath Mount Orford and surrounded by the **Parc du Mont-Orford**. It's scenic boat trips are the main draw, though, visiting the **Abbaie St.-Benoît** (monastery) on the lakeshore.

✚ 208 B1

#### Tourisme Cantons-de-l'Est
✉ 20 rue du Bosco Sud, Sherbrooke
☎ 819/820-2020 or 800/355-5755;
www.tourisme-cantons.qc.ca

#### Parc du Mont-Orford
✉ 3321 chemin du Parc, Canton d'Orford ☎ 819/843-9855 or 800/665-6527; www.sepaq.com 🎫 Inexpensive

Magog, in the Cantons-de-l'est, is on the shore of the beautiful Lake Maphremagog

#### Abbaie St.-Benoît
✉ St.-Benoît-du-Lac ☎ 819/843-4080;
www.st-benoit-du-lac.com 🕐 Daily,
year-round; store open Mon–Sat (closed
10:45–11:45 during Eucharist)

## 6 Trois-Rivières

Where it flows into the St. Lawrence, the St. Maurice River splits into three to flow around two islands, and it was here that Québec's second-oldest city was founded in 1634. Today, Trois-Rivières is the third-largest city in the province, and has a number of historic attractions. The suburb of **Cap-de-la-Madeleine** is famous for its **Sanctuaire Nôtre-Dame-du-Cap**, incorporating the beautiful octagonal Rosary Basilica, which attracts half a million pilgrims each year. **Les Forges du St.-Maurice**, a little way north, was Canada's first iron-smelting works, and is now a national historic site.

✚ 208 A1

#### Office de Tourisme et des Congrès de Trois-Rivières
✉ 1457 rue Nôtre-Dame ☎ 819/375-1123 or 800/313-1122; www.v3r.net

#### Sanctuaire Nôtre-Dame-du-Cap
✉ 626 rue Nôtre-Dame, Cap-de-la-

Manoir Mauvide-Genest is a stately building on the Île d'Orléans

Madeleine ☎ 819/374-2441; www.sanctuaire-ndc.ca ⏰ Daily for Mass

**Forges du St.-Maurice**
✉ 10,000 boulevard des Forges, Trois-Rivières ☎ 819/378-5116 or 800/463-6769; www.pc.gc.ca
⏰ Mid-May to mid-Oct daily
👐 Inexpensive

## 7 Île d'Orléans

Wedged like a giant cork in the St. Lawrence River as it widens beyond Québec City, this beautiful and fertile island preserves some fine French architecture from the 18th century. Farmhouses with steeply pitched roofs, ancestral mansions and old churches line the shores and dot the agricultural areas. The jewel among them is the **Manoir Mauvide-Genest**, which has been meticulously restored and populated with costumed guides, who re-create life here in former times.
➕ 208 B1

**Chambre de Commerce de L'Île d'Orléans**
✉ 490 Côte du Pont, St.-Pierre ☎ 418/828-9411 or 866/941-9411; www.iled orleans.qc.ca

**Manoir Mauvide-Genest**
✉ 1451 chemin Royal, St.-Jean
☎ 418/ 829-2330 ⏰ May–Oct daily
👐 Moderate

## 8 Les Laurentides

A land of sport, leisure, good food and *joie-de-vivre*, this is Montréal's "cottage country." The Laurentians, some of the oldest mountains in the world, are modest in height, rising to no more than 960m (3,150ft), but are very scenic, with trees clinging precariously to their rocky slopes. The highest point is Mont Tremblant, focal point of the **Mont Tremblant National Park**, where there is now a superb alpine-style ski resort. Longer-established as a ski resort is **St.-Sauveur-des-Monts**, which has some excellent restaurants, boutiques and craft shops. **Ste.-Agathe-des-Monts** is set on lovely Lac-des-Sables (Sandy Lake), and offers popular boat cruises.
➕ 208 A1

**Association Touristique des Laurentides**
✉ 14142 rue de la Chapelle, Mirabel
☎ 450/436-8532 or 800/561-6673; www.laurentides.com

## 9 Lac St.-Jean

Source of the mighty Saguenay River (► 131–132), this vast, saucer-shaped lake covers 1,350sq km (850sq miles) amid flat, fertile land known for its wild blueberries. The **Village Historique de Val-Jalbert** is dominated by the magnificent Ouiatchouan Falls. Abandoned in 1927, the village was restored in the 1960s to give a nostalgic reminder of better times, enhanced by theatrical performances in summer.
➕ 208 A2

**Fédératon Touristique Régionale du Saguenay-Lac-St.-Jean**
✉ 455 rue Racine Est, Bureau 101, Chicoutimi ☎ 418/543-9778 or 877/253-8387; www.tourismesaguenay-lacsaintjean.qc.ca

**Village Historique de Val-Jalbert**
✉ 95 rue Saint-George, route 169, Chambord ☎ 418/275-3132 or 888/675-3132; www.sepaq.com
⏰ Daily, mid-May to mid-Oct (full animation mid-Jun to late Aug)
👐 Expensive

# Where to... Stay

**Prices**
High season room-only rates, based on two sharing a double room, excluding taxes
$ up to $120    $$ $121–$260    $$$ more than $260

## MONTRÉAL

### ❤❤ Auberge Le Jardin D'Antoine $-$$

In the heart of the Latin Quarter, this is an elegant little European-style hotel in a 19th-century building, and the bilingual owners and staff offer a friendly welcome. Rooms and suites all have queen- or king-size beds, and some of the private bathrooms have whirlpool tubs. All but two of the rooms overlook the pleasant interior courtyard. Breakfast is included in the rates.

➕ 201 A1 ✉ 2024 rue St.-Denis ☎ 514/843-4506, 800/361-4506; fax: 514/281-1491; www.hotel-jardin-antoine.qc.ca

### ❤❤❤ Château Versailles $$$

This is a stylish historic hotel, with original plaster moldings and huge fireplaces standing out against bold-colored walls hung with Matisse reproductions. Bedrooms have cable TV, minibar, Nintendo and coffee-makers, and are provided with bathrobes and luxury toiletries.

➕ 201 A1 ✉ 1659 rue Sherbrooke ouest ☎ 514/933-3611, 888/933-8111; fax: 514/933-8401; www.versailleshotels.com

### ❤❤❤ Fairmont The Queen Elizabeth $$

This grand, luxury hotel hit the world's newsreels in 1969, when John Lennon staged his famous "bed in" (in Suite 1742) and wrote and recorded "Give Peace a Chance." Lennon wasn't the first celebrity to stay here – it's hosted the rich and famous since it opened in 1958. Premier rooms and suites offer the best views. There's a modern health club, an indoor swimming pool and direct access to the underground city.

➕ 201 A1 ✉ 900 Boulevard René-Levesque ouest ☎ 514/861-3511; fax: 514/954-2256; www.fairmont.com

### ❤❤❤ Hotel Ruby Foos $$-$$$

Just off the TransCanada, this is a good option for those who prefer to be out of the city. Rooms are modern and have cable TV and coffee-makers; some have kitchenettes, and two-bedroom suites are available. A choice of restaurants serve seafood, Continental cuisine and sushi, and there's a fitness center.

➕ 201 A1 ✉ 7655 boulevard Decarie ☎ 514/731-770. 800/361-5419; fax: 514/731-7158; www.hotel-rubyfoos.com

## QUÉBEC CITY

### ❤❤❤ Auberge St.-Antoine $$-$$$

Though it doesn't look it from the outside, this is a new hotel, converted from a derelict warehouse in 2003. The owners have done a superb job of creating a hotel that has enormous character, and made some bold choices in the process. You'll want to keep coming back, just to be able to stay in a different room each time.

➕ 208 B1 ✉ 8 rue St.-Antoine ☎ 418/692-2211; fax: 418/692-1177; www.saint-antoine.com

### ❤❤❤ Fairmont Le Château Frontenac $$$

Like a fairy-tale European château, with steep roofs, turrets and dormer windows, this magnificent hotel dominates its surroundings and is an integral part of the city scene. Particularly imposing seen from the lower town, it is without question the most prestigious place to stay

# Where to... Eat and Drink

## MONTRÉAL

### ⚐⚐ Ben's Montréal Deli $–$$

This whole place, started by the Kravitz family in 1908, harks back to a different age, from the soda fountain to the photographs of past celebrity patrons on the walls, but its no-frills appeal has never waned. The menu is strong on smoked meat sandwiches and platters, with burgers and pasta dishes thrown in for good measure.

➕ 208 A1  ⌑ 990 boulevard de Maisonneuve ouest  ☎ 514/844-1000  ⊙ Daily 7:30 am–2 am (Thu to 3 am, Fri–Sat to 4 am)

### ⚐⚐ Le Commensal $–$$

French cuisine, which naturally predominates in this city, is not particularly noted for providing vegetarian options, so this chain is a welcome relief to those who prefer a meat-free diet. Home-style dishes are set out buffet style and you pay by the weight of what's on your plate. There are well-labeled vegan options too, and the staff is very knowledgeable about what they are serving. Also on rue St.-Denis, just south of rue Ontario.

➕ 208 A1  ⌑ 1204 avenue McGill College  ☎ 514/871-1480  ⊙ Daily 11:30–10

---

and it's hard to believe that it was built as something so mundane as a railroad hotel. Inside it is as luxurious as you might expect of a place that has such a long list of royalty and movie stars among its clientele.

➕ 208 B1  ⌑ 1 rue des Carrières  ☎ 418/692-3861, 800/257-7455; fax: 418/692-1751; www.fairmont.com

### ⚐⚐ L'Hôtel du Vieux Québec $–$$

This is a fascinating building, with staircases leading this way and that before finally arriving at your room, which is likely to have sloping ceilings and exposed stone walls. It's in a great location within the old city walls and the friendly owners run free guided walks in summer.

➕ 208 B1  ⌑ 1190 rue St-Jean  ☎ 418/692-1850, 800/361-7787; fax: 418/692-5637; www.hvq.com

### ⚐⚐ Hotel Le Priori $–$$

The chic modern decor sets off to perfection the exposed brick and hardwood floors of this 18th-

---

century building in the Old Port. All bedrooms have ensuite bathrooms with massaging showers, but some also have an old-fashioned tub right in the room. Suites have whirlpools, fireplaces and kitchens. The restaurant is of a high standard and breakfasts (included in the price) are delicious and generous.

➕ 208 B1  ⌑ 15 Sault-au-Matelot  ☎ 418/692-3992; fax: 418/692-0883

## TADOUSSAC

### ⚐⚐ Hotel Le Beluga $

In the heart of Tadoussac, this is a lovely, traditional, clapboard building. Its 39 rooms are charmingly decorated with pretty fabrics and light-wood furniture set against plain walls, and each has cable TV. The restaurant, in a separate building next door, is equally attractive with an all-day à la carte menu and table d'hôte in the evening.

➕ 208 B2  ⌑ 191 rue des Pionniers  ☎ 418/235-4784; fax: 418/235-4295  ⊙ Closed mid-Dec–Mar

## L'Express $$

There's a real Parisian atmosphere in this Latin Quarter bistro, from its zinc bar to its lively clientele of regulars. The menu is full of classic French favorites, such as *bouillabaisse*, steak tartare, steak-frites and seafood, and the wines are exclusively French. It's extremely popular so reservations are essential – and make sure you get directions when you call, because it's not that easy to find.

🖪 208 A1 ⊠ 3927 rue St-Denis
🖀 514/845-5333 🕲 Daily
8 am–3 am

## Nuances $$$

If there's one thing you expect to find in Montréal it's excellent French cuisine, and this is one of the best places of all. Part of the casino complex, it's very formal and the presentation and flavors of the food is nothing short of artistic. Dishes might include an asparagus and lobster chartreuse appetizer, clay-baked loin of lamb with gnoc-

chi, or parmesan breaded eggplant (aubergine) and bell-pepper ratatouille. There's a dress code – business smart – and an age limit: diners here must be over 18.

🖪 208 A1 ⊠ 5th Floor, Casino du Montréal, 1 avenue du Casino
🖀 514/392-2708, 800/665-2274;
www.casino-de-montreal.com
🕲 Daily 5:30–11 (11:30 Fri–Sat)

## 3 Amigos Resto-Bar $–$$

In an easy-to-find, downtown location, this is a Mexican/Tex-Mex restaurant that offers deliciously authentic south-of-the-border cuisine. The daily specials are particularly good value.

🖪 208 A1 ⊠ 1657 rue Ste.-Catherine ouest 🖀 514/939-3329
🕲 11 am–midnight (1am Fri–Sat)

## Weinstein & Gavino's Pasta Bar Factory Co Ltd $–$$

On Montréal's busy nightclub street, this popular restaurant is always busy and always buzzing, spilling out onto the terrace in

warm weather. The menu features all the traditional Italian dishes, including an extensive *antipasti* selection, pastas, pizzas and entrées that include chicken, steak, seafood and lamb. Good value and good fun.

🖪 208 A1 ⊠ 1434 rue Crescent
🖀 514/288-2231;
www.weinsteinandgavinos.com
🕲 Daily 11–11 (midnight Thu–Sat)

# QUÉBEC CITY

## Restaurant Aux Anciens Canadiens $$

This is a gorgeous place – the oldest building in Québec City, dating back to 1675 – and the five separate dining rooms give it a very intimate atmosphere. The menu has some interesting dishes, such as caribou cooked with creamy blueberry wine sauce, and a ragout of boar and pig's knuckles, served with meatballs. There's lavish use of maple syrup in the desserts, completing the authentic Canadian experience.

🖪 208 B2 ⊠ 34 rue St-Louis,
Haute-Ville 🖀 tel: 418/692-1627;
www.auxancienscanadiens.qc.ca
🕲 Daily noon–10

## Restaurant le Parlementaire $$

Dine like a diplomat beneath glittering chandeliers in the National Assembly's imposing beaux-arts dining room. This restaurant is renowned for its regional cuisine using top-quality Québec produce, and the cost is surprisingly reasonable. Main courses might include paupillette de volaille au jambon, trout with cider and mint, or grilled steak with mushrooms and thyme. Breakfasts are good, too, including omelets and crêpes.

🖪 208 B1 ⊠ National Assembly (Door No. 3) 🖀 418/643-6640;
www.assnat.qc.ca 🕲 Mon–Fri from 9am, late Jun–early Sep: 8–11, 11:30–2:30 (also 5:30–8 Tue & Fri).
May and Dec (hours vary and the restaurant may be closed without notice for government reasons)

# Where to... Shop

Québec offers a different shopping experience from anywhere else in Canada, with its distinctive French chic combined with refreshing Canadian enthusiasm and First Nations traditions.

## MONTRÉAL

As Canada's second-largest city, Montréal has terrific shopping – and if you're here in winter, you'll be glad to know that much of it is sheltered from the bitter cold in the Ville Souterraine (underground city, ▶ 120). The **Complexe Desjardins** (150 rue Ste.-Catherine Ouest, tel: 514/281-1870) is the largest building in the network, centering on the huge Grande Place, and has more than 100 stores, but the **Montréal Eaton Centre** (705 rue Ste.-Catherine Ouest, tel: 514/288-3708) tops this with 175 units and is the main shopping destination in the city. **Place Montréal Trust** (1500 avenue McGill College, tel: 514/843-8000) is another bright and lofty mall in the underground city, with around 100 stores.

Montréal has three great traditional markets, each with a character all of its own. **Atwater Market** (138 avenue Atwater, tel: 514/937-7754), in a distinctive building with a tall clock tower, has fresh produce and gourmet foods; **Jean-Talon** (7075 avenue Casgrain, tel: 514/277-1588) is a cosmopolitan treasure in the heart of Little Italy; and **Maisonneuve Market** (4445 rue Montréal Est, tel: 514/937-7754) is a 1990s reincarnation of the original 1914 market, not only a place to buy local produce, but also a cultural center for festivals and entertainment.

The **Marché Bonsecours** (350 rue St.-Paul Est, tel: 514/872-7730), in a magnificent building in the Old City, is headquarters of the Design Council, with two galleries and 15 boutiques selling top-quality crafts. More top-quality crafts are on show at the **Canadian Guild of Crafts** (2025 rue Peel, tel: 514/849-6091), a non-profit (which doesn't necessarily mean inexpensive) outlet for Canadian artisans. Little **rue du Trésor** is where you'll find sidewalk artists selling their work.

If it's antiques you're looking for, stroll along **Antiques Row** (rue Notre-Dame Ouest, between Guy and Atwater), where down-to-earth vendors sell from decidedly unglamorous premises. There are bargains to be found.

## QUÉBEC CITY

This beautiful old city is home to a huge shopping mall – **Place Laurier** (2700 boulevard Laurier, tel: 418/ 651-7085), with around

## TADOUSSAC

### Le William ($$)

Within the landmark three-diamond rated Hotel Tadoussac, this intimate restaurant is renowned for excellent seafood, bought daily from local North Shore fishermen.

➕ 208 B2 ⊠ 165 rue Bord de l'Eau ☎ 418/235-4421, 888/222-3307 🕘 Daily

## PERCÉ

### ▼▼▼ La Normandie $$–$$$

This waterfront hotel dining room is renowned for some of the best food in the area – and it has great views of Rocher Percé and Île Bonaventure. There's a refined atmosphere and the four-course table d'hôte offers more than 20 main courses. You can also get a European-style breakfast buffet.

➕ 208 C3 ⊠ Hotel La Normandie, 221 Route 123 ☎ 418/782-2112; www.normandieperce.com 🕘 Daily 7:30–10 am, 6–9 pm, Jun–Sep

350 stores – but the city is better known for streets of individual stores that enhance the whole experience of a visit.

The Lower Town is chock full of artisan-owned craft boutiques and galleries. **Artisans du Bas-Canada** (30 Côte de la Fabrique, tel: 418/692-2109) is a long-established showcase for the work of around 500 Canadian artists and crafts-people, including Inuit and First Nations works. At **Verrerie la Mailloche** (58 rue Sous-le-Fort, tel: 418/694-0445), near the base of the funicular, you can watch the master glassblower making delicate works of art. Take the funicular up to visit the **Galeries d'Art Inuit Brousseau et Brousseau** (35 rue St-Louis, tel: 418/694-1828), next door to Le Chateau Frontenac, a gallery dedicated to promoting the work of Inuit artists from Arctic Canada, or call in at the **5 Nations Indian Art Gallery** (20 rue Cul-de-Sac, tel: 418/692-1009), representing First

Nations artists from across North America.

The city's **Public Market** (160 quai St.-André, tel: 418/692-2517) has a particularly good cheese selection and lots of maple syrup products alongside the usual fruit and vegetables.

Bookstores carry mostly French-language titles and some in English, but **La Maison Anglaise** (2600 boulevard Laurier, tel: 418/654-9523) only has books in English and specializes in fiction.

Montréal is the center for the Canadian fur industry, a contentious issue in many places, but seen here as a traditional means of supporting First Nations people who might otherwise be forced to give their land over to oil and mineral exploitation in order to survive, causing severe ecological consequences. Of many city furriers, **Dubarry Furs** (370 rue Sherbrooke Ouest, tel: 514/844-7483) has some original designs and will make to measure.

# Where to...
# Be Entertained

**Many of the theater productions here are in French, and you need a good understanding of the language to fully appreciate them, but there are some shows in English. Of course, music is universal and Québec offers some world-class performances in every genre.**

## MONTRÉAL

This city has everything you would expect from the second-largest French-speaking city in the world. The whole spectrum of entertainment is laid out for you, from the most prestigious classical performances to somewhat risqué night-

clubs, and everything in between. The **Place des Arts** (tel: 514/842-2112) is the showpiece venue, central to Montréal's cultural life, with five halls totaling 6,000 seats and a full schedule of classical music, ballet and opera. Mega rock concerts and massive classical events are staged at the **Bell Centre** (1260 rue de la Gauchetière Ouest, tel: 514/790-1245). More intimate is the **Centre Pierre Peladeau** (300 boulevard Maisonneuve Est, tel: 514/987-6919). Montréal theaters include the **Centaur** (453 rue St-François-Xavier, tel: 514/288-3161), home to the city's leading English-language company, with a reputation for ground-breaking productions. The **Théâtre du Nouveau Monde** (84 rue Ste-Catherine Ouest, tel: 514/878-7878) stages classical and modern drama, **La Chapelle** (3700 rue Ste.-Dominique, tel: 514/843-7738) stages drama in French, plus roots, jazz and classical music concerts, and the **Saidye Bronfman Centre for the Arts** (5170 rue Côte Ste.-Catherine, tel: 514/739-2301) is an internationally acclaimed venue offering a wide range of productions in English and Yiddish. One of the city's premier jazz clubs is the **House of Jazz** (2060 rue Aylmer, tel: 514/842-8656), with live music nightly from big-name and local performers, plus jam sessions.

Nightlife in Montréal is really buzzing, with a huge number of nightclubs and bars, and more than 100 gay venues, including the vast **Bourbon Complex** (1474 rue Ste.-Catherine Est, tel: 514/529-6969). The **Casino de Montréal** (1 avenue du Casino, tel: 514/392-2746 or 800/665-2274) in a spectacular waterfront location, offers gaming tables, slot machines and Las Vegas-style shows.

Montréal is also world-famous for comedy because of its annual "Just for Laughs" festival, and permanent comedy clubs include **Ernie Butler's Comedy Nest** (Forum Pepsi, 2313 rue Ste.-Catherine Ouest, tel: 514/932-6378) and **Comedy Works** (1238 rue Bishop, tel: 514/398-9661), both of which feature top comedy names and open mike sessions.

Every other year, you get the chance to see the spectacular **Cirque du Soleil** on home ground, when the Québec company sets up its distinctive striped marquees in Montréal. Check with the tourist office for information.

Sport gets an enthusiastic following here, especially when one of the teams is playing the city's great rival, Toronto. The **Montréal Canadiens** are the hockey team, playing at the **Bell Centre** (1260 rue de la Gauchetière Ouest, tel: 514/790-1245); the **Montréal Expos** are one of only two Canadian baseball teams in the American Major League (Toronto's Blue Jays is the other), and they play to rousing support at the Olympic Stadium (4549 avenue Pierre de Coubertin, tel: 514/8GO-EXPOS); and the **Alouettes** Canadian football team play at the **Percival Molson Memorial Stadium** (475 avenue des Pins, tel: 514/871-2266). The **Canadian Grand Prix** takes place at the Gilles Villeneuve circuit, accessible from the city on the métro system.

## QUÉBEC CITY

Entertainment in Québec City is more low-key, but it does have the province's premier theater, the **Grand Théâtre de Québec** (269 boulevard René-Lévesque Est, tel: 418/643-8131), home to the Opera de Québec and the Québec Symphony Orchestra. Its two concert halls provide a full schedule of dance, drama and music. The **Petit Champlain** (Maison de la Chanson, 68–78 rue du Petit-Champlain, tel: 418/92-4774) is an atmospheric little theater in a converted warehouse, staging concerts by French-speaking performers. There are a couple of places where you can experience a truly French evening listening to Québecois chansons: **Les Yeux Bleus** (1117 1/2 St.-Jean, tel: 418/694-9118), which also has some pop music; and the **Café des Arts** (1000 rue St-Jean, tel: 418/694-1499), where chansons shares the bill with jazz, poetry readings and mime.

The **Terrasse d'Orsay** (65 rue de Buade, tel: 418/694-1582) is a lovely old pub-restaurant with a small dance floor and a DJ or live music. If you're visiting in winter, drive out to the famous Ice Hotel's nightclub, **N'Ice** (143 route Duchesnay, Ste.-Catherine-de-la-Jacques-Cartier, tel: 418/875-4522) which is as hot as it can be at a constant -2°C (28°F). This remarkable hotel is built anew every winter from blocks of ice.

# Atlantic Provinces

# Getting Your Bearings

Add together the three mainland Atlantic provinces – New Brunswick, Prince Edward Island and Nova Scotia – and you wouldn't achieve the size of just one of the other provinces of Canada. And yet, here on the eastern seaboard, you will find a concentration of some of Canada's oldest settlements, a history that shaped the whole country, and a fascinating mixture of cultures that encompasses a large number of Acadian French and communities of Scottish descent (Nova Scotia means "New Scotland"). Put Newfoundland into the mix and you'll get evidence of the earliest Viking visitors, the first footfall of explorer John Cabot (though Nova Scotians may argue this point), and the great wave of immigrants who came here from Ireland during the Great Famine.

The character of this part of Canada is quite different from the rest of the country, with Atlantic salt in the air, fiddle music in the blood, and a slower pace of life, even on the city streets. The scenery is breathtaking, with rocky coastlines, beautiful beaches, dense forests, wide river valleys and vast stretches of wilderness in Newfoundland and Labrador. The land supports a variety of wildlife, including moose, bear and caribou, while whales, seals and dolphins inhabit the coastal waters. Quaint seaside towns of colorful clapboard buildings sit on pretty coves, and, aside from Halifax, the provincial capitals are small and low-rise, with quiet tree-lined streets and fascinating historic corners.

The climate is generally warm in summer, although coastal areas are prone to mists and strong winds. In winter it's milder here than in many parts of Canada, but snowfall is among the highest in the country, making it excellent for cross-country skiing, dog-sledding and snowmobiling. Winter and summer, the place is lively with festivals and other events.

*Bluenose II* recalls a glorious maritime past

## ★ Don't Miss

## At Your Leisure

The Cabot Trail around the north of Cape Breton Island features breathtaking coastal scenery

Page 141:
Flags maritime and national fly from the signal mast of the Citadel, Halifax

Marconi's historic radio signal is commemorated on Signal Hill, St. John's, Newfoundland

Get an overview of the Maritimes, including provincial capitals, national parks and historic settlements, spectacular coastlines, and a few oddities of nature along the way.

# Atlantic Provinces in Nine Days

## Day One

**Morning** Begin in **1** Halifax (➤ 146–147), up on the Citadel, then head down to the Water-front for a boat trip of the harbor (➤ right).
**Lunch** Have lunch at Salty's (➤ 160), with a great view over the harbor.
**Afternoon** Explore the Historic Properties, Maritime Museum and Pier 21 to get a feel for the city's maritime heritage.
**Evening** Sample some East Coast entertainment in one of the city pubs.

## Day Two

**Morning** Drive to **8** Annapolis Royal (➤ 156) and see its two National Historic Sites.
**Lunch** There's a good selection of restaurants in Annapolis Royal.
**Afternoon** Continue to Digby for the ferry across the Bay of Fundy to Saint John, New Brunswick, take a look at the Reversing Falls at low or high tide, then continue west to spend the night at Back Bay.

## Day Three

**Morning** Take the ferry to the **2** Fundy Islands (➤ 148), first to Deer Island, then on to Campobello to explore the **Roosevelt International Park**.
**Lunch** Have a picnic in the park.
**Afternoon** Return to the mainland and overnight at Saint John. Return to Reversing Falls (if the tide is right) to see them flow the other way.

## Day Four

**Morning** Drive east on Highway 1, then take the 114 down through the **Fundy National Park** to Alma, then east along the Fundy Coast Drive. Visit the Hopewell Rocks along the way, then continue to Moncton – stop off at Magnetic Hill, to experience the weird sensation of freewheeling "uphill".
**Lunch** At Magnetic Hill there's a re-created fishing wharf beside a duck pond, with a family restaurant.
**Afternoon** Take Highway 15 out through Shediac and Cap-Pele. Follow signs for **3** Prince Edward Island (➤ 149–150) and stop at the visitor center on the New Brunswick side for a great view of Confederation Bridge. Drive across the bridge and make your way up to Cavendish.

# Day Five

**Morning** Visit the **PEI National Park** and **Green Gables House**.
**Lunch** Opposite Avonlea, a charming re-creation of the
village in *Anne of Green Gables*, the Captain's Cove restau-
rant (tel: 902/963-2700; winter 902/566-4705, $$$) has
a good range of steaks, seafood and snacks.
**Afternoon** Drive down to the provincial capital of
**Charlottetown** for a quick look round, then head for Wood
Islands on the south coast and take the ferry to Caribou on
the Nova Scotia mainland.
**Evening** Drive east to spend the night at Antigonish.

# Day Six

**Morning** From Antigonish, continue on the 104 to cross
the Canso Causeway onto **4 Cape Breton Island**
(► 151–152). Visit the interesting little town of Baddeck, then follow the
Cabot Trail (► 188–190) northwest to Cheticamp.
**Lunch** Among Cheticamp's many restaurants, the Co-op Artisinale (tel:
902/224-3207, $$) is an interesting choice, on the site of an Acadian
craft center, serving traditional Acadian dishes.
**Afternoon** Continue on the Cabot Trail, passing through the spectacular
scenery of the **Cape Breton Highlands National Park**, looping around the top
of the island and down the other side through Ingonish.
**Evening** Spend the night in North Sydney and try to get to a Cape Breton
ceilidh.

# Day Seven

**Morning** Take the morning ferry from North Sydney to Port aux Basques,
Newfoundland (6 hours), and drive up to **Deer Lake** for the night.

# Day Eight

**Morning** Drive west into **5 Gros Morne National Park** (► 153), and at
Wiltondale take Highway 430 along the north shore of Bonne Bay.
**Lunch** Have lunch at Rocky Harbour.
**Afternoon** Retrace your steps to Deer Lake and drive across the island to
**6 St. John's** (► 154–155).
**Evening** At 9:30pm join the fun guided Ghost Tour (tel:709/685-3444).

# Day Nine

**Morning** Drive up **Signal Hill** for the spectacular view along the coast.
**Lunch** There are lots of pubs and restaurants in St. John's; the Hungry
Fisherman (tel: 726-5791, $$$) in the Murray Premises is strong on
seafood.
**Afternoon** Take a whale-watching trip from the harbor.
**Evening** Wander around the historic streets near the harbor, and let your
ears guide you into one of the many pubs with live Celtic music.

# ⓪ Halifax

The international gateway to the Maritimes, Halifax is a
lively city that sits on the second-largest natural harbor in
the world (after Sydney, Australia). Historic buildings line a
waterfront that has been bustling with activity since the
mid-18th century. Behind the waterfront, glittering modern
high-rise offices mark it as a prosperous provincial capital,
but it has a distinct East Coast laid-back atmosphere.

Begin your exploration up at the **Halifax Citadel National
Historic Site**, not just for its historic importance, but also for
the spectacular view over the city and harbor. The site was
fortified from the mid-18th century, when Halifax was one of
the four major overseas naval stations of the British Empire.
This was the nerve center of the city's defenses, a massive
star-shaped bastion that was completed in 1865, and despite
the development of the modern city it still dominates the
skyline. In summer you'll be greeted by guides in uniform and
hear the pipes and drums of a military band. You can tour the
restored buildings and talk with "inhabitants," who are
skilled at portraying military life of the 1860s.

Eventually, everyone gravitates toward the **waterfront**. A
4km (2.5-mile) walkway links the historic buildings,
restaurants, craft stores and museums, there's a little food
market and the renowned Alexander Keith brewery (tours
available), and always activity on the water.

Between 1928 and 1971 the Halifax waterfront was the
first thing seen by more than a million immigrants as they
disembarked from transatlantic vessels, and one of the immi-
gration sheds has been restored as the **Pier 21 National
Historic Site**. With the aid of a dramatic multimedia presen-
tation and interactive displays, it provides a wonderful evoca-
tion of the emotional experiences of wartime evacuees,
refugees, war brides and people who were just coming in
search of a better life.

The sea has always played a major part in the culture and
heritage of the city, and the **Maritime Museum of the
Atlantic** here is the largest and oldest of its kind in Canada.
Located in an 1879 chandlery, it has a collection of full-size
and model ships (some floating) and seafaring artifacts, plus
displays about maritime history. There's also an excellent film
about the Halifax Explosion in 1917, when a collision in the
harbor involving a French arms ship caused the greatest man-
made explosion the world had seen prior to Hiroshima.
Spending part of its time at the museum (otherwise in
Lunenburg, ► 156, or at sea) is *Bluenose II*, a replica of the
legendary schooner that appears on the Canadian dime.

*Actor-guides
bring to life the
military history
of the Citadel*

*Opposite: the
harbor is a
lively mix of
tourist and
working boats
in summer*

## TAKING A BREAK

**Salty's on the Waterfront** (► 160) has wonderful harbor
views and excellent seafood.

## HALIFAX: INSIDE INFO

**Top tips** Parking is very expensive on the waterfront, so leave your car at your hotel and use public transportation.
• The ferries that cross over to Dartmouth, on the opposite side of the harbor, provide a wonderful view back toward the city and cost less than the many sightseeing boat trips that are available from Halifax.

---

🔁 209 D2

**Nova Scotia International Visitors Centre**
✉ 1595 Barrington Street ☎ 902/424-4248; www.halifaxinfo.com

**Waterfront Visitor Info Centre**
✉ Sackville Landing ☎ 902/424-4248

**Halifax Citadel National Historic Site**
✉ P.O. Box 9080, Station A ☎ 902/426-5080; www.parkscanada.gc.ca ⏱ Daily 9–5, early May–Oct ( to 6 pm Jul–Aug)
🎟 Moderate

**Pier 21 National Historic Site**
✉ 1055 Marginal Road ☎ 902/425-7770; www.pier21.ca ⏱ Daily 9:30–5:30,

May–Nov; Tue–Fri 10–5, Sat noon–5, Dec–Mar (daily during March break); Mon–Fri 10–5, Sat noon–5, Apr
🎟 Moderate

**Maritime Museum of the Atlantic**
✉ 1675 Lower Water Street ☎ 902/424-7490; www.maritime.museum.gov.ns.ca
⏱ daily 9:30–5:30, Jun–Sep (also 5:30–8 Tue); Mon–Sat 9:30–5:30, Sun 1–5.30, May and Oct (also 5:30–8 Tue); Tue 9:30–8, Wed–Sat 9:30–5, Sun 1–5, Nov–Apr
🎟 Moderate

*Bluenose II*
✉ 1675 Lower Water Street ☎ 902/634-1963 or 1-800/763-1963; www.bluenose2.ns.ca ⏱ Call for details
🎟 Harbor cruise: expensive

# 2 Fundy Islands

The three Fundy Islands – Campobello, Deer Island and Grand Manan – provide a wonderful haven for wildlife and seabirds and are the perfect place to unwind in tranquil surroundings.

**The Roosevelt "Cottage" on Campobello is in Dutch Colonial style**

**Deer Island**, nearest to the New Brunswick shore, is home to about 900 residents who make their living from lobsters, clams and farmed salmon. If time is limited, head straight down to Deer Island Point on the southern tip to view the **Old Sow Whirlpool**, the largest in the Western Hemisphere.

**Campobello Island** sits right up against the US border and is famous as the vacation spot for the Roosevelt family. Young Franklin Delano spent childhood summers here and eventually acquired his own home, now the centerpiece of the **Roosevelt Campobello International Park**, with 1,130ha (2,800 acres) of parkland and rocky shores.

The third and largest island is **Grand Manan**, with lofty cliffs, rugged scenery and a dulse (edible seaweed) industry.

### TAKING A BREAK

Take a **picnic** – there are tables at Deer Island Point and in the Roosevelt Park.

🕂 208 C1

**Tourist information**
Deer Island: Lord's Cove, Deer Island
For ferryservice tel: 506/453-2600
Campobello: Roosevelt Campobello
International Park Visitor Centre,
tel: 506/752-2922
For ferry service tel: 506/747-2159 or
877/747-2159

Grand Manan: 130 Route 776, Grand Manan,
tel: 506/662-3442
For ferry service tel: 506/662-3724

**Roosevelt Cottage and Visitor Centre**
✉ Route 774, Campobello ☎ 506/752-2922
🕐 Daily 10–6, mid-May to mid-Oct, park and
grounds open daily during daylight hours
✋ Free

## FUNDY ISLANDS: INSIDE INFO

**Top tips** The **Old Sow Whirlpool** off Deer Island is at its peak three hours before high tide during the new and full phases of the moon.
• **Swimming** is not recommended anywhere on the Fundy Islands.

# ③ Prince Edward Island

Canada's smallest province is a rural idyll, with rolling farmlands, a gracious provincial capital, beautiful beaches washed by the warmest waters north of the Carolinas and succulent seafood. It's the home of Anne of Green Gables and the historic birthplace of the Confederation of Canada, and remains unassuming even though it's earned a place on the list of top ten islands in the world, alongside Hawaii and Bali.

Access to Prince Edward Island (generally shortened to PEI, or simply "The Island") is easier since the **Confederation Bridge** opened. The longest bridge over salt water in the world, at 13km (8 miles), it links the island to New Brunswick across the Northumberland Strait and makes for a thrilling drive. There's also a ferry from Caribou, Nova Scotia.

The provincial capital, **Charlottetown**, is a charming place with quiet tree-lined streets, historic buildings and a pleasant waterfront. It's here that you'll find **Founders' Hall**, which commemorates the foundation of the nation of Canada. It began with the arrival on this very spot in 1864 of 23 forward-looking politicians from across the land, now known as The Fathers of Confederation. Using modern technology, the exhibition here tells the story of Canada from its inception to the creation of the Territory of Nunavut in 1999.

Charlottetown is a stately and historic provincial capital

The main resort area on the island is **Cavendish**, a paradox of a place that has on the one hand a magnificently unspoiled section of protected coastline and on the other a cluster of brash, family-oriented attractions around the town itself. The **Prince Edward Island National Park** encompasses long, sandy beaches, grassy dunes, red sandstone cliffs, wetlands and forests.

You won't get far on the island without seeing a reference to *Anne of Green Gables*, the classic children's book by Lucy Maud Montgomery. Devotees come in droves to **Green Gables House**, within the national park, once owned by relatives of the author, and the inspiration for her graphic portrayal of rural life. **Avonlea** is re-created nearby and inhabited by actors taking the parts of Anne and her friends.

*Green Gables House reflects the popularity of the stories about Anne*

### TAKING A BREAK

Charlottetown's **Gahan House** (➤ 160) has above average pub food and six ales brewed on the premises.

---

✈ 209 D2

**Charlottetown Visitor Information Centre**
✉ 178 Water Street, Charlottetown
☎ 902/368-4444 or 888/734-7529

**Founders' Hall**
✉ 6 Prince Street, Charlottetown
☎ 902/368-1864; www.foundershall.ca
🕔 Mon–Sat 9–5, Sun 9–4, Aug to mid-Oct
👋 Moderate

**Prince Edward Island National Park**
✉ Off Route 2, between Cavendish and Dalvay ☎ 902/672-6350 🕔 Entrance kiosks: daily 9–7 (11–5in early Jun );

restricted services Sep to mid-Jun.
Greenwich Interpretation Centre: daily 10–4, mid-May to early Jun; 9–6, rest of Jun and late Aug to mid-Oct 👋 Day pass: moderate

**Green Gables House Heritage Place**
✉ Route 6, Cavendish ☎ 902/963-7874 or 888/773-8888 (Parks Canada) 🕔 May–Oct daily noon–4; Nov–Apr Wed–Sun noon–4
👋 Moderate

**Avonlea**
✉ Route 6, Cavendish ☎ 902/963 3050; www.avonlea.ca 🕔 Mid-Jun to Aug daily 9–5, first three weeks in Sep daily 10–4
👋 Expensive

---

## PRINCE EDWARD ISLAND: INSIDE INFO

**Top tips** You can get to PEI by airplane, train and bus, or by ferry, but once you are there there is **no public transportation** of any kind.
• In season you'll see billboards all over the island advertising **Lobster Suppers**, often run by the local church or community association. They are open to visitors, and offer great lobster (at low prices) and good company.

**Hidden gem** An unexpected find on the island is the **Rossignol Estate Winery** (tel: 902/962-4193), at Little Sands, where you can tour the winery, farm and vineyard, see a splendid collection of folk art in the gallery, and taste the wine.

# 4 Cape Breton Island

Cape Breton's most famous resident, Alexander Graham Bell, said about the island: "I have traveled the globe. I have seen the Canadian and American Rockies, the Andes and the Alps and the highlands of Scotland, but for simple beauty, Cape Breton outrivals them all." It is indeed one of the most beautiful islands in the world, with forest-clad mountains, glittering lakes and a spectacular coastline.

Cape Breton has an interesting blend of cultures, with its Mi'kmaq communities, its descendants of Scottish settlers, and its strong Acadian (French) presence. It also has a world-famous tradition of fiddle music and step-dancing.

At the very heart of the island is **Baddeck**, which Alexander Graham Bell made his home. The **Alexander Graham Bell National Historic Site** is a jaw-dropping exhibition illustrating the full extent of the man's genius, including his invention of the telephone, his part in the first manned flight in Canada, and the world speed record he achieved on nearby Bras d'Or Lake.

From Baddeck set out on the **Cabot Trail**, one of the most scenic drives in the world (▶ 188–190). On the way you'll pass through **Chéticamp**, a stronghold of Acadian French culture on the island and one of the places to get a whale-watching trip (also at Pleasant Bay, Bay St. Lawrence and

**The Cabot Trail features one magnificent view after another**

Ingonish). A little way north of Chéticamp, you enter the **Cape Breton Highlands National Park**, a spectacular area of densely wooded mountains and spectacular coastal vistas. At Pleasant Bay the **Whale Interpretive Centre** has life-size whale models and interactive displays. Another highlight of the Cabot Trail, over on the east coast, is **Ingonish**, with its superb beach.

The Fleur de Lis Trail along Cape Breton's southeastern coast leads to the remarkable **Fortress of Louisbourg**. Built by the French in 1713, this national historic site was a fortified town of several thousand settlers, an important trade center with a military stronghold protecting the approach to the Gulf of St. Lawrence. It was at the forefront of the struggle between the French and English and changed hands many times. About 25 percent of the original settlement has been reconstructed and more than 60 buildings are populated by costumed interpreters.

The Fortress of Louisbourg saw plenty of action in the French-English struggle for Canada

### TAKING A BREAK

On the west coast, call in at the **Rusty Anchor** ($) at Pleasant Bay for superb lobster; on the east coast, **Keltic Lodge** (tel: 800/565-0444, $$$) at Ingonish is a popular choice.

---

✚ 209 E2

**Cape Breton Tourism**
Information centers at Port Hastings, Baddeck, Louisbourg, Sydney and several other places around the island
☎ 800/565-0000

**Alexander Graham Bell National Historic Site**
✉ Chebucto Street, Baddeck ☎ 902/295-2069; www.pc.gc.ca 🕐 Daily 9–6, Jun; 8:30–6, Jul to mid-Oct; 9–5, mid-Oct to May
🚻 Moderate

**Cape Breton Highlands National Park**
✉ 902/224-2306; www.pc.gc.ca 🕐 year round; info centers: mid-May to mid-Oct
🚻 Moderate; free mid-Oct to mid-May

**Whale Interpretive Centre**
✉ Pleasant Bay ☎ 902/224-1411
🕐 Daily 9–5, Jun to mid-Oct
🚻 Inexpensive

**Fortress of Louisbourg National Historic Site**
☎ 902/733-2280; www.pc.gc.ca 🕐 Daily 9:30–5, May–Jun and Sep–mid-Oct; 9–6, Jul–Aug; May & Oct guided tours only
🚻 Expensive

---

### CAPE BRETON: INSIDE INFO

**Top tips** If you're planning to go on a **whale-watching trip**, look for one that offers guaranteed sightings. There's still a chance the whales won't cooperate, but if that happens, you get another trip for free.
• A great way to travel between Halifax and Sydney, Cape Breton is on board the *Bras d'Or*, a scenic, first-class, 10-hour train ride with observation cars, meals and commentary. Tel: 1-888/842-724 or visit www.viarail.ca.

# 5 Gros Morne National Park

Dramatic geological events created the spectacular land-scapes of Gros Morne National Park and it's global geological importance has made it a UNESCO's World Heritage Site.

This landscape can best be appreciated from the top of flat-topped, 806-m (2,650-ft) **Gros Morne Mountain**, a full day's hike. Other ways to enjoy the park include boat trips that dip in and out of fjords and sea caves or cross tranquil lakes, notably supremely beautiful **Western Brook Pond**, actu-ally a large lake. Scenic drives round Bonne Bay include the **Discovery Centre** on the southern stretch (Route 431), where you can learn more about the area and its wildlife, and the excellent **Visitor Centre** on the north-ern arm (Route 430), en route to Rocky Harbour.

## TAKING A BREAK

Try the **Seaside Restaurant**, Trout River (tel: 709/451-3461, $$$), or **Fisherman's Landing**, Rocky Harbour (tel: 709/458-271, $$).

Lobster Cove Head Light-house keeps shipping safe

---

➕ 209 D4

**Gros Morne National Park Headquarters**
✉ Rocky Harbour ☎ 709/458-2417;
www.pc.gc.ca/grosmorne ⏰ Mon–Fri 8–4:30;
park entrance kiosk mid-May to mid-Oct daily
10–6 💲 Moderate

**Discovery Centre**
✉ Woody Point ☎ 709/453-2490, ext 229

⏰ Daily 9–5, mid-May to mid-Jun and
Sep–mid-Oct; 9–6, mid-Jun–Aug (also 6–9 pm
Wed and Sun

**Visitor Centre**
✉ Route 430 ⏰ May and late Oct Mon–Fri
9–4; Jun–early Sep daily 9–9; mid-Sep to mid-
Oct daily 9–5. Closed Nov–Dec

---

## GROS MORNE NATIONAL PARK: INSIDE INFO

**Top tips** Gros Morne Mountain is **closed to hikers** until the beginning of July to let the soil dry out after the snow, and give plantlife a chance to establish itself.
• The boat trip on **Western Brook Pond** (☎ 709/458-2730) is unmissable.

# ⑥ St. John's

Out on the edge of the continent, the provincial capital of Newfoundland has a spectacular setting on a superb natural harbor. Here you follow in the wake of centuries of visitors, from the "discoverer" John Cabot (in 1497) to fishermen, merchants and others in search of rich pickings. Today's visitors find a strong sense of history, a vibrant culture and a very friendly welcome.

The narrow streets around the harbor are lined with brightly painted wooden houses, and the waterfront is always busy with ships from many nations. Seafaring is in the blood here, and the population, mainly of Irish descent, has a distinctive accent and a dry wit.

**Picturesque clapboard buildings rise steeply above the harbor**

At the entrance to the harbor, The Narrows is overlooked by the brooding mass of **Signal Hill**, which offers a magnificent view across the town and along the coastline. Because of its strategic position, the British fortified the hill during the 18th century after the town was captured by the French on three occasions, and military displays in summer commemorate those days. It was also an obvious choice for Marconi, when looking for a site to receive the first transatlantic wireless signal, beamed from Poldhu in Cornwall, England. Today, the hill is topped by Cabot Tower, erected in 1897 to mark the 400th anniversary of John Cabot's landing. There are some great walking trails leading from the tower.

**Above right: strategically placed Queen's Battery, above the Narrows and the Inner Harbour**

Tunneled into the rock beneath Signal Hill, the **Johnson Geo Centre** is a thrilling attraction that explores the geology of the planet with simulated earthquakes and volcanic eruptions. Newfoundland attracts scientists from all over the world to study the evidence of plate tectonics on the island, and to examine rocks that date back to the birth of the earth 4.5 billion years ago. Here you can see why they get so excited.

In June 2005, the Provincial Museum, the Art Gallery and the Provincial Archives will reopen in a new center, called **The Rooms**. The $40-million development provides a superb modern showcase for the province's museum and art collections. The building recalls the design of traditional "rooms" – buildings at the water's edge where fish processing was carried out.

St. John's has two cathedrals and both are worth a visit. The **Anglican Cathedral of St. John the Baptist**, designed

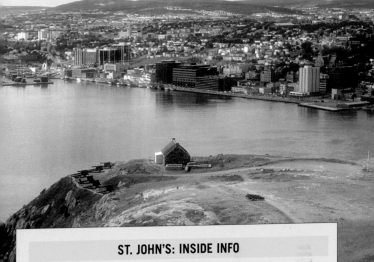

by Sir George Gilbert Scott, is a superb example of ecclesiastical Gothic, and the **Basilica Cathedral and Museum** has a splendid collection of church art and artifacts.

## TAKING A BREAK

Traditional Newfoundland food can be enjoyed anytime at **Oscar's** on Duckworth Street (tel: 709/579-4444, $$) – open 24 hours, 364 days a year.

✚ 209 F4

### St. John's Tourist Office
✉ 2nd Floor, City Hall Annex, 35 New Gower Street ☎ 709/576-8106 ⏰ Mon–Fri 9–4:30

### Signal Hill National Historic Park
☎ 709/772-5367; www.pc.gc.ca ⏰ Daily 8:30–4:30, mid-May to mid-Jun and Sep to mid-Oct; 8:30–8, mid-Jun to Labour Day; Mon–Fri 8:30–4:30, mid-Oct to mid-May 🎫 Inexpensive

### Johnson Geo Centre
✉ 175 Signal Hill Road ☎ 709/737-7880; www.geocentre.ca ⏰ Mon–Sat 9:30–5, Sun 1–5. Closed Mon mid-Oct to May 🎫 Moderate

### The Rooms
✉ 9 Bonaventure Avenue ☎ 709/729-0917; www.therooms.ca ⏰ Daily 9–9, mid-Jun to mid-Oct; call for hours rest of year 🎫 Not yet decided at time of going to press; call for information

### Anglican Cathedral of St. John the Baptist
✉ 16 Church Hill ☎ 709/726-5677; www.infonet.st-johns.nf.ca/cathedral or www.sji.ca/cathedral ⏰ Daily, Jun–Sep, off season by appointment

### Basilica Cathedral and Museum
✉ 200 Military Road ☎ 709/726-3660; www.stjohnsarchdiocese.nf.ca ⏰ Daily 9–4 by appointment

# At Your Leisure

Supremely beautiful, the little town of Lunenburg has a strong maritime heritage

## 7 Lunenburg

Lunenburg is just about the loveliest town in eastern Canada – if not in the whole country, and its historic core is now a UNESCO World Heritage Site. The town still adheres to its original plan, and the streets are lined by colorful, beautifully preserved buildings, many dating back to 1760.

It is for its fishing heritage that the town is best known, not least for the prowess of the schooner *Bluenose*, the unbeaten champion of the North Atlantic fishing fleet from 1921 to 1942, which features on the back of the dime coin. Sadly sold off when she retired from duty, she has been replaced by an accurate replica, **Bluenose II**, which divides its time between Lunenburg, Halifax (► 146–147) and the open sea, and sometimes offers coastal cruises.

On the waterfront you'll find the **Fisheries Museum of the Atlantic**, with three floors of displays and outdoor floating exhibits.

➕ 209 D1

### Visitor Information Centre
✉ Blockhouse Road ☎ 902/634-8100 or 888/615-8305; www.explorelunenburg.ca

### Bluenose II
✉ At the Fisheries Museum, when in Lunenburg ☎ 902/634-1963 or 800/763-1963; www.bluenose2.ns.ca
🕐 Cruises 9:30 am and 1 pm, Jun–Sep
💰 Expensive

### Fisheries Museum of the Atlantic
✉ 68 Bluenose Drive ☎ 902/634-4794; www.fisheries.museum.gov.ns.ca
🕐 Daily 9:30–5:30, May–Oct; Mon–Fri 8:30–4:30, Nov–Apr 💰 Moderate

## 8 Annapolis Valley

The Annapolis Valley is known for its apple orchards, charming small towns, and the site of the earliest permanent European settlement in North America. Its main attraction is **Annapolis Royal**, where you'll find the **Fort Anne National Historic Site**, built by the French in 1702 and further fortified by the British. It was the most fought-over settlement in the country during the struggle between the British and the French.

About 10km (6 miles) to the west, French colonists led by Samuel de Champlain settled in 1605, three years before Jamestown in the US was established. Here the **Port Royal National Historic Site** is a faithful reconstruction of the original settlement, where interpreters portray the lives of early colonists.

➕ 209 D1

**Fort Anne National Historic Site**
✉ PO Box 9, Annapolis Royal ☎ 902/532-2397 (532-2321 off season); www.pc.gc.ca/lhn-nhs/ns/fortanne
🕐 Daily 9–6, mid-May to mid-Oct
💲 Inexpensive

**Port Royal National Historic Site**
✉ P.O. Box 9, Annapolis Royal ☎ 902/532-2321; www.pc.gc.ca/lhn-nhs/ns/portroyal 🕐 Daily 9–6, mid-May to mid-Oct 💲 Inexpensive

## 9 St. Andrews-by-the-Sea
On a tiny promontory that juts out into Passamaquoddy Bay, this is Canada's oldest seaside resort, a pretty little town with a picturesque harbor, where whale-watching boats are moored alongside fishing charters and pleasure boats. Just back from the harbor, Water Street has remained largely unchanged for more than 200 years. It's lined with art and craft galleries, antiques stores and fashion boutiques, and intermingled with these are little cafés and restaurants. In the heart of town is the lovely 11-ha (27-acre) **Kingsbrae Garden**, with views over the bay and Minister's Island. You can visit **Minister's Island** by driving across the ocean floor at low tide.

➕ 208 C1

**Kingsbrae Garden**
✉ 220 King Street ☎ 506/529-3335 or 866/566-8687; www.kingsbraegarden.com 🕐 Daily 9–6, mid-May to early Oct 💲 Moderate

## 10 King's Landing
A 20-minute drive west of Fredericton on the Riverside Trail (Highway 2) leads to **King's Landing**, a superb reconstruction of a Loyalist settlement on a large riverside site. It has entire farms, complete with animals and workshops, furnished homes with cultivated gardens, a church, a working sawmill, and a splendid pub, the King's Arms, where you can taste a unique beer and eat traditional food in the upstairs restaurant. The whole place is populated by costumed interpreters, who engage visitors in authentic conversations of the day. If you get footsore exploring it all, take a wagon ride.

➕ 208 C2 ☎ 506/363-4999 or 506/363-4959 (info-line recording); www.kingslanding.nb.ca 🕐 Daily 10–5, Jun to mid-Oct 💲 Expensive

## 11 Fredericton
The provincial capital of New Brunswick is a lovely, compact city on the banks of the wide St. John River, and it's easy to explore on foot. The atmosphere is gracious small-town with a touch of importance and the downtown area is full of interesting little stores and good restaurants. In the heart of the city is the historic **Garrison District**, where the British army were quartered from 1784 until Canada's independence in 1867. The buildings have been adapted to house museums, artisans' workshops, craft stores, cafés and other amenities, all arranged around Officer's Square, which hosts Changing of the Guard ceremonies, open-air theater and free concerts. A short distance west, opposite the Legislative Assembly Building (open to the public), is the **Beaverbrook Art Gallery**, with a fine collection of works by Canadian and British artists.

➕ 208 C2

**Beaverbrook Art Gallery**
✉ 703 Queen Street ☎ 506/458-8545 🕐 Mon–Fri 9–6, Sat–Sun 10–5, Jun–Sep; Tue–Fri 9–5, Sat 10–5, Sun noon–5 rest of year 💲 Moderate

## 12 L'Anse aux Meadows
On the northern tip of Newfoundland a discovery was made in the 1960s

Vikings came to Newfoundland to harvest the plentiful lumber and fish its rich waters

that not only has national significance, but is important to the history of the entire continent – archeological evidence that the Vikings were here around 1,000 years ago. Excavations revealed three homes and a number of workshops, and the site is now a National Historic Site and a UNESCO World Heritage Site. The first Norsemen stayed for only a short time, but others came in their wake and used the dwellings they had built as a summer base for collecting the plentiful gifts of nature – fish, wild grapes and lumber.

The little Norse encampment has been accurately reconstructed, and is populated by costumed guides, who carry out demonstrations of ancient crafts. The log houses show how the Vikings would have lived, and the visitor center has a film about the excavations and some of the artifacts.

➕ 209 D5 ✉ PO Box 70, St-Lunaire-Griquet; 30km (18 miles) north of St. Anthony on Route 436 ☎ 709/623-2608; www.pc.gc.ca ⏰ Daily 9–5, Jun to mid-Oct (also 5–8 pm, mid-Jun to early Sep) 💲 Moderate

## 🅱 Bonavista Peninsula
*"Oh, buona vista!"* (Oh, happy sight!) were supposedly the words of explorer John Cabot when he made

his first landfall in North America here in 1497. Some dispute the actual location where he stepped onto the continent, but none would argue with the sentiment. Bonavista has breathtaking views, especially at the Cape, where waves pound the rocky shoreline beneath one of Canada's most picturesque lighthouses, hundreds of puffins flock around the nearby cliffs, and you can often see whales offshore. The **Cape Bonavista Lighthouse Provincial Historic Site**, fully restored after three lightning strikes set fire to it in 2001, has costumed guides to show you around.

In addition to sending news back across the Atlantic of his "New found land," Cabot alerted the fishermen of Europe to the huge shoals of cod that populated the waters here, starting off a centuries-long fishing industry. The **Ryan Premises National Historic Site**, in a restored, 19th-century fish-merchant's premises in Bonavista, tells the story.
➕ 209 F4

### Cape Bonavista Lighthouse
✉ PO Box 8700, St. John's ☎ 709/468-7444 ⏰ Daily 10–5:30, mid-Jun to early Oct 💲 Inexpensive

### Ryan Premises
✉ PO Box 1451, Bonavista ☎ 709/468-1600; www.pc.gc.ca ⏰ Daily 10–6, mid-May to mid-Oct 💲 Inexpensive

# Where to... Stay

**Prices**
High season room only rates, based on two sharing a double room, excluding taxes
$ up to $120      $$ $121–260      $$$ more than $260

## HALIFAX

### ☞☞☞ Halliburton House Inn $$

In the center of Halifax, this is a lovely and comfortable historic property, elegantly furnished with antiques. All rooms have private bathrooms (some with whirlpool) and goose-down comforters. In winter, the library is a great place to relax by the open fire. Innovative Canadian cuisine is served in the four-room restaurant. Less mobile guests should bear in mind that there's no elevator.

✚ 209 D2  ⊠ 5184 Morris Street
☎ 902/420-0658; fax: 902/423-2324;
www.halliburton.ns.ca

### ☞☞☞ Westin Nova Scotian $$

With views of the harbor or Point Pleasant Park, this modern hotel has a lovely waterfront site. Rooms feature pillow-top beds and there's an indoor swimming pool, spa and fitness suite. A free shuttle service to downtown is run on weekdays.

✚ 209 D2  ⊠ 1181 Hollis Street;
902/421-1000; 888/679-3784; fax:
902/422-9465; www.westin.ns.ca

## PRINCE EDWARD ISLAND

### ☞☞☞ The Inns on Great George $–$$$

Several properties in Charlottetown's National Historic District have been converted into this beautiful inn, which maintains a 19th-century style throughout. The best rooms have a Jacuzzi and fireplace, but all are elegant. The central building, called The Pavilion, houses the breakfast room and fitness center.

✚ 209 D2  ⊠ 58 Great George Street, Charlottetown ☎ 902/892-0606, 800/361-1118; fax: 902/628-2079; www.innsongreatgeorge.com

### ☞☞ Lakeview Lodge & Cottages ($)

In walking distance of all the Cavendish attractions, these housekeeping cottages, motel units and suites are family owned and run. Daily maid service and heated pool.

✚ 209 D2  ⊠ Highway 6, Cavendish
☎ 902/963-2436, 800/565-7550; fax:
902/963-2493; email: lakeview@pei.
sympatico.ca

## CAPE BRETON ISLAND

### ☞ Parkview Motel $

You get a real Acadian welcome at the Chiasson family's motel, which lies along the Cheticamp River at the entrance to the Cape Breton Highlands National Park. Rooms have two double beds, full bathroom and satellite TV, and deluxe rooms have better views and such extras as microwaves and refrigerators. The dining room serves fresh seafood and steaks.

✚ 209 D3  ⊠ 16546 Cabot Trail (PO Box 117), Cheticamp ☎ 902/224-3232, 877/224-3232; fax: 902/224-2596; email: parkview@ns.
sympatico.ca

## ST. JOHN'S, NEWFOUNDLAND

### ☞☞☞ Leaside Manor Heritage Inn $$

Named one of the most romantic destinations in Canada, this inn has exceptionally pretty rooms, many with four-poster beds and Jacuzzis. Wonderful breakfasts and 24-hour complimentary beverages.

✚ 209 F4  ⊠ 39 Topsail Road
☎ 709/722-0387, 877/807-7245; fax:
709/739-1835; www.leaside.nf.ca

# Where to...
## Eat and Drink

### Prices

Based on the cost of a three-course dinner, excluding drinks and service

$ under $25    $$ $26–$50    $$$ more than $50

## HALIFAX

### ▽▽▽ Bish World Cuisine $$

A chic modern decor and a mouth-watering menu distinguish this fine waterfront restaurant. International influences are applied to local ingredients to create such dishes as Thai lobster and coconut corn chowder, butter poached lobster on a Romesco fish stew, or cornbread-stuffed roasted pork loin with pecan butternut squash hash. Delicious desserts include maple walnut tart with cinnamon creme fraiche. The extensive wine list features New World and European bottles.

✚ 209 D2 ⊠ Bishop's Landing, 1475 Lower Water Street ☎ 902/425-7993; www.bish.ca ⏰ Mon–Fri 11:30–2:30, 5:30–10, Sat 5:30–10. Closed Sun

### ▽▽▽ Salty's on the Waterfront $$–$$$

Right on the waterfront, on a 19th-century wharf, this restaurant has a spectacular view across the harbor. The decor is suitably nautical and fresh Atlantic seafood is the focus, including Nova Scotia lobster. Lighter meals available downstairs.

✚ 209 D2 ⊠ 1869 Upper Water Street ☎ 902/423-6818; www.saltys.ca ⏰ Daily 11:30–10

## PRINCE EDWARD ISLAND

### ▽▽ Gahan House Brewery $–$$

This great brewpub not only has a half-dozen excellent ales brewed on the premises, it also serves up some of the best pub food in the Maritimes. The signature dish is the Brown Bag Fish and Chips, with batter made using their own ale. Groups of more than four can get a brewery tour (call in advance).

✚ 209 D2 ⊠ 126 Sydney Street, Charlottetown ☎ 902/626-2337; www.peimenu.com/brewing ⏰ Mon–Sat 11–closing time, Sun 4–10

## CAPE BRETON ISLAND

### ▽ Baddeck Lobster Suppers $–$$

The Maritimes are famous for their lobster suppers, and here the authentic experience is available in a friendly informal restaurant that offers excellent value. In addition to fresh Atlantic lobster, the specialties are oven-poached salmon and baked ham, and all entrees come with unlimited (yes, really) amounts of fresh seafood chowder, mussels, potato salad and homemade bread.

✚ 209 E3 ⊠ 17 Ross Street, Baddeck ☎ 902/295-3307 ⏰ Daily 11:30–1:30, 4–9, early Jun to early-Oct

## ST. JOHN'S, NEWFOUNDLAND

### ▽▽▽ The Cabot Club $$

Traditional Newfoundland cuisine gets gourmet treatment here. Jumbo scallop saute with lobster butter, baby greens and grapefruit vinaigrette might be followed by pepperberry-crusted loin of Labrador caribou with redcurrant jus. The elegant dining room has picture windows with spectacular views – in winter you'll even see icebergs floating by.

✚ 209 F4 ⊠ Fairmont Newfoundland, Cavendish Square ☎ 709/726-4980; www.fairmont.com; ⏰ Mon–Sat 6–10

# Where to... Shop

There's really only one big city in the Maritimes, and that's Halifax, but it doesn't have a monopoly on great shopping. Each of the provincial capitals has at least one good shopping mall, plus interesting individual and specialty stores.

## NOVA SCOTIA

**Halifax** is the international gateway to the region for many visitors, and it has excellent shopping. The hub is around Spring Garden Road and South Park Street, lined with fashion stores, galleries and craft shops. The **Historic Properties** on the water-front include specialty boutiques, and Cable Wharf has Canada's only traditional crystal factory, **Nova**

**Scotia Crystal** (Lower Water Street, tel: 902/492-0416).

For reading matter, seek out **John W. Doull** (1684 Barrington Street, tel: 902/429-1652), with a huge stock of books. Farther along this street are two stores that reflect different aspects of "New Scotland." The **Plaid Place** (1903 Barrington Street, tel: 902/429-6872) sells kilts, sweaters and other Highland goods, and the **Micmac Heritage Gallery** (tel: 902/422-9509) has First Nations art and craft.

Halifax's biggest shopping mall is the **Halifax Shopping Centre** (7001 Mumford Road, tel: 902/453-1753). More interesting, perhaps is the **Granville Mall** near the harbor, in a group of 19th-century buildings.

## PRINCE EDWARD ISLAND

A popular souvenir is the PEI Dirt Shirt, a T-shirt dyed using the famous red soil. It looks better than it sounds. Another PEI product is the delicious Cow's Ice Cream.

The capital, **Charlottetown**, has a historic, low-rise downtown area, based on Queen Street, with lots of individual stores. On Richmond Street, traffic-free in summer, **Victoria Row** has craft and gift stores. The **Confederation Court Mall** (tel: 902/894-9505) is the largest mall (more than 90 stores), while down on the waterfront, **Peake's Wharf** offers clothing, craft and gift stores. Farther out is the **Charlottetown Mall** (670 University Avenue, tel: 902/368-8854) and the **PEI Factory Shops** (TransCanada Highway, North River Causeway), discount outlets offering low prices on big-name lines.

## NEWFOUNDLAND AND LABRADOR

**St. John's** is where you'll find Newfoundland's best shopping, with masses of craft shops and art galleries, including the **Craft Council** (49 Duckworth Street, tel: 709/753-2749). Look especially for textile crafts, available at a number of workshops and stores. On the harbor, the **Murray Premises** are home to several boutiques, while the city's main shopping mall is the **Avalon Mall** (48 Kenmouth Road, tel: 709/753-7144).

## NEW BRUNSWICK

**Fredericton** is a charming city that has preserved its downtown area as a pleasant place to wander among individual stores. The historic Garrison District includes **River Valley Crafts and Artisan Gift Shops** (tel: 506/460-2837) and **Botinicals** (65 Shore Street, tel: 506/454-7361), great for quality souvenirs. **Boyce's Farmers' Market** (665 George Street, tel: 506/451-1815) has more than 200 vendors. Of the malls, **Regent Mall** (1381 Regent Street, tel: 506/452-1005) is the brightest and best, with more than 115 stores and services. However, the biggest mall in the Atlantic Provinces is **Champlain Place** over at **Moncton**.

# Where to...
## Be Entertained

### NOVA SCOTIA

Halifax is the prime spot for entertainment in Nova Scotia, but many towns have good theaters: the lovely, historic **King's Theater** at Annapolis Royal (209 St. George Street, tel: 902/532-7704); the **Bauer** at Antigonish (St. Francis-Xavier University, tel: 902/863-4921); the grand **Savoy** at Glace Bay, Cape Breton (116 Commercial Street, tel: 902/564-6668); the **Decoste Entertainment Centre** at Pictou (Water Street, tel: 902/485-8848); and **Th'Yarc** in Yarmouth (76 Parade Street, tel: 902/742-8150).

In Halifax, the principal venues are the **Dalhousie Arts Centre** (6100 University Avenue, tel: 902/494-3820), home of Symphony Nova Scotia, and the 1915 **Neptune**

**Theatre** (1593 Argyle Street, tel: 902/429-7070 or 800/565-7345).

Nightlife in Halifax ranges from the **Casino Nova Scotia** (1983 Upper Water Street, tel: 902/425-7777), to places like the **Lower Deck Pub** (Upper Water Street, tel: 902/425-1501), for traditional Maritimes music. The **Velvet Olive** (1770 Market Street, tel: 902/492-2233) and **Reflections Cabaret** (5184 Sackville Street, tel: 902/422-2957), the latter predominantly a gay club, are popular nightclubs.

### PRINCE EDWARD ISLAND

PEI draws visitors for its tranquility and rural charm, but it is certainly not devoid of entertainment. One of the island's biggest attractions is a musical based on *Anne of Green*

*Gables*, a perennially popular feature of the **Charlottetown Festival**. For live music in the provincial capital, try **Myron's Cabaret** (51 Kent Street, tel 902/892-4375) for classic rock, or the **Olde Dublin Pub** (131 Sydney Street, tel: 902/892-6992) for traditional Celtic music.

### NEWFOUNDLAND

With its strong Irish and English heritage, this province is reeling (literally) with traditional Celtic music. In **St. John's** on any night of the week, you can stroll along the main streets (George Street in particular) and hear it wafting from many of the pubs. There are pubs that feature country or rock music, too. **O'Reilley's** (15–17 George Street, tel: 709/722-3735) is one of the best.

Big concerts are staged at **Mile One Stadium** (tel: 709/576-7657), in the heart of downtown, and at **St. John's Memorial Stadium** (King's Bridge Road at Lake Avenue,

tel: 709/576-7688). The **Arts and Culture Centre** (Allandale Road and Prince Philip Drive, tel: 709/729-3900) has a varied program, while classical music is staged at the **Cochrane Street United Church** (tel: 709/722-3023). **Bowring Park Amphitheatre** (off route 1, tel: 709/576-8601) has varied open-air entertainments.

### NEW BRUNSWICK

**Fredericton** is a lively provincial capital with lots to do. The main theater is the modern **Playhouse** (686 Queen Street, tel: 506/458-8344). In summer there's outdoor entertainment in **Officers' Square** (575 Queen Street, tel: 506/460-2129). Nightlife is provided by city bars such as **Dolan's** (349 King Street, tel: 506/454-7474) and the the **Right Spot/20-20 Club** (403 Regent Street, tel: 506/457-9887) in the old station building, which has a pool room, a sports bar and a venue featuring 1960s music.

# The North

# Getting Your Bearings

The North is a vast area of rugged mountains, endless wilderness, forests, lakes and waterways, even desert, as well as impressive highways running through some truly remarkable scenery. The area is divided into the Yukon, adjoining the American state of Alaska, the Northwest Territories, and Nunavut, Canada's newest territory, created in 1999 from the eastern part of the Northwest Territories. The Yukon is gold-rush country, where at the end of the 19th century prospectors rushed in to stake their claim to the riches hidden in the gold fields of the Klondike. Many of the attractions – the cities, the museums, the highways – owe their existence to this incredibly brief period in history.

Melville Island

Banks Island

Beaufort Sea

Amundsen Gulf

Tukluk Nogait National Park
**6** Inuvik

Eagle Plains

Peel

Fort Good Hope

Coronation G
Kugluktuk (Coppermine)

**1** Dawson City

Stewart Crossing

Yukon

YUKON

Great Bear Lake

Kluane National Park
**4** Alaska Highway

Haines Junction

Mackenzie Mts

Mackenzie

NORTHWEST TERRITORIES

Wrigley

**2** Whitehorse and White Pass

Skagway

Teslin

Watson Lake

Liard

**5** Nahanni National Park

**3** Yellowknife

Great Slave Lake

Fort Providence

Fort Smith

But nature has provided more than enough of its own attractions in the North. This is the land of the *aurora borealis* and the midnight sun; a land where temperatures range from an icy -40°C (-40°F) in winter to a very respectable 25°C (77°F) in summer. The wildlife is wonderful, the sport varied and plentiful, the shopping unique – the craftwork of the First Nations peoples is treasure indeed.

And as if that wasn't enough, throughout the year there are entertainments in the form of festivals, sporting events, celebrations of the changing of the seasons and First Nations' gatherings.

Opposite: Driving the Alaska Highway is still an adventure

Right: First Nations art and crafts reflect the nature of the northern lands

Ellesmere Island

Axel Heiberg Island

Queen Elizabeth Islands

Parry Islands

Devon Island

Lancaster Sound

Somerset Island

Prince of Wales Island

Gulf of Boothia

Boothia Peninsula

Melville Peninsula

**Baffin Island** 7

Auyuittuq National Park

Nettilling Lake

Cumberland Sound

Baffin Bay

Davis Strait

Foxe Basin

NUNAVUT

Southampton Island

Hudson Strait

Hudson Bay

Nueltin Lake

Arviat (Eskimo Point)

0 _____ 500 km
0 _____ 250 miles

Page 163: it's not always the "frozen North," but severe winters only add to the spectacular beauty

The North is a huge area with vast distances between the main sites, so travel by small plane is the best option. The only major Yukon airport is at Whitehorse, so this is the best place to use as your base. As attractions in the Yukon are seasonal, the itinerary suggested here is for the summer season, mid-May to mid-September.

# The North in Eight Days

## Day One

**Morning** Fly from **2** Whitehorse (➤ 170) up to **1** Dawson City (➤ 168–169) via the local air service.

**Lunch/Afternoon** You're here to experience Gold-Rush fever, so do it in style with lunch at Klondike Kate's (➤ 175, above left), then wander around the historic buildings.

**Evening** Visit **Diamond Tooth Gertie's** casino, even if you don't want to gamble, then take a drive up to the **Midnight Dome** to enjoy the sunset and the view.

## Day Two

**Morning** Still in Dawson City, visit the **Tr'ondek Hwech'in Danajo Zho Cultural Centre** for a taste of life before the Gold Rush. Catch a reading of the works of Jack London or Robert Service in the cabins where they lived.

**Lunch** Buy picnic food at Bonanza Market (2nd Avenue and Princess; tel: 867/993-6527) and eat it by the Yukon River in town or up on Midnight Dome, with magnificent views.

**Afternoon/Evening** Return to Whitehorse and see the **Frantic Follies** show (➤ 176).

## Day Three

Leave Whitehorse very early to follow the **Golden Circle Drive** (➤ 191–192, right). Aim for an overnight stop in Haines City.

# Day Four

Continue on the Golden Circle Drive. Allow yourself time to explore **Skagway** (➤ 170) before driving over the White Pass back to Whitehorse.

# Day Five

Fly to **3 Yellowknife** (➤ 171) and enjoy a leisurely pre-prandial stroll along the shores of Great Slave Lake.

**Evening** Try some northern food creatively cooked at L'Heritage Restaurant Français (➤ 175), then walk it off in one of the city parks.

# Day Six

**Morning** Visit the **Diavik Diamond Mines Visitor Centre** in Yellowknife.

**Lunch** All kinds of food, from light snacks to meals based on caribou or Arctic char can be enjoyed at L'Attitudes (Yellowknife Inn, Central Square Mall, tel: 867/873-2603)

**Afternoon** Stroll around the Old Town – make sure you soak up the atmosphere along Ragged Ass Road, and finish up at the Pilots' Monument, the highest point, for views over the city and the Great Slave Lake.

**Evening** Enjoy the food and more views at the Wildcat Café (➤ 175).

# Day Seven

**Morning** Visit the **Prince of Wales Northern Heritage Centre** (➤ 171).

**Lunch** Eat at the Heritage Café within the heritage center (Mon–Fri 11:30–2; tel: 867/873-0205)

**Afternoon** Treat yourself to some shopping, then relax by taking a trip on a river steamer.

**Evening** Have supper at The Prospector (3506 Wiley Road, tel: 867/920-7639, $), right on the water's edge – you might be treated to the sight of float planes landing or taking off right in front of you.

# Day Eight

Fly back to Whitehorse or carry on to your next destination.

# Dawson City

Dawson is an extraordinary city, where the few short years that saw the Yukon Gold Rush at the end of the 19th century are frozen in a collection of meticulously preserved historic buildings. Here is the stuff of old black-and-white movies – you'll find clapboard houses, costumed characters and a casino with the irresistible name of Diamond Tooth Gertie's.

Above and right: visitors still pan for gold nuggets

To get a real feel of those manic years of feverish endeavor, imagine arriving in Dawson via the "Gold Rush Route" – the Klondike Highway – followed by the 100,000 or so prospectors who virtually stampeded their way north to pan for gold. Stretching from Skagway in Alaska, it was covered on foot or horseback as far as Whitehorse (▶ 170), then the final leg to the Klondike gold mines – more than 500km (300 miles) – was by boat on the Yukon River.

Gold was discovered here in 1896, but the rush was over within three years, and Dawson almost died with it, even losing its status as capital of Yukon Territory to Whitehorse in 1950. However, its immense importance as a part of Canadian heritage was recognized, and a rescue operation began on more than 30 of its historic buildings, including **Diamond Tooth Gertie's**, a Gold-Rush style saloon and gambling casino with can-can dancers and traditional poker, blackjack and roulette. The name commemorates dancing girl, Gertie Lovejoy, a colorful character with a diamond set into her front tooth.

Dawson is not just about the Gold Rush. It has a thriving First Nations tribe, the Han Hwech'in, celebrated at the **Tr'ondek Hwech'in Danajo Zho Cultural Centre**; downstream on the Yukon River, the annual Moosehide Gathering is a festival of the tribe's traditions. And if you're a fan of the writer Jack London – whose novels include *The Call of the Wild* (1903) and *White Fang* (1905) – or the poet Robert Service, whose fondness for alliteration inspired him to write, among others, *Songs of a Sourdough* (1907) and *Rhymes of a Rebel* (1952), you might like to catch a reading of their works in the re-created cabins where they lived on 8th Avenue.

## TAKING A BREAK

**Klondike Kate's** (▶ 175) offers Canadian and ethnic food in an original Gold-Rush building.

## DAWSON CITY: INSIDE INFO

**Top tips** The **best time to visit** Dawson is during the summer months, from mid-May to mid-September. This is mainly because the attractions, and some of the hotels and restaurants, are only open during this period, and also there are some great annual events to enjoy, such as the **Yukon Gold Panning Championships**, a music festival and some fun happenings at Diamond Tooth Gertie's, where the opening and close of the season are celebrated in style.
• **Follow the Dome Road** out of Dawson for 8km (5 miles) to the top of the Midnight Dome (884 meters/2,900 feet), for a wonderful view over the city and the surrounding mountains, sunlit until late at night. On June 21, the summer solstice, you can see the sun at midnight.

The view from Midnight Dome over Dawson City and the Yukon River

➕ 210 B4

**Klondike Visitors' Association**
✉ P.O.Box 389  ☎ 867/993-5575, 1-877/465-3006; www.dawsoncity.org

**Tourism Yukon Visitor Reception**
✉ Corner of Front and King streets  ☎ 867/993-5566  🕐 Daily 8–8, mid-May to late Sep

**Parks Canada**
✉ PO Box 390  ☎ 867/993-7237; www.pc.gc.ca

**Jack London Cabin**
✉ 8th Avenue  🕐 Daily at 11:30 and 2:15, mid-May to mid-Oct; check times with the Klondike Visitors' Association (above) rest of year  💲 Inexpensive

# ② Whitehorse and White Pass

Whitehorse may not be the prettiest place in the world, but it's an excellent base for exploring the Yukon. It's another Gold-Rush town, where prospectors stopped off to negotiate the troublesome obstacles of Miles Canyon and the Whitehorse Rapids. The problem was solved by building a railway, and the town continued to do well even after the Gold Rush was over. There are some good museums to visit and a fantastic range of artists live and work here – including painters, sculptors, potters, carvers and quilters.

Follow the **Golden Circle Drive** (➤ 191–192) from Whitehorse, and you will eventually find yourself climbing up to White Pass, a narrow, steep ravine heading southwest between Whitehorse and Skagway. It's pretty impressive, especially Dead Horse Gulch, where – as the name suggests – there are the bones of more than 3,000 pack horses, which were unable to survive the harsh conditions.

**Skagway**, in Alaska, is in a glorious position at the head of the Lyn Canyon waterway, and it's been preserved much as it was a hundred years ago,

*A dog-sled race sets off from the main street in Whitehorse*

when prospectors arrived here by sea to start the journey to the Klondike gold fields. Part of it (the Klondike Goldrush National Historic Park) is a living museum.

### TAKING A BREAK

The **Talisman** (➤ 175) on Whitehorse's 2nd Avenue is family-friendly café, serving home baking

✚ 210 B2

---

## WHITEHORSE AND WHITE PASS: INSIDE INFO

**Top tips** If you're not from North America, you'll need your **passport** to visit Skagway, which is over the border in Alaska.

# **3 Yellowknife**

If you like diamonds with your gold, head for the vibrant, cosmopolitan city of Yellowknife, on the northeast shore of the Great Slave Lake, dubbed "the Diamond Capital of North America." Once a boom town for gold prospectors, it switched to diamond-mining as its main industry in the 1990s.

Yellowknife, capital of the Northwest Territories, was named by a traveler in 1770, after the "yellow knives" (copper-blades) used by the native Dongrib Dene peoples. In spite of the industry, it's not all modern tall buildings – a stroll around the **Old Town**, where miners once lived in tents or wooden shacks, takes you right back through history.

This is the place to connect with **nature** – the forests and wilderness around Yellowknife are unspoiled and great for wildlife watching – and to view the midnight sun in summer and the *aurora borealis*. It's fabulous, too, for fresh-air activities – walking, cycling, sailing, swimming, fishing, canoeing – or you can take a leisurely trip on a river steamer and just soak it all up.

To get a good feel of the whole area, from the traditions and lifestyles of the local First Nations peoples to life after the discovery of gold and diamonds, head for the **Prince of Wales Northern Heritage Centre**.

First Nations culture is evident throughout the North region

### **TAKING A BREAK**

Take your camera and head for the **Wildcat Café** (▶ 175) in an original log building overlooking Back Bay – the views are as good as the northern specialties.

➕ 211 F2

**Prince of Wales Northern Heritage Centre**
✉ PO Box 1320; off Highway 4 near Northern

Frontier Visitors' Centre ☎ 867/873-7551; http://pwnhc.learnnet.nt.ca 🅒 Daily 10:30–5:30 (also 5:30–9 Thu & Fri), Jun–Sep; Mon–Fri 10:30–5, Sat–Sun noon–5, rest of year 🎟 Moderate

---

### **YELLOWKNIFE: INSIDE INFO**

**Top tips** Learn all about the mining, cutting and polishing of diamonds at the **Diavik Diamond Mines Visitor Centre** (5007 50th Avenue; tel: 867/669-6500; Mon–Fri 10:30–5, Sat–Sun noon–5)

# At Your Leisure

The "signpost forest" at Watson Lake continues to grow as visitors add their home towns

## 4 Alaska Highway

The Alaska Highway starts at the Mile Zero marker in Dawson Creek, BC and runs for 2,400km (1,488 miles) to Delta Junction, Alaska, USA. It was built at incredible speed (it took just over seven months to complete) as a joint Canadian/US venture during World War II to protect Alaska by linking it to mainland America.

It's a marathon journey to cover the whole highway, so if time is limited you could just drive a short stretch. If you head southeast of Whitehorse, after 420km (262 miles) you'll reach **Watson Lake**, where there's an interpretive center, a Northern Lights Centre and an amazing "forest" of signposts. The first one was "planted" by a homesick US Army soldier in 1942, pointing his way home, and the idea has been taken up by more than 42,000 travelers since.

On the way you'll pass through **Teslin** – take a look in the town museum, where there's a wonderful collection of early 20th-century photographs of the local Tlingit people, taken by George Johnston (1884–1972).

🚪 210 C2

Northern Rockies Alaska Highway Tourism Association
✉ PO Box 6850, 9923 96 Avenue, Fort St. John, British Columbia ☎ 250/785-2544

## 5 Nahanni National Park

Some planning is needed to visit this glorious wilderness in the southwest Northern Territories, because you can only reach it by chartering a seaplane. You'll get a fantastic view of the sheer rocky peaks of the **Cirque of the Unclimbables**, the 92-m (302-ft) **Virginia Falls** (twice the height of Niagara), and the deep canyons.

This remote national park protects sections of the Mackenzie Mountains and was the first designated UNESCO World Heritage Site. The park is centered around the **South Nahanni River** – the place to go for whitewater-rafting. There are incredible hot springs here, such as **Rabbitkettle**, which is at a constant 20°C (68°F).

🚪 211 D2 ✉ P.O. Box 348, Fort Simpson ☎ 867/695-3151 🕐 Daily: mid-Jun to mid-Sep; Park Office: daily 8–noon, 1–5, mid-Jun to mid-Sep; Mon–Fri 8:30–noon, 1–5, rest of year

# Farther Afield

The aptly-named Igloo Church is a unique landmark in Inuvik

## 6 Inuvik

You reach Inuvik by plane from Yellowknife or, if you're adventurous, via the 735-km (455-mile) **Dempster Highway**. Inuvik lies in the delta of the Mackenzie River, and is the largest Canadian settlement north of the Arctic Circle. The delta's mass of islets and channels attract migratory wildfowl and fish; herds of caribou migrate here to calve, and polar bears live in the vast tundra.

Inuvik's small population of 3,400 – mostly First Nations Inuvailut and Gwich'in – live by hunting, sport hunting and ecotourism. Visitor attractions include white-water-rafting, kayaking, hiking or wildlife viewing, and in winter there are snowmobile, dogsled or snowshoe trips and *aurora borealis* viewing.

You won't be able to miss the town's biggest landmark, the circular **Igloo Church of Our Lady of Victory** on Mackenzie Road. Built in 1958, the white walls are marked to resemble blocks of ice. Inside you'll see the *Stations of the Cross* by local Inuit artist, Mona Thresher.

🕀 211 D5

**Western Arctic Visitor Centre**
✉ Mackenzie Road ☎ 867/777-8618

## 7 Baffin Island

Baffin Island forms the major part of **Nunavut**, which means "our land" in the Inuit language. Three-quarters of the island's land mass lies north of the Arctic Circle, and the landscape is wild, rugged and glaciated, with vast areas of tundra. Here again, you'll find great opportunities for sport and wildlife spotting. The Inuit have lived here for 5,000 years, but you'll be disappointed if you're expecting to see them living their traditional lifestyle – they have mostly shunned their nomadic existence in favor of conventional homes and offices. As a tourist, however, you can stay in a igloo, if you wish!

🕀 213 D3

**Nunavut Tourism**
✉ PO Box 1450, Iqaluit, Nunavut
☎ 867/979-6551

### Wildlife to Spot on a Boat Trip
Polar bears
Whales
Narwhals
Seals
Walruses

# Where to... Stay

## Prices

High season room only rates, based on two sharing a double room, excluding taxes
$ up to $120     $$ $121–$260     $$$ $more than $260

If you're visiting in the summer, it's best to book ahead, and remember that some attractions and a number of hotels are only open from around mid-May to mid-September.

## DAWSON CITY

### Bombay Peggy's $$

The name alone may tempt you to stay in this luxurious hotel, built in 1900 and once notorious as a brothel – if you really want a taste of this (in the decor, at least), ask for the Lipstick Room, with its red walls and black velvet bedding, or the Purple Room with exotic fabrics

and a mind-boggling 2-meter (7-ft) high carved headboard. Elsewhere the decadence is a little more discreet – hardwood floors, huge claw-foot baths and rich colors.

🕂 210 B4 ⊠ PO Box 411, 2nd Avenue ☎ 867/993-6969; fax: 867/993-6199

## WHITEHORSE

### ▼▼▼ Hawkins House $$

If you like Victorian style coupled with modern comforts, you'll enjoy this pretty, two-story B&B. It was built in 1994 with high ceilings, hardwood floors and stained glass to give an old-fashioned feel, but each room has a queen-size bed and

private bathroom. The rooms (there are only four) are themed: there's the opulent and romantic Tea Rose Room, the Fleur de Lys Room with a French feel, the Wild Sage Room with First Nations decor, and the Fireweed Room styled as a Yukon log cabin. There are also vacation apartments available.

🕂 210 B2 ⊠ 303 Hawkins Street ☎ 867/668-7638; fax: 867/668-7632

### ▼▼ High Country Inn $–$$

This inn has four floors of rooms with great views, from standard doubles to luxurious suites with Jacuzzis or kitchenettes, but it still manages to retain a country atmosphere. Other facilities include private bathroom, cable TV and a modem outlet. You'll know you're at the right place when you spot the 12-m (40-ft) wooden Mountie guarding the door. There's a good menu of northern specialties – fresh fish, caribou steak, venison – served in the restaurant or the less formal bar.

🕂 210 B2 ⊠ 4051 4th Avenue; ☎ 867/667-4471; fax: 867/667-6457

## YELLOWKNIFE

### ▼▼▼ Chateau Nova $$

This is a fine modern hotel with big-city standards of comfort twinned with such up-to-the-minute facilities as internet connection and telephones with voice mail in the rooms. All the rooms are large and elegant and have private bathrooms. The walls of the hotel are adorned with wonderful archive images of early explorers, emphasizing how lucky guests are that the days are gone when travelers had to sleep outside with the mosquitoes. The Mill Wright Restaurant serves excellent Northern food and is famed for its Sunday brunches. The hotel has a fitness center where you can work out, or you can indulge yourself with a relaxing treatment in the spa.

🕂 210 B2 ⊠ 4401 50th Avenue; ☎ 867/873-9700, fax: 867/873-9702

# Where to... Eat and Drink

## Prices

Based on the cost of a three-course dinner, excluding drinks and service

$ under $25    $$ $26–$50    $$$ more than $50

## DAWSON CITY

### Jack London Dining Room $$

This period-style restaurant in the Downtown Hotel is a great place to get a filling breakfast or a light lunch, and the evening meals are particularly satisfying, with a menu featuring pasta, stir-fries, steaks, fish and grills. The fresh Yukon salmon is especially good, and the best of the desserts is the cheesecake. There is a special BBQ "patio" menu for outdoor eating.

✚ 210 B4 ⊠ Downtown Hotel, P.O. Box 780 V ☎ 867/863-5221 ⓦ Sun–Thu 6 am–10 pm, Fri–Sat 6 am–11 pm

### Klondike Kate's $

It's fun to eat in this authentic Gold-Rush building (1904), which opens early (try the $4.99 breakfast special) and closes late. Canadian and ethnic dishes can be enjoyed inside or on the covered, heated patio.

✚ 210 B4 ⊠ Corner of 3rd Avenue and King Street ☎ 867/993-6527 ⓦ Mid-May to mid-Sep daily 6:30 am–11 pm

## WHITEHORSE

### The Cellar $$$

An elegant dining room in the Edgewater Hotel serving imaginative steaks, chicken, seafood and pasta – look for the Fillet Neptune, a tenderloin steak topped with crab, asparagus and hollandaise sauce, and the Alaska king crab (don't miss this if you're a fan of crab) with lemon and clarified butter.

✚ 210 B2 ⊠ Edgewater Hotel, 101 Main Street ☎ 867/667-2572 ⓦ Tue–Fri 11:30–1:30, 5–10, Sat 5–10

### Talisman Café $–$$

This lovely little café, voted one of the top ten vegetarian places to eat in Canada, has good meat dishes too, and is particularly good for families. It offers generous portions of international dishes, hearty breakfasts are also served and there's a take-out service, to cover pretty much all the options. Original works by First Nations artist Ivan Sawrenko (who also designed the café logo) are on display on the walls.

✚ 210 B2 ⊠ 2112 2nd Avenue ☎ 867/667-2736 ⓦ Daily 9–8, Sat 10–5

## YELLOWKNIFE

### L'Heritage Restaurant Français $$–$$$

The place to go for elegant French dining in downtown Yellowknife. Traditional Northern foods such as caribou, muskox and arctic char are given a French twist with exotic sauces, and there's an excellent range of wines to go with them.

✚ 211 F2 ⊠ 5019 49th Street, 2nd level ☎ 867/873-9561 ⓦ Tue–Sat 5–10

### Wildcat Café $

Good food and fabulous views in this original log cabin overlooking Back Bay. It's tiny and gets very crowded, but it's a Yellowknife must. The menu changes daily, but usually includes Northern specialties such as caribou, muskox and local fish; the fresh pie and coffee are legendary.

✚ 211 F2 ⊠ 3904 Wiley Road; ☎ 867/873-8850 ⓦ Mon–Fri 11–10, Sat–Sun 10–10. Closed mid-Sep to May

# Where to... Shop

As you might expect, the shopping opportunities in this area tend to center around local gold and crafts and keeping warm. Whitehorse, Dawson City, Yellowknife and Iqaluit are the principal oases amid this vast retail wilderness.

## CLOTHING

For really unique knitted items, **Folknits** (2151 2nd Avenue, Whitehorse, tel: 867/668-7771) has garments that are made from such unusual fibers as qiviut (muskox down), dog hair, arctic fox fur and mountain goat wool, as well as the more familiar sheep wool; **Unique Tailors** (4101 4th Avenue,

Whitehorse, tel: 867/633-6088) have great winter clothing and a selection of First Nations clothing and jewelry.

In Iqaluit, the Inuit culture is reflected in the exclusive sealskin garments at **Rannva Design** (Apex Beach, Old Hudson Bay Building 3606, Iqaluit, Nunavut, tel: 867/979-0333).

## GOLD

For genuine gold nuggets, original jewelry designs and other souvenirs, try **Rivers of Gold** (952 2nd Avenue, Dawson City, tel: 867/993-6909) or **Goldsmiths** (106 Main Street, Whitehorse, tel: 867/667-7340).

## BOOKS

**Mac's Fireweed Books** (203 Main Street, Whitehorse, tel: 867/668-6104) has a wide selection of books about the Yukon.

# Where to... Be Entertained

## FOLLIES AND FESTIVALS

Though it's not all can-can dancers and old-style humor – the **Yukon Arts Centre** (Yukon College Campus, Whitehorse, tel: 867/667-8574) has an eclectic program of dance, drama and music – the Gold-Rush theme is definitely to the fore in the Yukon's entertainment scene. You can catch the Gaslight Follies at the restored 1899 **Palace Grand Theatre** (King Street, Dawson City, tel: 867/993-6217), or gamble the night away at **Diamond Tooth Gertie's** (Queen Street, Dawson City, tel: 867/993-5525). Vaudeville is also the theme at **Frantic Follies** (Westmark Whitehorse Hotel, 200 Wood Street, Whitehorse, tel: 867/393-9700).

Music festivals take place year-round, from the **Frostbite Music Festival** (www.frostbitefest.com) – cool in every way – to the **Dawson City Music Festival** (www.dcmf.com), which takes place under the midnight sun.

## SPORT

There are plenty of sporting events throughout the year. In winter, time your visit to coincide with a **sled dog race** (www.yukonquest.com or www.thepercy.com); the long days of summer are ideal for such events as **midnight sun golf tournaments** (www.topoftheworldgolf.com) or the Yukon River Quest, the longest **canoe and kayak race** in the world (www.polarcom.com/riverquest).

# Tours

# 1 INSIDE PASSAGE CRUISE

*Tour*

Canada's western coast is dotted with islands, and early explorers soon found a way through these safe, sheltered waters. Today, it is one of the most spectacular cruise routes in the world, with rocky mountains rising straight out of the ocean, prettily wooded islands and magnificent glaciers breaking into the waves. Whales, dolphins, porpoises, sea lions and seals inhabit the waters, bald eagles are among about 100 species of bird that fly overhead, and you may spot bears on the mainland shore. In summer the entire trip is completed in daylight.

**DISTANCE** 288km (180 miles) **TIME** 15 hours
**START POINT** Port Hardy, Vancouver Island; ferry departs 7:30 am 🕀 202 B2
**END POINT** Prince Rupert, arrival 10:30 pm 🕀 202 B4

## 1–2

At the northern tip of Vancouver Island, **Port Hardy** is your departure point, the largest town in the area and a center for all kinds of outdoor activities. It's worth arriving a day early to explore its waterside nature path, take a forestry industry tour, or browse its art and craft galleries. Sailing out of the harbor, you soon enter the Queen Charlotte Strait, the only stretch of open ocean on the voyage. It can be rough at times, but it doesn't last for long and the ferry soon enters the calmer waters of Fitzhugh Sound (also known as the Discovery Coast).

The first island on the left side is Calvert Island, 32km (20 miles) long and between 3 and 16km (2 and 10 miles) wide. It is thickly wooded on its western side, its highest point is Mt. Buxton (1,045m/3,430ft), and to the north is the Hakai Provincial Recreation Area, for marine activities such as sea-kayaking, salmon-fishing and wilderness camping. It's British Columbia's largest marine park, encompassing a group of islands of outstanding natural beauty. The town you will see on

**There is a resident population of orca off Vancouver Island**

## 3-4

Milbanke Sound is a prime fishing spot, with shoals of herring and salmon on their spawning runs. Fishing boats vie with the resident orca (killer whale), visiting humpback whales, Steller sea lions, northern fur seals and bald eagles for the catch. From here, the ferry soon tucks into the lea of Price and Swindle islands, where forests inhabited by bears grow right down to the high tide mark, reflecting prettily in the water. Narrow Meyers Pass separates Swindle from the larger **Princess Royal Island**, which has a much-indented coastline and a dense growth of rain forest. But the island is most famous as a habitat of the white Kermode bear that is only found in this region.

## 4-5

Continuing north between Gill and Gribbell islands, the ferry enters the 89-km (55-mile) long Grenville Channel, only 600m (1,970ft) wide at its narrowest point, for the most dramatic scenery of the entire voyage. Thickly forested mountains rise steeply from water that is so deep the boats can get close inshore. Finally, the ferry enters the harbor at **Prince Rupert** (▶ 66).

the right is **Namu**, which had a thriving cannery until the 1980s. You can still see the cannery buildings, built out over the water.

## 2-3

The ferry snakes between King Island, Hunter Island and Campbell Island on its way north. On Campbell Island, **Bella Bella** is the biggest settlement in the area, home to the Heiltsuk First Nations, who have an interpretive center here. Beyond Campbell Island, the ferry sails into Milbanke Sound.

**There are huge numbers of bald eagles in British Columbia**

### Information

**BC Ferries:** ✉ 1112 Fort Street, Victoria, ☎ 250/386-3431 or 888/223-3779; www.bcferries.bc.ca 🕐 Mid-May to mid-Sep $82-$102.50, child (5–11) $41-$51.25, under 5 free; reduced rates in off season. Vehicles are charged in addition to passenger fares – call for rates. All quoted prices are subject to change.

# 2 THE ICEFIELDS PARKWAY

*Drive*

**DISTANCE** 292km (181 miles) **TIME** 1 day
**START POINT** Lake Louise village ⊞ 203 E2
**END POINT** Jasper ⊞ 203 D3

Traversing the Banff and Jasper national parks (▶ 60–64), the Icefields Parkway is one of the most spectacular drives in the world, opening up ever-changing vistas of vertiginous peaks, strings of dazzling blue lakes, glittering waterfalls, great river valleys and the glaciers that give the parkway its name. Just driving this route is enough to take your breath away, but the route also provides easy access to some of the highlights of the Banff and Jasper national parks, many of which are just a short walk from the designated parking areas.

## 1–2

Start at **Lake Louise** village (stock up with snacks and water here). Take Route 1 north, then turn right onto Route 93 (Icefields Parkway). After a couple of kilometers you'll pass through the national park entry point (stop to buy a park pass, if you don't already have one) before embarking on the Parkway.

## 2–3

Beginning in the Bow Valley, the route climbs steadily for the first 16km (10 miles), and scenic treasures begin to unfold when tiny Herbert Lake, backed by Mt. Temple, then **Hector Lake** appear to the left. Both have parking with viewpoints. Some 34km (21 miles) from Lake Louise you'll catch sight of **Crowfoot Glacier**, so named because it looked like a giant, icy claw gripping the rocks. Soon, Bow Lake (with a pleasant lakeshore walk) and Bow Glacier comes into view. When you reach the Bow Summit, at 2,088m (6,850ft) the highest point on the parkway, turn left for the **Peyto Lake viewpoint**, with a panorama sweeping out over pine forests to the azure lake below.

## 3–4

Descending beyond the Bow Summit, there are wonderful views of the peaks of the Continental Divide, with Upper Waterfowl Lake in the foreground. When you have driven

72km (45 miles) from the beginning of the parkway, you'll reach the start of a short trail leading into the narrow **Mistaya Canyon**. Drive another 5km (3 miles) north to cross the wide, rocky valley of the North Saskatchewan River (fuel up here – it's the last until Jasper 130km/81 miles).

**There are spectacular lake and mountain views all along the Icefields Parkway**

follows the course of the river through the narrow gorge. Later come the even more spectacular **Athabasca Falls**. The Athabasca contains the greatest volume of water of any river in the Rockies, and here it cascades about 21m (70ft).

Continue for 30km (19 miles) to end your journey at **Jasper** (➤ 63–64).

## When to Go

The road is open all year, weather permitting, but many services along the way are only open April through October. Avoid high summer, when the route is busy with tour buses.

## Places to Visit

**Icefield Centre** ☎ 877/423-7433 ◷ Daily 9–5, Apr to mid-Oct, (2 to 6 pm, Jun 27–Sep).

## Taking a Break

The **Crossing Resort** (tel: 403/761-7000, $$$) at Saskatchewan River Crossing has food all day.

### 4–5

Beyond the river are views of the yellowish-hued Mt. Wilson, and then the valley narrows, with waterfalls tumbling down its rocky flanks, before reaching the Big Bend. Viewpoints here look out over Cirrus Mountains and Bridal Veil Falls, and there's a path to the Panther Falls. Up on the plain above, there's a steep 2.5km (1.5-mile) walk along Parker Ridge for a breathtaking view of the Saskatchewan Glacier.

### 5–6

The parkway exits Banff National Park at **Sunwapta Pass** and goes directly into the Jasper National Park and the Columbia Icefield. Beneath the snow-capped mountains is a moonscape of rocks and moraine interspersed with huge glaciers, with streams that grow into rushing rivers and waterfalls and feed turquoise lakes. Call in at the Icefield Centre, which has masses of information. It's worth stopping here, especially for the two-hour Snocoach Tour (tel: 877/423-7433; expensive) onto the **Athabasca Glacier**, 6km (4 miles) long and 1km (0.6 mile) wide. Alternatively, you can walk to the glacier's edge from the parking lot at **Sunwapta Lake**,

where marker posts show how the glacier has retreated over the years.

### 6–7

Farther north the road follows the wider flood plain of the Sunwapta River, and the two main attractions are waterfalls. The first is the **Sunwapta Falls**, where a trail

# 3 NIAGARA PARKWAY

*Drive*

**DISTANCE** 53km (33 miles), including stops for sightseeing
**TIME** 1 day, including stops for sightseeing
**START POINT** Old Fort Erie ⊞ 207 F1
**END POINT** Niagara-on-the-Lake ⊞ 207 E1

This beautiful drive opens up wonderful sights and interesting contrasts. There's the world-famous Niagara Falls, of course, with its thundering waters and power plants (and huge numbers of visitors), but there are also tranquil stretches of water, delightful old towns and villages full of history, and large areas of vineyards and orchards producing the Niagara region's renowned wines and fruits.

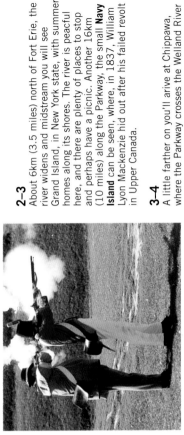

Old Fort Erie recalls the days of British-American hostilities during the War of 1812

## 1–2

The drive begins at the Mather Arch by the **Peace Bridge**, the border crossing from the Buffalo, New York state, US, which links Fort Erie, Canada with Buffalo, New York across the Niagara River. It is one of four international bridges across the river. Close by is **Old Fort Erie** (➤ 108), a reconstruction of a British fort that was built during the War of 1812 and destroyed by the Americans in 1814. It has a wonderful site, with views over Lake Erie and Buffalo.

## 2–3

About 6km (3.5 miles) north of Fort Erie, the river widens and midstream you will see Grand Island, in New York state, with summer homes along its shores. The river is peaceful here, and there are plenty of places to stop and perhaps have a picnic. Another 16km (10 miles) along the Parkway, the small **Navy Island** can be seen, where, in 1837, William Lyon Mackenzie hid out after his failed revolt in Upper Canada.

## 3–4

A little farther on you'll arrive at Chippawa, where the Parkway crosses the Welland River near its confluence with the Niagara. The Dufferin Islands are a cluster of islets linked by bridges, forming a park with lovely walks. After this, you'll see the control works that

Lake Ontario

Niagara-on-the-Lake

0 ____ 10 km
0 ____ 5 miles

opposite Table Rock, and explore all that **Niagara Falls** has to offer (▶ 107).

## 6–7

Drive the 2km (1.2 miles) to the **Rainbow Bridge,** another crossing to the US. Soon the Parkway passes the Whirlpool and White Water Walk (▶ 108), where you can get close to the turbulent waters below the falls. If you continue for another 3km (2 miles), you can hike down into the gorge for free at **Niagara Glen**. A short distance farther on are the Niagara Parks Botanical Gardens and Butterfly Conservatory, maintained by the students of the School of Horticulture here. Covering 40ha (100 acres), the gardens are a riot of color in summer.

## 7–8

Some 2km (1.2 miles) beyond here the Parkway passes impressive **generating stations** on both banks of the river. More attractive is the Floral Clock, a 12-m (40-ft) working clock with 20,000 small plants decorating its surface. Another 1km (0.6 mile) along is Queenston Heights Park and the Brock Monument, on the top of the Niagara escarpment.

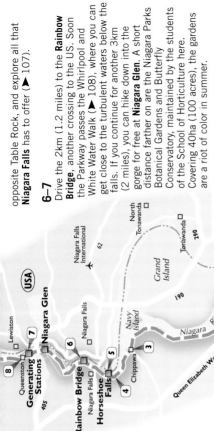

**The botanical gardens at Niagara are a testament to the favorable summer climate of southern Ontario**

divert the river below ground to the hydro-power plants beyond Niagara Falls.

## 4–5

The Niagara River picks up pace north of Chippawa, traveling at nearly 100kph (60mph) in its downhill journey through great rapids toward the falls. Excitement builds too, with the anticipation of the sights to come, espe-cially when the spray starts to hit the windshield.

## 5–6

Just 2km (1.2 miles) beyond Chippawa, you arrive at Table Rock and the **Horseshoe (Canadian) Falls** (▶ 107). You can park

Here, during the War of 1812, British commander Isaac Brock was killed in battle and his monument stands 50m (150ft) tall above the site. A little farther on, you can detour into Queenston (▶108) to visit the home of Canadian heroine, Laura Secord, who embarked upon a long walk to warn the British that an American attack was imminent after they ransacked her home.

### 8–9

Beyond Queenston Heights, the vast orchards and vineyards of the Niagara wine region open out, and you can detour to a number of wineries for tours and tastings. Eventually, the Parkway ends in **Niagara-on-the-Lake** (▶108), one of the loveliest towns in Ontario. Settled by Loyalists after the American Revolution, it was the first capital of Upper Canada, but was burned to the ground by the Americans during the War of 1812. Visit nearby Fort George National Historic Park (▶108) for a glimpse of military life in those days. The town was rebuilt soon afterwards, and it is this era that is recalled in its gracious homes and wide, tree-lined streets. The town is also well known for its summer Shaw Festival (see ▶116).

**Niagara-on-the-Lake** is a delightful set-piece of charming homes and craft and antiques shops

### Taking a Break

There are a number of options with views of the falls at Niagara Falls. One of the best for families is the **Victoria Park Restaurant** (tel: 905/356-2217) within a lovely floral park. In Niagara-on-the-Lake, the **Epicurean Restaurant and Bistro** (tel: 905/468-0288) has a great selection of made-to-order sandwiches, salads and entrées.

### When to Go

June and September are the best months, when the weather is good and the biggest summer crowds have not yet built to their peak. The falls are impressive in winter, but if you drive the route after October and before late May, some of the attractions will not be open.

**Places to Visit** ▶ 107–109

### Information
**Niagara Parks Commission** (▶ 109)

**Niagara Economic and Tourism Corporation**
⊠ 2201 St David's Road (PO Box 1042), Thorold; ☎ 905/984-3826 or 800/263-2988; www.tourismniagara.com or discoverniagara.com

**Niagara-on-the-Lake Chamber of Commerce** (▶ 109)

**Shaw Festival** ☎ 905/468-2172; www.shawfest.com

# 4 GASPÉ PENINSULA

*Drive*

This drive follows the spectacular coastline of the Gulf of St. Lawrence, with deep coves, craggy capes and pretty little fishing villages along the way. It explores the extraordinary cliffs of the Forillon National Park, with later views of the famous pierced rock at Percé. At the very beginning of the route, just before the descent into the town of Grande-Vallée, there is a wonderful view over the village and its bay.

## Places to Visit
**Manoir Le Bouthillier** ✉ 578 Boulevard Griffon (CP 37), L'Anse-au-Griffon ☎ 418/892-5150 🕒 Daily, Jun to mid-Oct 💲 Inexpensive

**Forillon National Park** ✉ B122 Boulevard de Gaspé, Gaspé ☎ 418/368-5505; www.parkscanada.gc.ca/forillon 💲 Inexpensive

**DISTANCE** 236km (147 miles), not including detours
**TIME** 1 day, 2 to allow sufficient time in Percé
**START POINT** Grande-Vallée ⊞ 208 C3
**END POINT** Grand-Rivière ⊞ 208 C3

### 1–2
As you drive through **Grande-Vallée**, notice the covered bridge across the Grande-Vallée River and the parish church, high on the cape. From the village, take Route 132 east, twisting and turning around the coast. Waves smash on the rocks, seagulls fly overhead, and one tiny fishing village succeeds another, all clustered in sheltered coves. After 65km (40 miles) you reach **Rivière-au-Renard**, an important fishing center.

### 2–3
Here the route enters the **Forillon National Park**, which preserves 245sq km (95sq miles) of the peninsula, encompassing mountains and coastline with seabird colonies. Continue for 10km (6 miles) to **L'Anse-au-Griffon**, a small agricultural and fishing community. Here, Le Manoir Le Bouthillier, built in the 1850s for a wealthy cod merchant, is open to the public.

Covered bridges, sometimes quite lengthy, are a feature of French Canada

### 3–4
From here it's 11km (7 miles) to **Cap-des-Rosiers**. Samuel de Champlain visited the cape in 1631 and made a note in his journal about the wild rose bushes, and they still flourish here. Canada's tallest lighthouse, 34m (112ft) high, is here. The route turns

inland through the national park. Make a left onto a park road, signed Cap Bon Ami, for a round-trip detour of 12km (7.5 miles). Stop at the Interpretive Centre after 2km (1.2 miles) to walk the short Discovery Trail (about 20 minutes). You can also get boat trips from the wharf to view seabirds and seals. Then continue to **Cap Bon Ami** to view the tilted limestone cliffs.

### 4–5

Return to Route 132, turn left and continue across the peninsula through the mountains. There's a great viewpoint after 8km (5 miles), looking out toward Percé. When you've driven 11km (7 miles) from Cap-des-Rosiers, turn left on a park road, signed Grande Grave for a 13-km (8-mile) round-trip detour to this former cod-processing center. Some of the buildings have been restored and are open to the public (daily, mid-Jun to mid-Oct). The detour continues to Anse aux Sauvages for a hike out to the tip of Cap Gaspé (8km/ 5 miles round trip).

### 5–6

Return to Route 132 and continue for 11km (7 miles) to the Penouille Peninsula and Information Centre, where there is a fine

sandy beach and you can stretch your lets on a 4-km (2.5-mile) trail. After this, the route exits the national park to wind around the Baie de Gaspé, crossing a long bridge over the Dartmouth River estuary. There are some terrific backward views as you climb away from the river. Eventually, 20km (12 miles) beyond Penouille, you'll enter **Gaspé**, the commercial heart of the peninsula and a historic spot, where French explorer Jacques Cartier claimed the land for France.

## Boat Trips

**Bateaux de Croisières Julien Cloutier (Forillon and Ile Bonaventure)** ⊠ 395 Route 132 Ouest (CP 467), 9 rue de Quai, Percé ☎ 418/782-5606 (Cap-des-Rosiers in season) or 877/782-2161 (Percé) ◷ Daily, mid-May to mid-Oct ◗ Expensive

**Les Bateliers de Percé (Ile Bonaventure)** ⊠ 162 Route 132 (CP 278), Percé ☎ 418/782-2974 or 877/782-2974

**Les Croisières les Traversiers de l'Ile Inc. (Ile Bonaventure)** ⊠ Jean-Pierre Cloutier, 878 Route 132, Percé ☎ 418/782-5526 (in season) or 866/782-5526

The road down into Percé has a wonderful view, with the whale-like Bonaventure Island offshore

## Information

**Association Touristique Régionale de la Gaspésie** ⊠ 357 rue de la mer, Ste.-Flavie ☎ 800/463-0323; www.tourisme-gaspesie.com

**Office du Tourisme et des Congrès du Gaspé** ⊠ 27 Boulevard York, Gaspé ☎ 418/368-8525; www.gaspe-forillon.com

**Information Touristique de Percé** ⊠ 142 Route 132, PO Box 99, Percé ☎ 418/782-5448; www.rocherperce.com

88m (289ft) high and 438m (1,437ft) long, with a hole right through it. You can walk out to the rock at low tide.

## 8–9

Leaving Percé, halt awhile at the viewpoint on Cap Blanc, 2km (1.2 miles) out of town, for another magnificent view of the rock and Mont-Ste.-Anne. In another 7km (4.3 miles) you will reach the little town of **L'Anse-à-Beaufils,** and 7km (4.3 miles) beyond here is **Cap d'Espoir,** with a final view of Rocher Percé.

Then the route heads west to end at **Grande-Rivière,** known for its salmon-rich waters.

## 6–7

Leave Gaspé via the bridge over the York River, then turn left with Route 132, with views across the bay. The route detours inland around the St.-Jean River estuary and continues to Douglastown, 25km (15.5 miles) from Gaspé, and, in another 23km (14 miles), **Pointe-St.-Pierre.** Here, make a left opposite the Episcopal church on to rue du Quai, which leads to the water's edge for a fine view of the Rocher Percé (Percé Rock) and Île Bonaventure (Bonaventure Island).

## 7–8

Back on the main route, there's a scenic 7-km (4.3-mile) stretch to Barachois, with constant views of the rock, then it disappears as you begin the steep, winding descent into **Percé.** Finally, and dramatically, you breach the last hill and the great rock is directly below. In this spectacular area that shows its geological upheavals all too clearly, there is none so impressive as the Rocher Percé, a massive chunk of limestone

# 5 THE CABOT TRAIL

*Drive*

**DISTANCE** 292km (181 miles)
**TIME** Allow 2 days
**START/END POINT** Baddeck ⊞ 209 E3

Cape Breton (▶ 151–152) is one of the most beautiful islands in the world, and the Cabot Trail encircles one of the most scenic parts of the island, incorporating the mountains and forests of the Cape Breton Highlands National Park and a spectacular coastline. It is named after the 15th-century explorer, John Cabot, who is said to have landed on the northern tip of the island in 1497.

## 1–2

Leave **Baddeck** (▶ 151) on Highway 105 west in the direction of the Canso Causeway, to skirt the lovely Bras d'Or Lake. At Nyanza, reached after 8km (5 miles), make a right, signed "Cabot Trail" and drive for 52km (32 miles) through agricultural countryside, following the Margaree River to **Margaree Harbour**. Here, where the river flows into the Gulf of St. Lawrence, you turn north along the coast. The

character of the drive changes markedly, and you will notice that all the place names are in French here, for this area is populated largely by French-speaking Acadians. Look for their flag – a French tricolor with a gold star.

### Information

**Cape Breton Highlands National Park**
⊠ Ingonish Beach ☎ 902/285-2535 (seasonal) and 902/224-2306 (year-round); www.pc.gc.ca/capebretonhighlands ◉ Visitor centre: daily, mid-May to mid-Oct; park: always accessible ◉ Park fee moderate (applies mid-May to mid-Oct only)

## 2–3

Continue north for 24km (15 miles) until you reach **Chéticamp**, the center of Acadian culture – visit the Coopérative Artisinale Acadienne (Acadian Crafts Cooperative), which has a good selection of locally produced hooked rugs (made by a group of ladies known as "Happy Hookers") and other items. With its sheltered harbor, Chéticamp is one of the places where you can go whale-watching.

## 3–4

About 8km (5 miles) north of Chéticamp, the route enters the **Cape Breton Highlands National Park** (▶ 152), with an excellent information center. From here, the highway winds around the coast on one of the most spectacular parts of the drive, with stunning views, then curves inland, up through thickly forested mountains. There are regular parking areas where you can stop for a walk. The highest ground is at French Mountain (455m/1,495ft) and Mackenzie Mountain (355m/1,165ft), and after this, a series of dramatic hairpin bends winds down to **Pleasant Bay**. This is another whale-watching center, with a Whale Museum above the harbor.

Cape Breton's renowned fall colors are just beginning to appear as a backdrop to the lovely Neil's Harbour

## 4–5

The Cabot Trail leaves the coast here, heading inland for 14km (8 miles) and climbing the slopes of North Mountain (457m/1,500ft) to the **Lone Shieling**, a tiny stone replica of a Scottish croft amid a beautiful maple forest. The cottage is a reminder of the many Scottish settlers who came to the island following the Highland Clearances during the 18th and 19th centuries. Their presence on the island has given it a strong culture of music and dance – and a whiskey distillery. Beyond here, the route descends into the Aspy Valley and follows the river to **Aspy Bay** on the northeast coast.

## Taking a Break

A good place to eat on the northwest stretch of the Cabot Trail is the **Rusty Anchor** (tel: 902/224-1313, $), just south of Pleasant Bay. It has a lovely ocean-view terrace. Along the other coast, the **Atlantic Restaurant** at the Keltic Lodge resort (tel: 902/285-2880 or 800/565-0444, $$) is a good place for lunch.

### 5–6

Turning inland once again, the chances of spotting a moose are good, especially at dawn or dusk. After 34km (21 miles) there's a very worthwhile detour to the charming fishing village of **Neil's Harbour**, and 6km (4 miles) beyond here is pretty **Black Brook Cove**, with a lovely beach and coastal walks. In another 6km (4 miles) Lakies Head Lookout has wonderful views of Cape Smokey and Middle Head. For the next 20km (12 miles) the lovely communites and beaches of the **Ingonish** (▶ 152) area are dotted along the coast, with Ingonish Island offshore.

**The wooded mountains sweep down to the sea between Presquile and Petit Etang**

### 6–7

After 22km (13.5 miles) you'll begin the dramatic drive up over **Cape Smokey**, rising 366m (1,200ft) out of the ocean, its summit often obscured by the swirling mists that give it its name. From the lookout at the top, there's a spectacular view over the Ingonish villages around the bay. The drive down the other side of the cape is even more dramatic, returning you to sea level. From here, the route continues southward along the Gaelic coast, another recognition of the strong Scottish heritage on the island. The Bird

school on the North American continent to teach the Gaelic language and traditional Scottish arts and crafts. This was also home to the Cape Breton Giant – Angus MacAskill (d.1863), who grew to be 2.35m (7ft 9in) tall. From here it's just 19km (12 miles) back to **Baddeck**.

### When to Go

Cape Breton, jutting out into the Atlantic Ocean, is famous for the dense fog that rolls in off the ocean. Wait for a clear day to see the island at its most spectacular. The fall colors are spectacular, and the roads are less busy at this time (except during the Celtic Colours Festival in October).

### Places to Visit

**Coopérative Artisanale Acadienne** 🖂 15067 Main Street, Chéticamp 🕿 902/224-2170; www.co-opartisanale.com 🕒 Daily mid-May to mid-Oct; Tue–Thu pm off-season

**Museum of the Gaelic College of Celtic Arts and Crafts** 🖂 PO Box 80, Englishtown 🕿 902/295-3411; www.gaeliccollege.edu 🕒 Mid-Jun to Sep 💷 Inexpensive

Islands can be seen offshore, and they are aptly named, forming a safe nesting ground for a huge numbers of birds.

### 7–8

After 23km (14 miles) take a detour on Route 312 and cross a narrow inlet by ferry to join Highway 105 (the TransCanada Highway) and rejoin the Cabot Trail. You can simply stay on the Cabot Trail, but this is a more scenic alternative. Either way, you will end up in **South Gut St. Ann's**, which is home of the only

# 6 GOLDEN CIRCLE

*Drive*

This route follows in the footsteps of the prospectors of the Klondike Gold Rush through some of the most unspoiled landscapes in the world, with high mountain peaks, glaciers, bright blue lakes and even a tiny desert.

**DISTANCE** 483km (300 miles)
**TIME** At least 2 days, more to allow for hiking
**START/END POINT** Whitehorse ➕ 210 B2

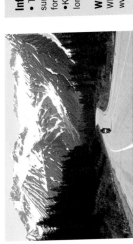

**Haines Highway is never too crowded with traffic**

## 1–2

Leave **Whitehorse** (➤ 170) via 4th Avenue and Two Mile Hill to join Route 1, the **Alaska Highway** (➤ 172). The initial section – by Yukon standards at least – is not that special, but as you approach Haines Junction, after 160km (100 miles), the horizon becomes jagged with the peaks of the St. Elias Mountains. **Haines Junction** is a popular base for the **Kluane** (pronounced *kloo-wa-nee*) **National Park**.

## 2–3

From Haines Junction, head south on the Haines Highway (Route 3), skirting the east-

ern edge of the Kluane National Park. After 27km (16.5 miles) turn right to **Kathleen Lake**, where there's a wonderful 10-km (6-mile) hike into the mountains. Stay on Route 3 for 17km (10.5 miles) to access the short Rock Glacier Trail. From here it's 7km (4.3 miles) to **Klukshu**, a First Nations camp that's only occupied June through early November (best visited during the salmon run).

## Information

• The route crosses the US border, so make sure you have all the necessary documentation for the vehicle and its passengers.
• Keep your fuel topped up – there are some long distances between filling stations.

**Whitehorse Tourism** ✉ 2121 Second Avenue, Whitehorse ☎ 867/667-6401; www.visitwhitehorse.com

**Skagway Convention and Visitors Bureau**
☎ 907/983-2854; www.skagway.org

**Haines Convention and Visitors Bureau**
☎ 907/766-2234; www.haines.ak.us

## 3–4

In another 40km (25 miles) or so, the route crosses into British Columbia amid superb mountain scenery, climbing steadily to the

## Taking a Break
The **Talisman Café** in Whitehorse (▶ 175) is a good place to stop. In Skagway, the **Haven Café** (tel: 907/983-3553) at 9th and State streets, has good coffee and light meals.

**Chilkat Pass**, 57km (35 miles) farther along. At an altitude of 1,065m (3,495ft), the pass saw much human traffic during the 1890s Gold Rush.

### 4–5
Continuing south, the route crosses the US border into Alaska 32km (20 miles) beyond the pass. The customs post is open between 7 am and 11 pm Alaska time (one hour ahead of local Canadian time). From here, it's 33km (21 miles) to the **Chilkat Bald Eagle Preserve**, 19,420ha (48,000 acres) of river-bottom land populated by as many as 4,000 bald eagles. There are lots of designated parking/viewing areas. From here it's just 35km (22 miles) to **Haines City**, a good place to break the journey and stay overnight.

### 5–6
Taking the ferry from here to **Skagway** (▶ 170) cuts a 563-km (350-mile) drive down to a one-hour trip. The most northerly town on the Alaskan Inside Passage, Skagway is a splendidly preserved Gold Rush town, containing the US-Canadian Klondike Gold Rush National Historical Park. Head north on the

Klondike Highway, climbing steadily to **White Pass**. In the late 1890s this was busy with prospectors on foot, and you can see their path from the highway, which was only finished in 1978. Cross back into Canada just before the summit (the customs post is another 12km/8 miles away and is open 24 hours in summer).

### 6–7
Beyond White Pass, Tushti Lake is followed for some distance. Back in the Yukon, you reach **Carcross**, which is most famous as the site of the world's smallest desert, covering just 260ha (642 acres). Some 157km (98 miles) farther, the Klondike Highway meets the Alaska Highway. Turn left for the short drive back to Whitehorse.

# Practicalities

## GETTING ADVANCE INFORMATION

**Websites**
- British Columbia: www.hellobc.com
- Alberta: www.travelalberta.com
- Saskatchewan: www.sasktourism.com
- Manitoba: www.travelmanitoba.com
- Ontario: www.ontariotravel.net
- Quebec: www.bonjourquebec.com
- New Brunswick: www.tourismnbcanada.com
- Newfoundland/Labrador: www.gov.nf.ca/tourism
- Nova Scotia: www.noviascotia.com
- Prince Edward Island: www.peiplay.com
- Northwest Territories: www.explorenwt.com
- Yukon: www.touryukon.com
- Nunavut: www.nunavuttourism.com

## BEFORE YOU GO

### WHAT YOU NEED

- ● Required
- ○ Suggested
- ▲ Not required
- △ Not applicable

Some countries require a passport to remain valid for a minimum period (usually six months) beyond the date of entry – contact their consulate or embassy or your travel agent for details.

| | UK | Germany | USA | Canada | Australia | Ireland | Netherlands | Spain |
|---|---|---|---|---|---|---|---|---|
| Passport/National Identity Card | ● | ● | ● | ● | ● | ● | ● | ● |
| Visa (regulations can change – check before booking) | ▲ | ▲ | ▲ | ▲ | ▲ | ▲ | ▲ | ▲ |
| Onward or Return Ticket | ● | ● | ▲ | ▲ | ● | ● | ● | ● |
| Health Inoculations (tetanus and polio) | ▲ | ▲ | ▲ | ▲ | ▲ | ▲ | ▲ | ▲ |
| Health Documentation (▶ 198, Health) | ▲ | ▲ | ▲ | ● | ▲ | ● | ● | ▲ |
| Travel Insurance | ● | ● | ● | ○ | ● | ● | ● | ● |
| Driver's Licence (national) | ● | ● | ● | ● | ● | ● | ● | ● |
| Car Insurance Certificate | △ | △ | ● | ● | △ | △ | △ | △ |
| Car Registration Document | △ | △ | ● | ● | △ | △ | △ | △ |

Anyone convicted of a drunken-driving or other offense within the last ten years, may not be allowed into Canada without submitting a "Ministers Permit" to show they are deemed "rehabilitated." Information available at: www.cic.gc.ca/english/applications/rehabil.html

### WHEN TO GO

**Toronto**

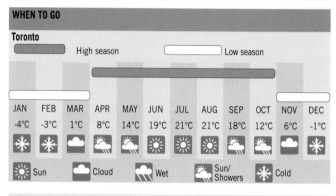

| | JAN | FEB | MAR | APR | MAY | JUN | JUL | AUG | SEP | OCT | NOV | DEC |
|---|---|---|---|---|---|---|---|---|---|---|---|---|
| | -4°C | -3°C | 1°C | 8°C | 14°C | 19°C | 21°C | 21°C | 18°C | 12°C | 6°C | -1°C |

High season / Low season

☀️ Sun  ☁️ Cloud  🌧️ Wet  ⛅ Sun/Showers  ❄️ Cold

Weather varies considerably between the different climatic zones in this huge country. In most parts **summers** are reliably warm and can get very hot – in southern Ontario, for instance, it often exceeds 30ºC (86ºF). It's pleasantly fresher on the coasts, though these areas are prone to sea mists. Even in the far north it's warm in summer, and there's the added bonus of 24-hour daylight. **Winters** are punishingly cold in most areas. BC is the only province in which the average winter temperature remains above freezing point, with little snowfall along the coast (but a good deal of rain); there's plenty of snow up in the Rockies and Coast Mountains, though. The Atlantic Provinces have relatively mild winters too, but also get some of Canada's highest levels of snowfall, and coastal regions may be battered by North Atlantic storms.

**In the UK**
**Visit Canada**
P.O. Box 170, Ashford,
Kent TN24 OZX
☎ 020 7408-1254
www.travelcanada.ca

**In the US**
**Canadian Tourism
Commission**
550 South Hope Street,
9th Floor, Los Angeles CA
90071-2627
☎ 1-323/937-5657

**In Australia**
**Canadian Tourism
Commission**
Suite 105, Jones Bay
Wharf, 19–21 Pirrama
Road, Pyrmont NSW 2009
☎ 02-9571-1766

## GETTING THERE

**By Air** The major international airports in Canada are in Toronto, Montréal and
Vancouver, with international flights also handled at Ottawa, Québec City, Halifax,
Edmonton, Winnipeg and Calgary. **Air Canada** (tel: 888/247-2262; www.aircanada.ca)
is the national airline.
**From the US**: A number of US airlines have scheduled flights to the major Canadian
cities, including American Airlines, Continental Airlines, Delta, Northwest Airlines,
United Airlines and US Airways.
**From the UK**: **British Airways** has regular scheduled flights to Vancouver, Toronto and
Montréal, and **Air Canada** has flights from London Heathrow to all the major
Canadian cities.
**From the rest of Europe**: From France, **Air France** flies from Paris to Montréal, Ottawa
and Toronto, and **Corsair** operate a summer service from Paris direct to Moncton,
New Brunswick. From Germany, **Lufthansa** have direct flights from Frankfurt to
Toronto, Montréal and Vancouver and from Munich to Toronto and Montréal. They
also offer code-share flights to such destinations as Ottawa, Calgary and Québec
City.
**From Australia and New Zealand**: **Qantas** flies to Toronto, Ottawa, Québec City,
Montréal, Winnipeg, Calgary and Vancouver.
**Air New Zealand** have scheduled flights to Toronto and Vancouver.

## TIME

Canada spans six time zones: Atlantic Standard Time (GMT+4); Eastern
Standard Time (GMT+5); Central Standard Time (GMT+6); Mountain
Standard Time (GMT+7); Pacific Standard Time (GMT+8); Newfoundland
and part of Labrador are a half-hour ahead of Atlantic Standard.
**Daylight Saving Time** operates in all provinces except Saskatchwewan from the first
Sunday in April until the last Sunday in October.

## CURRENCY AND FOREIGN EXCHANGE

**Currency** Canada's currency is the Canadian dollar, divided into 100 cents. **Bills** are
printed in English and French in the following dollar denominations: $5, $10, $20, $50
and $100 (the latter can be hard to use – people are suspicious because of forgeries).
**Coins** come in denominations of 1, 5, 10 and 25 cents, and 1 and 2 dollars. The dollar
coin is called the "loonie" after the bird featured on one face; the two-dollar is called the
"twonie." US dollars are often accepted on a one-for-one basis, but as the US dollar is
worth more it makes sense to exchange it for Canadian currency.
  The best way to take money is as **travelers' checks** made out in Canadian dollars, which
are widely accepted as cash and change is given in cash.
  **Exchange** rates are best in banks, and there is no limit to the amount of Canadian or
foreign currency that can be exchanged or brought into and out of the country. You can
withdraw money from most Canadian **ATMs** with a credit or debit card, but you'll need to
know your PIN – this is also useful in those Canadian stores that have machines for you to
enter your PIN rather than sign a sales slip.

## TIME DIFFERENCES

| GMT | Canada (Ottawa) | USA New York | Germany | Spain | Australia |
| --- | --- | --- | --- | --- | --- |
| 12 noon | 7 am | 7 am | 1 pm | 1 pm | Sydney 10 pm |

## WHEN YOU ARE THERE

### CLOTHING SIZES

| UK | Rest of Europe | Canada/USA | |
| --- | --- | --- | --- |
| 36 | 46 | 36 | |
| 38 | 48 | 38 | |
| 40 | 50 | 40 | |
| 42 | 52 | 42 | Suits |
| 44 | 54 | 44 | |
| 46 | 56 | 46 | |
| 7 | 41 | 8 | |
| 7.5 | 42 | 8.5 | |
| 8.5 | 43 | 9.5 | |
| 9.5 | 44 | 10.5 | Shoes |
| 10.5 | 45 | 11.5 | |
| 11 | 46 | 12 | |
| 14.5 | 37 | 14.5 | |
| 15 | 38 | 15 | |
| 15.5 | 39/40 | 15.5 | |
| 16 | 41 | 16 | Shirts |
| 16.5 | 42 | 16.5 | |
| 17 | 43 | 17 | |
| 8 | 34 | 6 | |
| 10 | 36 | 8 | |
| 12 | 38 | 10 | |
| 14 | 40 | 12 | Dresses |
| 16 | 42 | 14 | |
| 18 | 44 | 16 | |
| 4.5 | 38 | 6 | |
| 5 | 38 | 6.5 | |
| 5.5 | 39 | 7 | |
| 6 | 39 | 7.5 | Shoes |
| 6.5 | 40 | 8 | |
| 7 | 41 | 8.5 | |

### NATIONAL HOLIDAYS

| 1 Jan | New Year's Day |
| --- | --- |
| Mar/Apr | Good Friday |
| Third Mon in May | Victoria Day |
| 1 Jul | Canada Day |
| First Mon in Sept | Labour Day |
| Second Mon in Oct | Thanksgiving |
| 25 Dec | Christmas Day |

In addition, Easter Monday, Remembrance Day (Nov 11) and Boxing Day (Dec 26) are celebrated in different parts of the country, when government offices and banks are closed, but some stores are open. Various provincial holidays are also observed.

### OPENING HOURS

○ Shops
● Offices
● Banks
● Post Offices
● Museums/Monuments
● Pharmacies

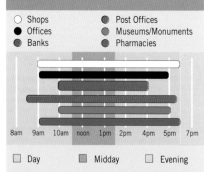

☐ Day  ■ Midday  ☐ Evening

**Stores** Most open Mon–Fri 10–9, Sat 9:30–6, Sun noon–6. Shopping malls don't usually close until after 7:30 pm.

**Banks** Usually open Mon–Fri 10–4, but hours can vary and some stay open until 5 or 6 some days.

**Post offices** Generally open Mon–Fri 8:30–5:30; some open Sat 9–noon.

**Museums** Hours can vary widely, but are usually Tue–Sun 10–5; closed on public holidays. Some museums have late opening one evening a week, with free admission after 5:30 on that day.

**Pharmacies** Most open Mon–Sat 9–6; 24-hour or at least a late night service is usually available somewhere in major towns and cities.

**EMERGENCY NUMBERS**

POLICE 911

FIRE 911

AMBULANCE 911

NOTE:
In Yukon, Northwest Territories, Nunavut and Vancouver Island, dial 0 for operator and and say you have an emergency

## PERSONAL SAFETY

Canada is a low-crime country and visitors need not be overly concerned about personal safety, but a few precautions can avoid unfortunate incidents.

- Carry money in a belt.
- Don't leave bags or other valuables visible in your car.
- Don't wear expensive jewelry or carry large amounts of cash.
- Leave your passport and valuables in the hotel safe.
- At night walk only along well-lit streets and avoid parks and train stations.
- Report any crime to the police and note the crime reference number.

**Police assistance:**
 **911** from any phone

## TELEPHONES

Local calls cost 25 cents for any length call from public pay phones; longer-distance calls, which generally need to be prefixed with a "1", connect to an operator who will tell you how much the call will cost. Within a province you only dial the area code if the province has more than one.

Public phones are widely available and accept coins, credit cards and pre-paid phone cards. US telephone credit cards are also accepted.

**International Dialing Codes**
**Dial 011 followed by**

| | |
|---|---|
| US: | no country code required |
| UK: | 44 |
| Ireland: | 353 |
| Australia: | 61 |
| Spain | 34 |

## POST

Post offices are usually open Mon–Fri 8:30–5:30 and some larger stores and train stations have mail outlets; you can buy stamps in some convenience stores. Canada is not noted for speedy mail delivery, but Priority Post offers a next-day delivery within Canada.

## ELECTRICITY

The power supply is 110 volts AC (60 Hz), the same as in the US Sockets take two-prong, flat-pin plugs. An adaptor is needed for appliances with two-round-pin and three-pin plugs. European appliances also need a voltage transformer.

## TIPS/GRATUITIES

Tipping is widespread; it's usually calculated on the pre-tax amount for food service. As a general guide:

| | |
|---|---|
| Restaurants (service not included) | 15 percent |
| Bar Service | 15 percent |
| Tour guides | optional ($1 per person) |
| Hairdressers | 15 percent |
| Taxis | 15 percent |
| Chambermaids | optional |
| Porters | optional ($1 per bag) |
| Room service | 10 percent |

## CONSULATES and EMBASSIES

**UK**
☎ 613/237-1303

**USA**
☎ 613/238-5335

**Australia**
☎ 613/236-0841

**Germany**
☎ 613/232-1101

**Spain**
☎ 613/747-2252

## HEALTH

**Insurance** Visitors needing medical treatment while in Canada must pay for it, and the cost can be expensive. It is essential that you take out travel insurance before your visit. If you are ill, you will be treated and charged later.

**Dental Services** As with all medical services in Canada, dental services are of an excellent standard, but you must ensure that your travel insurance covers this. Your hotel should be able to recommend a dentist; or consult *Yellow Pages*.

**Weather** Depending on when you travel, you can suffer frostbite and hypothermia, or heatstroke and sunburn. Dress accordingly. Remember: water increases the effect of the sun by reflection. Carry mosquito repellant in summer.

**Drugs** Medicines can be bought at drugstores and most towns and cities have at least one 24-hour pharmacy. Bring sufficient supplies of regular medications, but bring your prescription too, in case you need further supplies. It's also wise to note the generic name of any prescription medicines that you take, because they may be sold under a different name in Canada.

**Safe Water** Tap water is safe, except in some campgrounds. Boil back-country spring water (10 mins) – it may contain parasites.

## CONCESSIONS

**Students/children** Many hotels offer reductions or free accommodations for children sharing parents' rooms; many restaurants have a children's menu or provide smaller portions. **Via Rail** offers free travel for under 2s and half-price for children 2–11; student rail passes give discounts of 10–50 percent. There are discounts on admission to museums and attractions, though age categories vary.

**Seniors** Many museums and attractions offer discounts to seniors; age limits range from over 55 to over 65 years. There are also concessionary fares on public transportation.

## TRAVELING WITH A DISABILITY

Facilities and access for wheelchair-bound visitors is generally good throughout Canada, and many hotels have specially adapted rooms, but it is always wise to check in advance. A good source of information is the **Access to Travel** website (www.accesstotravel.gc.ca), set up by the government to assist people with disabilities to travel around Canada. You can also contact the **Canadian Paraplegic Association** (CPA) (1101 Prince of Wales Drive, Suite 230, Ottawa, Ontario K2C 3W7; tel: 613/723-1033; fax: 613/723-1060; www.canparaplegic.org).

## CHILDREN

Hotels and restaurants are generally child-friendly, but diaper-changing amenities are by no means universal.

## RESTROOMS

These can be found in public buildings, museums, malls and transportation terminals. Patrons can use restrooms in bars and restaurants.

## CUSTOMS

Wildlife souvenirs sourced from endangered species may be illegal. Check your country's regulations.

## CANADIAN LANGUAGES

Canada has two official languages—English and French. The reasons for this are historical. French settlement in the St. Lawrence Valley started in the early 17th century. No English-speaking settlers arrived until after the British conquest of 1760. At the time of Canadian Confederation in 1867, the English- and French-speaking populations were more or less equal in size. Today, less than a quarter of Canadians speak French as their mother tongue (6.7 million out of 31 million).

The country has large communities of peoples of other nationalities and languages, but none has official recognition.

### FRENCH SPEAKING-COMMUNITIES

French Canadians are in every province, but their greatest concentration is in the province of Québec, where they comprise more than 85 percent of the population. These are the people known as the Québécois. French-speaking people form more than a third of the population of New Brunswick, and are also prominent in Nova Scotia and Prince Edward Island—these are the Acadiens, the first European settlers to colonize this part of Canada. Following dispersal by the British, many Acadiens wound up in Louisiana in the US, where they became know as "Cajuns."

Ontario has a sizable French-speaking population distributed between Toronto and in the eastern part of the province, who are known as Franco-Ontariens.

Manitoba's distinct French-speaking community is in St.-Boniface, and these people are known as Franco-Manitobins. There are also small French-speaking communities in Saskatchewan, Alberta and British Columbia.

### THE FRENCH LANGUAGE

If you speak the French of France, you will find that the language of Québec has a strong and highly recognizable accent—as close to the language of the mother country as the Texas accent is to the English spoken in the UK.

The French spoken by the Acadiens is different again. For instance, *oui* sounds like "why," and *non* is pronounced "nah." The word for "and" is more likely to be *pi* than *et*. If you have a good ear, you can detect other differences and a softer accent. It resembles the French of old France more than the dynamic language that you will hear in French Montréal.

Differences of vocabulary that can cause unfortunate misunderstandings include words used for meals. In Québec, you eat *déjeuner* first thing in the morning, *dîner* at lunchtime, and *souper* in the evening. In France, breakfast is *petit-déjeuner*, the lunchtime meal is *déjeuner*, and *dîner* is the evening meal. You need to know the origin of your French-speaking hosts if you are invited for *dîner* or you may arrive for the wrong meal.

### OTHER LANGUAGES

The official Canadian census of 2001 recorded a population of just over 31 million, of whom more than 17.4 million spoke English as their mother tongue and 6.7 million spoke French. The third-largest language group was Chinese, with over 850,000 people (with a great concentration of these in British Columbia), followed by Italian and German, with just under half a million each.

Polish, Spanish, Portuguese, Punjabi, and Arabic were the mother tongue of about 200,000 people each. Dutch, Filipino, Greek and Vietnamese are each spoken by about 100,000 individuals.

Of First Nations languages, Cree has the most speakers, with 73,000. Inuktitut (the language of the Inuit) is spoken by about 29,000 people.

## USEFUL WORDS AND PHRASES

| FRENCH | ENGLISH |
|---|---|
| bonjour / bonsoir / bon nuit | good day / good evening / good night |
| au revoir | goodbye |
| oui / non | yes / no |
| merci / bienvenue | thank you / you're welcome |
| s'il vous plaît | please |
| Comment ça va? | How are you? |
| Très bien, merci | Very well, thank you |
| Ça va? | How's it going? (more colloquial) |
| douanes / frontière | customs / international border |
| autoroute / chemins / rue | highway / road / street |
| arrêt | stop (road sign) |
| aéroport | airport |
| métro / autobus / taxi | subway / bus / taxi |
| gare / train / billets | station / train / tickets |
| entrée / sortie | entrance / exit |
| droit / gauche | right / left |
| tout droit | straight ahead |
| nord / sud / est / ouest | north / south / east / west |
| matin / après-midi | morning / afternoon |
| soir / nuit | evening / night |
| Où est le restaurant / l'hôtel? | Where's the restaurant / the hotel? |
| le menu / table d'hôte | the menu / table d'hote (fixed-price meal |
| L'addition / la facture, s'il vous plaît | The check (bill), please |
| Combien? | How much? |
| déjeuner / dîner / souper / le thé | breakfast / lunch / dinner / tea |
| banque | bank |
| toilettes | washrooms / toilets |
| cinéma / théâtre / concert | cinema / theater / concert |
| librairie / bibliothèque | bookstore / library |
| cathédrale / église | cathedral / church |
| musée / galerie d'art | museum / art gallery |
| centre d'achat / boutique de souvenirs | shopping mall / souvenir store |
| édifice / place | building / city square |
| hôtel de ville / palais de justice | city hall / courthouse |
| fontaine / chute(s) | fountain / waterfall |
| rivière / fleuve | river / major river |
| ruisseau / lac | stream / lake |
| montagne / colline / vallée / falaise | mountain / hill / valley / cliff |
| baie / champ / île | bay / field / island |
| ville / cité / village | town / city / village |
| maison / pont / jardin | house / bridge / garden |
| salle / porte / fenêtre | room / door / window |
| moulin / belvédère | mill / viewpoint |

| INUKTITUT | PRONUNCIATION | ENGLISH |
|---|---|---|
| Qanuipit? | Ka-nwee-peet? | how are you? |
| Qanuingittung | Ka-nweeng-ni-toon-ga | I'm fine |
| Qujannamiik | Coo-yan-na-mee-ick | thankyou |
| Ilaali | Ee-lah-lih | you're welcome |
| Ii | Ee | yes |
| Aakka or aagaa | Ah-ka or Ah-ga | no |
| Qatsituqqa? | Cat-see-to-kaw? | how much is it? |

# Atlas

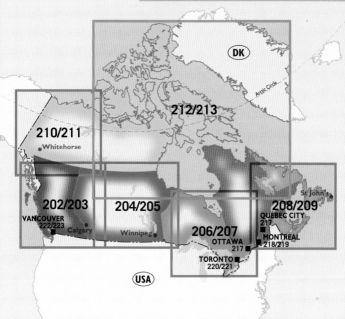

To identify the regions, see the map on the inside of the front cover

## Regional Maps

- ▬▬ Major route
- ▬▬ Motorway (Expressway)
- ▬▬ Main road
- ▬▬ Other road (MEX)
- ┄┄ International boundary
- ─ ─ State boundary

- ▫ City / Town
- National park
- ▣ Featured place of interest
- ▪ Place of interest
- ✈ Airport
- ▲ Peak

**202/211**  |  0 — 150 km  |  0 — 75 miles

**212/213**  |  0 — 300 km  |  0 — 150 miles

## City Plans

- ▬▬ Motorway (Expressway)
- ▬▬ Major route
- ▬▬ Other road
- ▬ Important building
- ▬ Park
- ▣ Place of interest
- [i] Tourist information
- ● Metro
- ✝ Church

**218/219**  |  0 — 150 metres  |  0 — 150 yards

**220/221**  |  0 — 300 metres  |  0 — 300 yards

**222/223**  |  0 — 300 metres  |  0 — 300 yards

Scales for Ottawa and Québec are shown within the plan frames

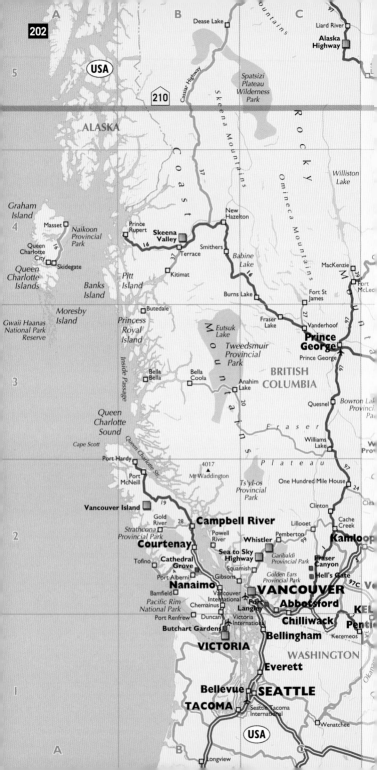

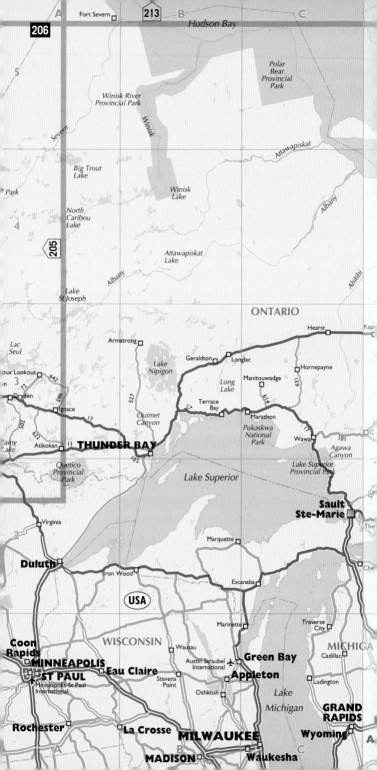

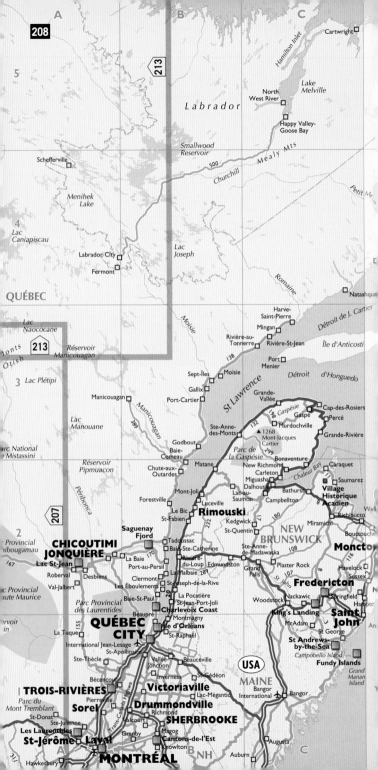

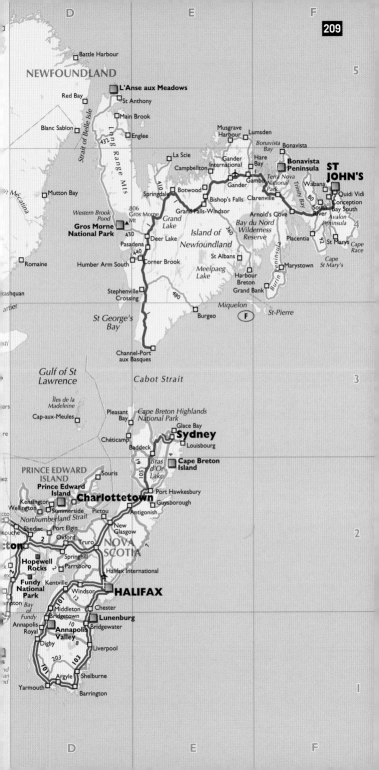

**NEWFOUNDLAND**

Battle Harbour

L'Anse aux Meadows

Red Bay

St Anthony

Blanc Sablon

Main Brook

Englee

Musgrave
Harbour

Lumsden

La Scie

Campbellton

Bonavista
Bay

Bonavista

Mutton Bay

Springdale

Botwood

Gander
International

Gander

Hare
Bay

Gambo

Bonavista
Peninsula

**ST
JOHN'S**

Wabana

Terra Nova
National
Park

Clarenville

Quidi Vidi

806
Gros Morne
Mt

Bishop's Falls

Grand Falls-Windsor

Conception
Bay South

Western Brook
Pond

Grand
Lake

**Gros Morne
National Park**

Arnold's Cove

South
River

Avalon
Peninsula

Deer Lake

Island of
Newfoundland

Bay du Nord
Wilderness
Reserve

Pasadena

Trinity Bay

Placentia

Romaine

Humber Arm South

Corner Brook

St Albans

Harbour
Breton

St Marys

Cape
Race

Meelpaeg
Lake

Marystown

Cape
St Mary's

Stephenville
Crossing

Grand Bank

Burin
Peninsula

St George's
Bay

Burgeo

Miquelon

**F**

St-Pierre

Channel-Port
aux Basques

Gulf of St
Lawrence

Cabot Strait

Îles de la
Madeleine

Cap-aux-Meules

Pleasant
Bay

Cape Breton Highlands
National Park

Glace Bay

**Sydney**

Chéticamp

Baddeck

Louisbourg

**PRINCE EDWARD
ISLAND**

Souris

Bras
d'Or
Lake

**Cape Breton
Island**

**Prince Edward
Island**

**Charlottetown**

Port Hawkesbury

Kensington

Summerside

Pictou

Guysborough

Wellington

Northumberland Strait

Antigonish

Shediac

Port Elgin

Oxford

Truro

New
Glasgow

**Hopewell
Rocks**

Springhill

Parrsboro

**NOVA
SCOTIA**

**Fundy
National
Park**

Kentville

Halifax International

Bay
of
Fundy

Windsor

**HALIFAX**

Middleton

Chester

Bridgetown

**Lunenburg**

Annapolis
Royal

**Annapolis
Valley**

Bridgewater

Digby

Liverpool

Yarmouth

Argyle

Shelburne

Barrington

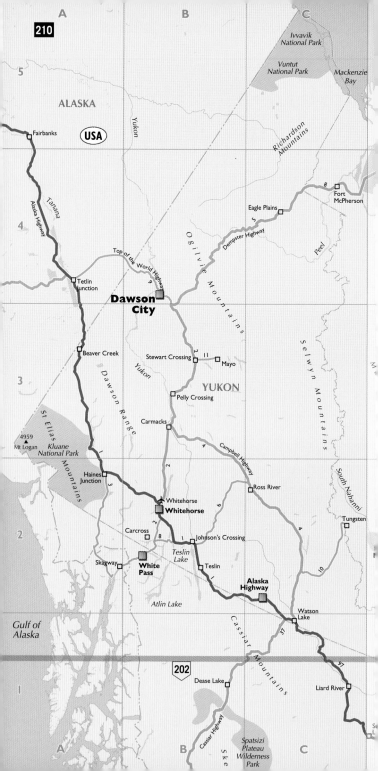

D        E        F

Sachs
Harbour

Banks
Island

**211**

*Beaufort
Sea*

*Amundsen
Gulf*

Tuktoyaktuk

*Cape
Parry*

**212**

Holman

**Inuvik**

*Tukluk Nogait
National Park*

5

Paulatuk

4

Fort
Good Hope

Kugluktuk
(Coppermine)

*Franklin
Mountains*

*Mackenzie*

*Great Bear
Lake*

Port
Radium

3

*Mackenzie Mountains*

**NORTHWEST TERRITORIES**

Wrigley

**212**

**Nahanni
National
Park**

2

Rae-Edzo

Fort
Simpson

Yellowknife

**Yellowknife**

*Liard*

Fort
Providence

*Great Slave
Lake*

**203**

Fort
Resolution

I

Hay
River

Enterprise

5

6

Summit
Lake

Fort
Nelson

**D**

E

35

F

Fort
Smith

*Wood Buffalo
National Park*

*Caribou*

A        B        C

5

*Ellesmere Island*

*Axel Heiberg Island*

4

*Queen Elizabeth Islands*

*Melville Island*

*Parry Islands*

*Devon Island*

Qausuittuq (Resolute)

*Lancaster Sound*

Pond Inlet

*Banks Island*

*Victoria Melville Sound*

*Somerset Island*

Ikpiarjuk (Arctic Bay)

...dsen ...ulf

*Prince of Wales Island*

*Gulf of Boothia*

3

*Victoria Island*

*Boothia Peninsula*

Igloolik

Taloyoak

Kugluktuk (Coppermine)

*Coronation Gulf*

Ikaluktutiak (Cambridge Bay)

*King William Island*

Ursuqtuq (Gjoa Haven)

*Melville Peninsula*

211

Naujat (Repulse Bay)

2

*Back*

*Garry Lake*

NUNAVUT

Southam... Island

Cor... Harbou...

Qamanittuaq (Baker Lake)

*Aylmer Lake*

*Thelon*

*Dubawnt Lake*

Rae-Edzo ✈ Yellowknife

NORTHWEST TERRITORIES

Yellowknife

*Great Slave Lake*

River

204

205

Fort Resolution

Arviat (Eskimo Point)

6

Fort Smith

*Nueltin Lake*

1

*Wood Buffalo National Park*

Uranium City

*Lake Athabasca*

Stony Rapids

*Wollaston Lake*

*Reindeer Lake*

*Cape Churchill*

Churchill

*Churchill*

ALBERTA

SASKATCHEWAN

MANITOBA

Fort McMurray

A

Lynn Lake

B

*Southern Indian Lake*

C

GREENLAND

DK

Baffin
Bay

4

Kangiqlugaapik
(Clyde River)

Davis Strait

Baffin
Island

Auyuittuq
National Park

3

Nettilling
Lake

Pangnirtung

Prince
Charles
Island

Cumberland Sound

Foxe
Basin

lle
sula

Amadjuak
Lake

Apex

Frobisher Bay

Labrador
Sea

Kingait
(Cape Dorset)

Kimmirut

Hudson Strait

Cape Chidley
1729
▲Mt Caubvick

2

outhampton
Island

Coral
Harbour

Quaqtaq

Fisher
Strait

Ivujivik

Ungava
Bay

Coats
Island

Mansel
Island

Péninsule
d'Ungava

N

Kuujjuaq

Hudson
Bay

Inukjuak

QUÉBEC

Caniapiscau

Schefferville

Lac
Caniapiscau

Lac
Bienville

Labrador City

1

Fort
Severn

Kuujjuarapik

D

E

F

Reservoir

# Atlas Index

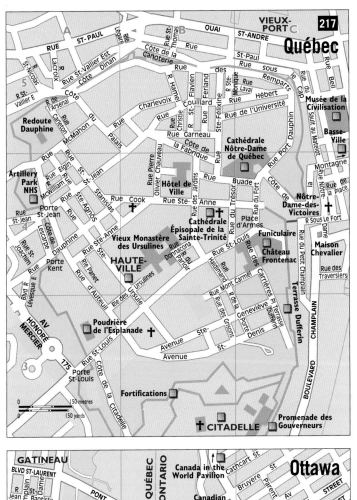

VIEUX-PORT C

QUAI ST-ANDRÉ

# Québec

A RUE ST-PAUL
B QUAI

Rue Ste-Thomas

Côte de la Canoterie

Rue Dinan

Côte Dinan

R St-Nicolas

Lacroix

Rue St-Vallier Est

Rue

Rue sous le Cap

Rue du Sault au Matelot

Rue Bell

St-Paul

Rue Laval

des Remparts

Hébert

**Musée de la Civilisation**

R St-Vallier E

R de l'Arsenal

Côte du Palais

McMahon

Carleton

Charlevoix

Rue Hamel

Rue Couillard

Rue Christie

R St-Félixine

Rue Ste-Monique

Rue de l'Université

Rue Garneau

Dauphine

Rue Port

**Basse-Ville**

**Redoute Dauphine**

Rue Garneau

Côte de la Fabrique

Rue Pierre Olivier Chauveau

**Cathédrale Nôtre-Dame de Québec**

Rue du Fort

Rue Port Dauphin

Montagne

Côte de la Montagne

**Artillery Park NHS**

Rue Elgin

Rue St-Jean

Rue McWilliam

Rue Ste-Agnès

Rue Stanislas

**Hôtel de Ville**

Rue des Jardins

Buade

Côte de la Fabrique

Rue Ste-Anne

Rue du Trésor

Place d'Armes

**Nôtre-Dame-des-Victoires**

Rue de la Place

Porte St-Jean

Rue St-Jean

Côte Ste-Geneviève

Rue Cook

Rue Ste-Anne

**Cathédrale Épiscopale de la Sainte-Trinité**

Rue Ste-Anne

Rue du Parloir

Rue Donnacona

**Vieux Monastère des Ursulines**

**Funiculaire**

**Château Frontenac**

R Sous Le Fort

**Maison Chevalier**

Porte Kent

Rue St-Joachim

Rue Dauphine

Rue Ste-Ursule

Rue d'Auteuil

Rue Panet

**HAUTE-VILLE**

Rue des Ursulines

Rue Mont Carmel

Rue des Grisons

Rue des Carrières

Pl Terrasse

Terrasse Dufferin

Rue des Traversiers

Blvd R Lévesque E

**Poudrière de l'Esplanade**

Rue Ste-Geneviève

Rue St-Denis

**AV HONORÉ MERCIER**

175

Rue St-Louis

Porte St-Louis

Côte de la Citadelle

Avenue Ste-

Avenue St-

CHAMPLAIN

BOULEVARD

3

0 / 150 metres
0 / 150 yards

**Fortifications**

✝ **CITADELLE**

**Promenade des Gouverneurs**

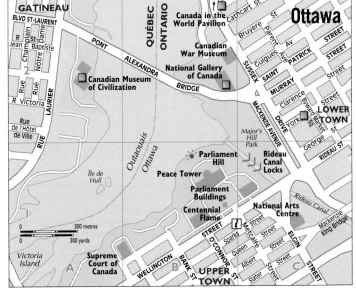

# Ottawa

GATINEAU

BLVD ST-LAURENT

QUÉBEC ONTARIO

R Champlain

Jean

St-Baptiste

Nôtre Dame

**Canada in the World Pavilion**

Cathcart St

Bruyere St

St

PATRICK STREET

PONT ALEXANDRA

**Canadian War Museum**

Guigues Av

SAINT

MURRAY STREET

2

Rue Victoria

Rue

LAURIER

**Canadian Museum of Civilization**

BRIDGE

**National Gallery of Canada**

SUSSEX

Clarence Street

ward Market St

**LOWER TOWN**

Rue de l'Hôtel de Ville

Outaouais

Ottawa

Île de Hull

MACKENZIE AVENUE

Major's Hill Park

York St

George St

RIDEAU

● **Parliament Hill**

**Peace Tower**

**Rideau Canal Locks**

Rideau Canal

**Parliament Buildings**

**National Arts Centre**

Mackenzie King Bridge

Victoria Island

**Centennial Flame**

WELLINGTON STREET

O'CONNOR ST

Sparks Street

Metcalfe Street

ELGIN STREET

i

0 / 300 metres
0 / 300 yards

A

**Supreme Court of Canada**

B

BANK ST

**UPPER TOWN**

Queen Street

Albert Street

Slater Street

C

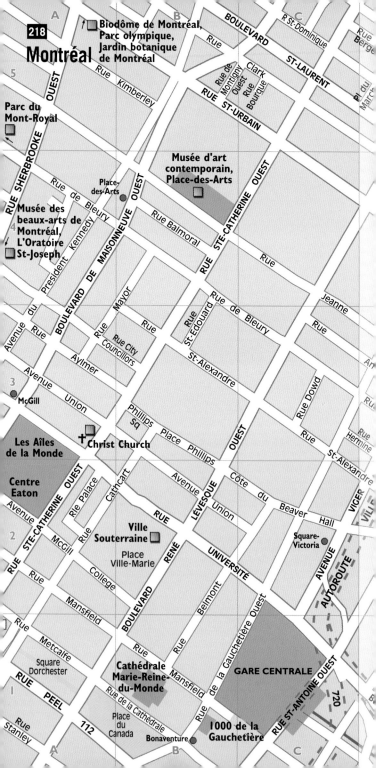

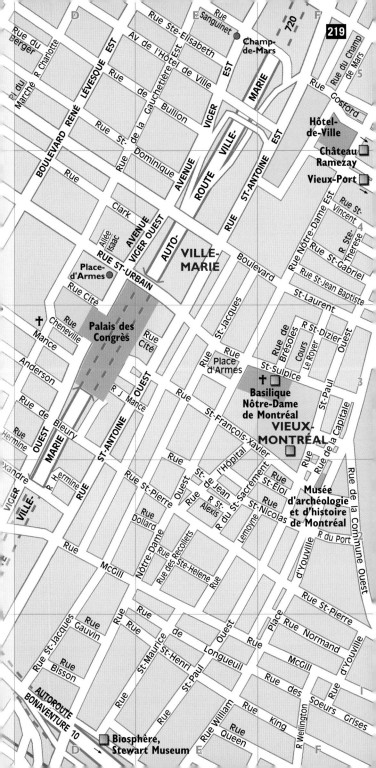

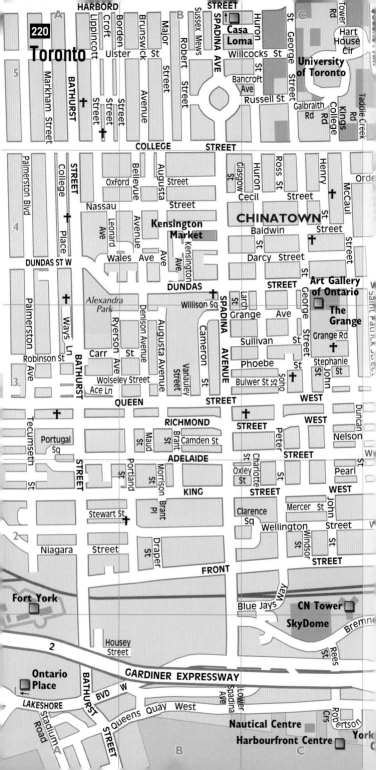

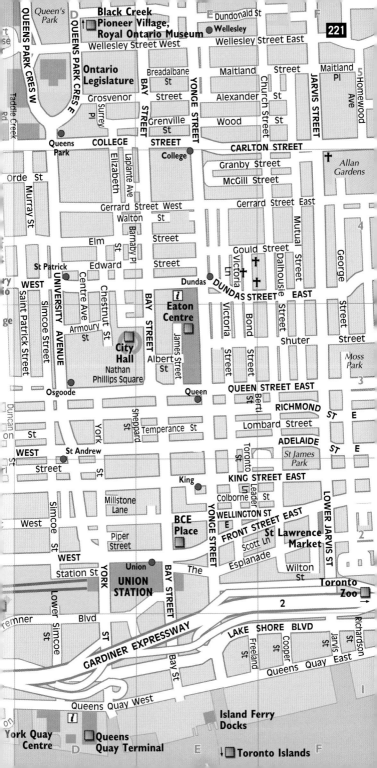

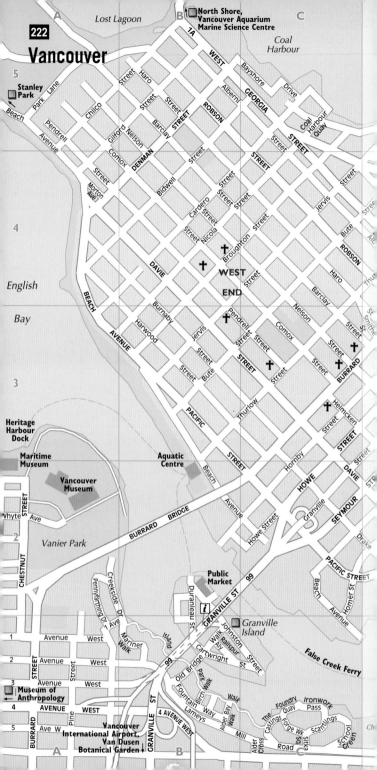

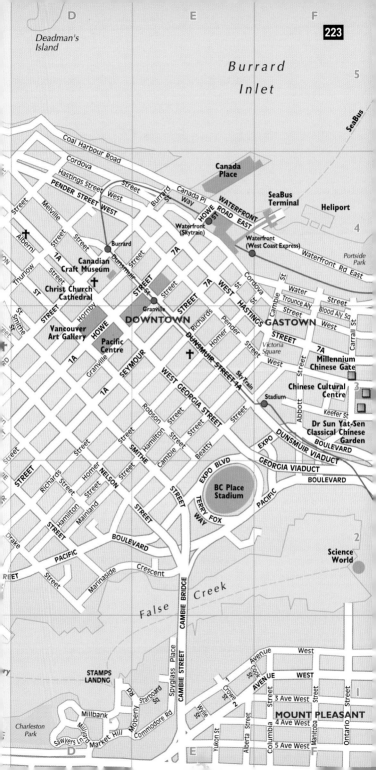

# City Plan Street Indexes

## QUÉBEC

# Index

## Picture credits

The Automobile Association wishes to thank the following photographers, libraries, associations and tourist organizations for their assistance in the preparation of this book.

Front and Back Cover: (t) **AA World Travel Library/ J Beazley**, (ct) **AA World Travel Library/N Sumner**, (cb), (b).

**1000 Islands International Tourism Council** 94, 96b, 101, 102; **Alamy** 3(ii) (Dinodia Photo Library Pvt. Ltd), 13t (Bruce Coleman Brakefield), 13b (ImageState), 14bl (Robert E Barber), 15bl (Martin Harvey), 22b (xela), 163 (Dinodia Photo Library Pvt. Ltd), 173 (Peter Llewellyn), 178 (Brandon Cole Marine Photography), 179 (Chris Cheadle); **Calgary Stampede** 2(iv), 27, 71, 76; **Canadian Museum of Civilization** 30t (Spirit of Haida Gwaii, artist Bill Reid, catalogue no. 92-51, photographer Harry Foster), 30/1 (main builder Cesar Newashish, catalogue no. 111-P-21, photo Merle Toole); **Canadian Tourism Commission, Pierre St-Jacques** 24; **City of Saskatoon Imagebank** 86, 87; **Corbis** 14br, 15br, 32; **Dan Lavoie (Studio Odeyssée)** 20b; **Department of Tourism and Culture, Yukon Territorial Government** 29, 165, 166b, 167, 170, 171, 172, 191; **Festival International de Jazz de Montréal** 28. 28/9; **Getty Images** 10/11; **Getty Images/Hulton Collection** 16/17, 17t, 18t, 18b; **Kelly clark fotography:typical girl.com** 9b; **Michel Julien, ATR Gaspésie** 185, 186; **Musee Marguerite-Bourgeoys** 21; **Photodisc** 14/15; **RCMP** 7t; **John E. Sokolowski** 12; **Tourism Calgary** 26/7; **Tourisme Montréal, Stéphan Poulin** 120l, 122/3.

All remaining pictures are held in the Association's own library (AA World Travel Library) with contributions from the following photographers:

**J Beazley** 106; **P Bennett** 22t, 22/23, 57; **C Coe** 2(iii), 3(iii), 9t, 45, 52, 58, 60/1, 77, 164, 168l, 168c, 169, 177; **J Davison** 104, 105t, 105b, 184; **M Dent** 48, 50; **M Lynch** 148; **J F Pins** 2(vi), 6b, 7b, 20t, 25t, 98, 99, 103, 117, 120b, 124, 125, 126/7, 127, 128, 143t, 143b, 154/5, 158; **C Sawyer** 7t, 31t, 47, 49, 51, 54/5, 56t, 56b, 57, 62, 63, 64, 74cl, 180, 197l, 197r; **N Sumner** 2(i), 2(v), 3(i), 5t, 6/7, 8/9, 8, 25b, 93, 95t, 95b, 96t, 97t, 97b, 100, 107, 108/9, 110, 111, 118, 119, 121t, 121b, 129, 120, 131, 132, 133, 134, 141, 142, 144, 145, 146, 147, 149, 150, 151, 152, 153, 154, 156, 182, 183, 189, 190; **P Timmermans** 2(ii), 33, 46, 61cr, 65.

## Acknowledgements

The author would like to thank the following for their invaluable assistance: Nim Singh (Canadian Tourism Commission), Kevin Johnston (Air Canada), and all of the provincial tourist boards.

# Questionnaire

**Dear Traveller**

Your comments, opinions and recommendations
are very important to us. So please help us to improve
our travel guides by taking a few minutes to complete
this simple questionnaire.

You do not need a stamp (unless posted outside the UK). If you do not
want to remove this page from your guide, then photocopy it or write your
answers on a plain sheet of paper.

*Send to:* The Editor, Spiral Guides, AA World Travel Guides,
FREEPOST SCE 4598, Basingstoke RG21 4GY.

---

## Your recommendations...

We always encourage readers' recommendations for restaurants, night-life or shopping
– if your recommendation is used in the next edition of the guide, we will send you a
FREE AA Spiral Guide of your choice. Please state below the establishment name,
location and your reasons for recommending it.

_____

_____

_____

_____

_____

**Please send me AA Spiral** _____

(see list of titles inside the back cover)

---

## About this guide...

Which title did you buy?

_____ **AA Spiral**

Where did you buy it?_____

When? m m / y y

Why did you choose an AA Spiral Guide? _____

_____

_____

_____

Did this guide meet your expectations?

Exceeded ☐   Met all ☐   Met most ☐   Fell below ☐

Please give your reasons _____

_____

_____

_____

_____

continued on next page...

**SPIRAL GUIDE**

**Were there any aspects of this guide that you particularly liked?**

_____
_____
_____
_____
_____

**Is there anything we could have done better?**

_____
_____
_____
_____

## About you...

**Name (Mr/Mrs/Ms)** _____

**Address** _____

_____

_____ **Postcode** _____

**Daytime tel no** _____ **email** _____

Please _only_ give us your email address and mobile phone number if you wish to hear from us about other products and services from the AA and partners by email or text or mms.

**Which age group are you in?**

Under 25 ☐   25–34 ☐   35–44 ☐   45–54 ☐   55–64 ☐   65+ ☐

**How many trips do you make a year?**

Less than one ☐   One ☐   Two ☐   Three or more ☐

Are you an AA member? Yes ☐   No ☐

---

About your trip...

**When did you book?** mm/ y y     **When did you travel?** mm/ y y

**How long did you stay?** _____

**Was it for business or leisure?** _____

**Did you buy any other travel guides for your trip?** ☐ Yes  ☐ No

**If yes, which ones?** _____

_____

**Thank you for taking the time to complete this questionnaire. Please send it to us as soon as possible, and remember, you do not need a stamp (unless posted outside the UK).**